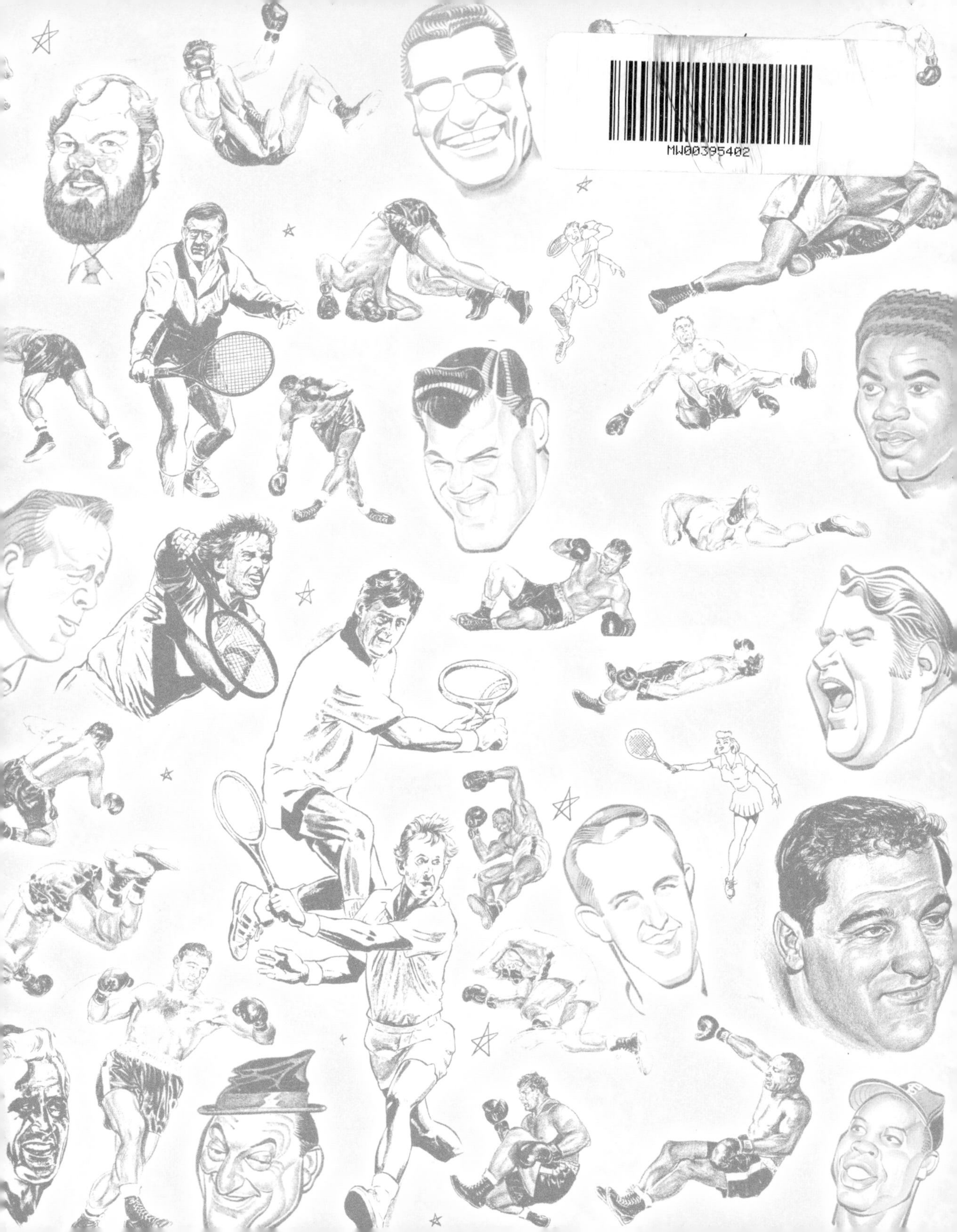

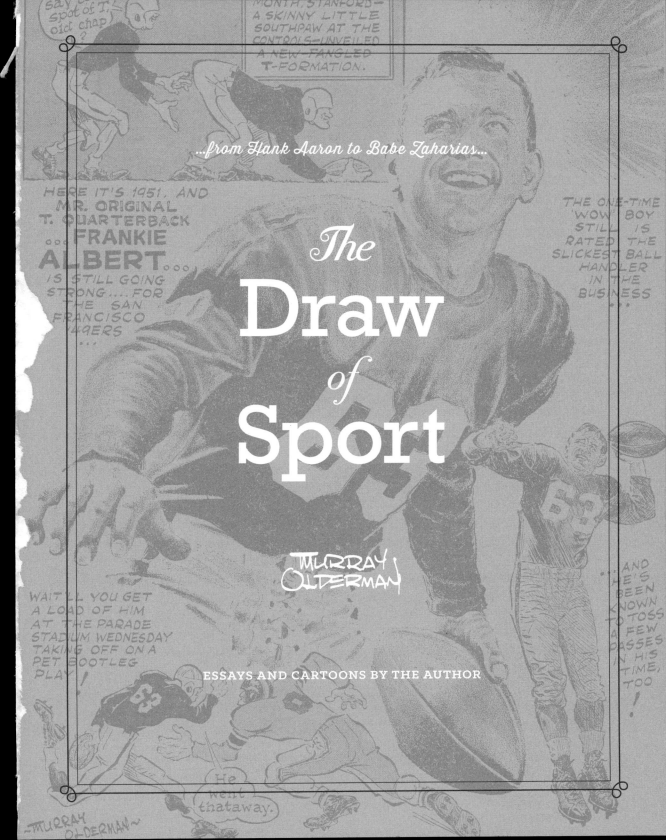

...from Hank Aaron to Babe Zaharias...

The
Draw
of
Sport

Murray Olderman

ESSAYS AND CARTOONS BY THE AUTHOR

FANTAGRAPHICS BOOKS INC.
7563 Lake City Way NE
Seattle, Washington 98115

Editor and Associate Publisher: ERIC REYNOLDS
Book Design: SEAN DAVID WILLIAMS
Production: PAUL BARESH
Publisher: GARY GROTH

ISBN 978-1-60699-995-0
Library of Congress Control Number: 2016947805

First printing: MARCH 2017
Printed in China

PREFACE

THE SPORTS CARTOON flourished as an art form during the middle of the twentieth century. Many metropolitan newspapers had their own full-time cartoonists to decorate their sports sections, and feature syndicates supplied sports cartoons nationally. With the advent of television and the resultant death of afternoon newspapers that had the space to display sports art, plus the digital revolution that brought color photo spreads to newspaper pages, the sports cartoon was virtually eliminated. I am among the last of this vanished media species. I was different than the other sports artists. I was trained as a journalist, and over my career that extends back professionally to 1947, I also wrote conjunctively about the subjects of my cartoons. As a nationally syndicated columnist and sports author, I had the opportunity to meet and get to know the greatest sports personalities of the last seven decades such as Jesse Owens, Red Grange, and Bobby Jones and saw Babe Ruth and Jim Thorpe perform. This book is a compilation, in art and text, of 118 outstanding figures in the world of athletics as I perceived them, culled from the estimated 6,000 sports cartoons and illustrations I produced in my career. The full-page drawings are accompanied by written personal reminiscences of those illustrious stars, (Hank) Aaron to (Babe) Zaharias, stressing my interaction with them.

—MURRAY OLDERMAN

ALL-AMERICAN

INTRODUCTION

AFTER A LIFETIME (or what seems like it) at the drawing board, I have for the most part put a capper on my inkwell and now sit back to ruminate about the people and experiences that have come within my purview as a cartoonist who concentrated primarily on the arena of sports. In the process, I came in contact with a broad range of the most exciting, interesting, and provocative personalities in all of sports, going back to the middle of the twentieth century, who shaped my work and left me with indelible memories. It is my purpose here to put my own spin on them and share them with you.

(Opposite:) the artist at work, c. 1960.

IN THE BEGINNING...

AN OLD FRIEND named Edwin Pope was the sports editor and columnist for the *Miami Herald* over more than five decades, and we used to encounter each other frequently in our fun-and-games travels chasing athletes around the globe. Invariably, Edwin would ask me in his Georgia drawl, "You still gettin' paid for drawing them li'l 'pitchers'?"

"Pitchers" was Pope-talk for pictures, or drawings, and distinguished me from other sports journalists. I was a rare double-threat in the business, both writing and drawing, a facility that developed from my schoolboy days doodling in class. People have accused me rashly of inherent talent. Bah, humbug, to borrow an old, printable epithet. I could draw a line no straighter than the next guy. And my scribbled signature would defy any pharmacist. I just liked the looks of a cartoon on a sports page. And seduced by the art style, I was willing to put in the time to try to learn it.

I have now been a practitioner of sports cartooning for more than six decades, in addition to dealing with the greatest athletes of our time, going back professionally to 1947. These are my observations on how that craft has evolved for me and where it is today.

During the Depression days of the 1930s, my father used to commute on the Rockland bus lines from Spring Valley, a hamlet thirty miles northwest of New York City, to lower Manhattan. Pop was making eighteen dollars a week in a sweatshop job in the garment industry, measuring cloth, feeding a family of five. Pennies were precious. On arrival at the bus station back home at night he'd gather up the New York newspapers left on the seats by the other riders and bring them to me to pore over. At the time, there were twelve dailies in the city, and every one of them, except the very august *Times* and the almost-august *Herald-Tribune*, had a sports cartoonist whose work was prominently displayed on the first page of the sports section, which I turned to immediately.

So I became familiar with the dramatic realism of Burris Jenkins Jr.'s flowing drawings in the *Journal-American,* the little lion of Leo O'Mealia cavorting in the *Daily News,* the brush strokes of John Pierotti in the *Post,* the precise portraits surrounded by goomies (little sketches) of Pap (Tom Paprocki) in the *Sun* (they were also distributed nationally by *Associated Press Features*), and Willard Mullin's sprawling pen-action figures rambling across the columns of the *World-Telegram.* Even the home county Nyack *Journal-News* featured syndicated sports panels by Alan Maver of Central Press, a Hearst newspaper syndicate.

I tried to emulate them in my naive way, copying their cartoons and illustrations in pencil on plain paper, later on heavier stock, and improved enough, doodling my way through high school and college classes, to get my work published occasionally in college and city newspapers. My very first sports cartoon committed to print was in the fall of 1941 when I did a drawing of Bob Steuber, a running back at the University of Missouri, that appeared in the *Columbia Missourian*, a city newspaper produced by the School of Journalism, where I was in my junior year. There was no theme other than to extol the athlete, which was the basic attitude toward sports in that era. The design was amateurish, an ink-and-crayon portrait of Steuber, accompanied by wobbly lettering and a crude little action figure. But the faculty was tolerant and encouraged me to do more drawings over the next couple of years. I even did a cover in January 1942 of Darold Jenkins, the Tigers' All-American center, for *Showme*, the college humor magazine. (On its staff was a freshman, Mort Walker, who achieved later fame with his comic strip, *Beetle Bailey*.)

That same year, home from school on summer break, I produced drawings of local sports stars for the Nyack *Journal-News*. But my cartooning aspirations were interrupted by three years of army service during World War II, though I continued to draw intermittently—the *Stanford Daily* while I was stationed at that university in an army language program and in division newspapers. And after my discharge from the army in 1946, I enrolled in the Medill School of Journalism at Northwestern University in Evanston, Illinois, to study for a master's degree in journalism and on the side contributed sports cartoons to the *Northwestern Daily*. My big coup, however, was getting a couple published in the *Chicago Daily News*, a reputable big city newspaper. I brashly went to the newspaper's office in downtown Chicago and offered them to Joe Rein, an assistant sports

Olderman and Sandy Koufax (right) honor Carl Yastrzemski for being named to the 1967 All-Major League Team.

editor. I wasn't paid anything.

In the spring of 1947, with graduation approaching, I sat down at an ancient portable typewriter that I'd had since high school and wrote seventy job applications for a sports writer position to newspapers around the country. This was in the Dark Ages of communications technology, before scanners or copy machines or personal printers. Not a hint of the coming computer revolution. In each letter I enclosed three 3x5 inch glossy photographs of my cartoons. I simply put the drawings on a wall and shot them with a 35mm Leica camera that I had "liberated" in Europe, then had prints made at a drugstore.

Walter Jones, the editor of the *Sacramento Bee* in California's capitol, responded with a job offer—as a sports cartoonist. First, however, I had to go downtown to the office of an independent headhunting agency in the Loop of the Windy City for a personal interview. They gave me a Rorschach test, a psychological exam of personality based on how the subject interprets ink blotches. They asked me if I beat my wife and other personal questions. Nothing about journalism. Certainly no mention of cartooning. I must have passed muster because in June, diploma tucked in an envelope, we got in a Chevrolet I purchased with my G.I. savings and drove west, turning north in Iowa to avoid floods and cruising across South Dakota, past the Corn Palace in Mitchell and the Badlands, then the Mormon Temple in Salt Lake City and the desert vista of Nevada, and finally over the High Sierra to Northern California to report for my first fulltime newspaper job.

I was to be the sports cartoonist for all three McClatchy newspapers—the *Sacramento*, *Fresno*, and *Modesto Bees*—but based in California's capital city, which was the head-quarters of the chain. I also worked on some feature writing for the Sacramento paper and even covered a high school football team as a reporter. All this for sixty dollars a week, which was twenty dollars more than I was offered by the *Des Moines Register*.

LEARNING ON THE JOB

MY FIRST PUBLISHED sports cartoon as a professional, on July 3, 1947, was of Eddie Fitz Gerald, a young player with the Sacramento Solons of the Pacific Coast League. A year later, Eddie was sold to the Pittsburgh Pirates and remained in the major leagues for twelve seasons but never made a great impact, spending most of his time as a backup catcher with several other teams. After I made it to New York, I'd look up Eddie at the ballpark when his team was in town, and he was genuinely happy to see a familiar face from his younger days. We remained friends until he left baseball. I cringe as I look at the drawing.

I had a facility for rendering the main figure, using a photograph as my guide. The rest of the art, created out of my head, is substandard, with no flow, sense of anatomy, or the drape of clothing, and the design is terrible. I had much to learn about cartooning and developing a style.

I was helped by the presence of two colleagues on the paper's staff. Courtney Alderson was a nasal Arkansan with a high-pitched twang who headed the *Bee*'s bullpen, a veteran staff artist whose only ambition was to produce a successful comic strip, which he never did. But Courtney introduced a young rookie artist to the different art materials available and how to use them and was there to answer questions about how to produce art for publication. Newton Pratt was editorial cartoonist for the McClatchy chain, a brilliant draftsman who quit his job as an engineer for the state of California to start a new career in the newspaper field. He was a superb artist with tremendous control of a fine brush. He was the one lone cartoonist I met who disdained a pen and lettered with his sable brush. On a bigger city paper he would have had a national reputation. And he was helpful in encouraging me to try new ideas. We kept in touch for years after I moved on. The publisher of the three *Bee*s was a spinster lady, Eleanor McClatchy, youngest daughter of the founder of the papers, going back to the Gold Rush days of California. That first year she came by my drawing board and in her low-key, polite way said she would like me to do cartoons of the leading Californian historical figures. They ran in the place of the editorial cartoon in the Saturday edition.

The research was provided by the California state library, and I became thoroughly immersed in the legends of Captain John Sutter, Kit Carson, Mariano Vallejo, General John Fremont, Snowshoe Thompson, Joaquin Murrieta (a particular bandit favorite of mine who robbed the rich to help the poor), and anyone else who mattered in the state's development. I did portraits surrounded by lettered legends and drawings of their exploits. At one point, Miss McClatchy had a collection of them bound in a booklet that was distributed to school systems.

My focal point was still sports, and Sacramento in the mid-twentieth century was a somnambulant little city without a major league team in any sport or a major university. It had only the Sacramento Solons in the Pacific Coast League. That wasn't going to hold me after four years. I started looking for a bigger market and was hired by the *Minneapolis Star* and *Tribune*—larger city, greater circulation, with the George Mikan-led Minneapolis Lakers the top team in the National Basketball Association, and big-time college football at the University of Minnesota. After my arrival in the spring of 1951, the Minneapolis Millers, a Triple-A farm team of the New York Giants, brought up from Trenton a young outfielder named Willie Mays. There was no shortage of interesting cartoon subjects. I was assigned to the *Star,* the afternoon newspaper, as its sports cartoonist, also working the desk part-time, and in the fall did a football tour of Big Ten universities, doing drawings and features on the top Big Ten players.

The one factor I didn't take into account was the weather. In January 1952, I flew to New York to visit my brother after a long absence. There was a mid-winter thaw with temperatures in the 60s. In the city, I landed an assignment to do an Olympic art layout for *True* magazine. The editor, Bill Wise, suggested I look up a sports writer friend at Newspaper Enterprise Association (NEA), a Scripps-Howard newspaper service. I was standing in the doorway telling this friend that I had recently written to the NEA editor, Boyd Lewis, about syndicating my work. A man walking by, poked his head in, and said, "I am Boyd Lewis." We had an amiable conversation. When I flew back to Minneapolis the next morning, my wife picked me up at the airport. The temperature was twenty below zero. We looked at each other. Simultaneously: "Let's get out of here." I went home and immediately wrote a letter to Lewis, applying for a position, and took it to the post office. The mail was going through in those days. The following morning, I received a phone call from Boyd Lewis in New York. "Do you believe in fate?" he asked. I thought he was into mythology. "We just decided," Lewis said, "that we want to develop a sports comic strip." And, having received my application, he instantly offered me a job at NEA, which I accepted. My learning curve didn't end.

TRICKS OF THE TRADE

NEWSPAPERS WERE PRINTED on high-speed cylinder presses, and line art, with only the black areas showing, was the most reliable technique for faithful reproduction of a drawing. I discovered coquille board and Ross board, papers with special grains. When you rubbed a black crayon pencil over them (in

my case, it finally became a Prismacolor 935 that didn't smudge), the result to the naked eye was shades of gray, depending on how much pressure you exerted with the pencil. Through a magnifying glass, you saw that the engraving camera picked up only the black specks left on the nibs of the grainy surface, dropping out all the white areas. In a newspaper half-tone photo, dots varying in intensity covered the entire surface of the printed picture; line art, leaving empty spaces white, offered greater contrast. I learned to manipulate a flexible Gillott 290 pen point dipped in India ink to vary the width of the pen strokes. I used Winsor & Newton Series 7 sable brushes (they were and are expensive) moistened to a fine point for delicate black lines. On close inspection of Mullin's drawings, I perceived that if you flattened the brush and wiped off excess ink, it produced a split line that imparted looseness, action, and spontaneity. My drawings weren't the result of God-given talent; they were the end product of hundreds of hours of trial-and-error labor and experimentation at the drawing board. Of course, your personality and perception helped to determine what was put on paper, just as they reflected your printed words.

I took the next logical step: a close study of the work of other sports cartoonists to improve my technique and draftsmanship. I wrote to fine sports artists in the hinterlands such as Lou Darvas of the *Cleveland Press* and Karl Hubenthal of the *Los Angeles Examiner*, requesting original drawings, and also sought advice and information on the technical aspects of drawing for publication. Karl was especially helpful and encouraging to me. Besides sending originals of his cartoons, he tipped me off to the Esterbrook 312 pen point that had a little bit of a square end and

made lateral strokes a shade thicker than the vertical. It was ideal for lettering. Later, when I couldn't find that particular nib in art supply stores, he sent me a few from his supply. I still use that same pen point for lettering.

Darvas, Hubenthal, and Willard Mullin were the big three of sports cartooning in the United States, and their work received national exposure in *The Sporting News*, the baseball bible published weekly in St. Louis. Mullin, the pacesetter for the craft and the most influential, won a 1954 Reuben Award given by the National Cartoonists Society to the number one cartoonist in the country in any medium.

Willard was a bustling, stocky man with a bit of the poet in him. His drawings oozed vitality. He had an agile mind. He went to a game at Ebbets Fields to see the Dodgers and grabbed a cab to get back to the office. The driver turned around and asked Willard, "How did dem bums do today?" The proverbial light bulb flashed in Willard's head. Thus was born the Brooklyn Bum, his unique cartoon creation. Like most cartoonists, he couldn't spell. But he could drink with anybody I've ever met. We went on a press jaunt to Miami that was arranged by a racetrack, Gulfstream Park, and for three days a glass with ice cubes and a steady supply of Scotch was glued to his drawing hand. He didn't slow up a lick but mused to me on the final night that he couldn't remember the cards he held in a game of gin rummy, which cost him $140 in losses.

Karl Hubenthal was a Mullin disciple and lived with him in New York for a while after he got out of the Marines. He drew in the same style and with cleaner lines that produced prettier drawings, but without Willard's vivid imagination. The *Los Ange-*

les Examiner hired Karl and gave him a featured niche in sports until William Randolph Hearst himself personally converted him to an editorial cartoonist. I visited Karl at his home in Encino, overlooking the San Fernando Valley, and in his studio on a small table next to his taboret was piled a huge stack of his original cartoons. I asked him what he was going to do with them. "Oh," he said with a shrug, "throw them out." Originals today are worth hundreds of dollars each to sports memorabilia collectors. (Like Hubenthal, Mullin had a large pile of his originals in his *World-Telegram* office. "Take whatever you want," he said to me. I grabbed a half dozen. Mullin originals today are highly prized and worth considerably more than Hubenthal's.)

The middle of the twentieth century was a flourishing time for sports cartoonists nationwide. There were a flock of them in Boston, led by Gene Mack, Bob Coyne, Jim Dobbins, and Vic Johnson. Howard Brodie went from a G.I. artist for *Yank* magazine to producing beautiful, huge sports illustrations for the *San Francisco Chronicle*. Pittsburgh,

With the cartoonist standing in the Yankee dugout, Joe Pepitone (center) and Mickey Mantle admire one of Olderman's cartoons (c. mid-'60s).

Cincinnati, St. Louis, Detroit, Seattle, Denver, Dallas—you name the city—all had their own sports cartoonists whose primary métier was decorating the local blatts with punchy action drawings. They sure as hell beat a stale photo at the top of the leading sports page of a base runner sliding into second base.

Yet as far back as 1952, when I arrived at NEA, the nabobs felt that the traditional sports cartoon was passé for syndication (my predecessor, Al Vermeer, had switched to doing a comic strip, *Priscilla's Pop*). Ostensibly, as noted previously, I was hired to develop a daily strip with a sports theme and began to create a character on my drawing board, going so far as to develop finished dailies. As a child of the depression, however, to justify my early paychecks, I also started doing general sports cartoons, and they gained enough acceptance from our 600-plus client newspapers to help keep me on the payroll until retirement age. The noodling for the development of a sports strip was relegated to an old file cabinet, where it still resides. Besides I relished the idea of going out to the ballpark for research instead of being cooped up perennially in an office or barn studio.

The genre, in my case, improved with experience. The early sports cartoons consisted of a portrait or full-length action, rendered in a realistic style, and surrounded by goomies, with text blocks to tell the story. Sharing an office with John Fischetti, the editorial cartoonist who would later win a Pulitzer Prize (at the *Chicago Daily News*), I expressed my frustration at not putting any meaning into my drawings. Fischetti nursed me through a cartooning thought process. I wanted to do something on Rocky Marciano, the heavyweight champion who had tired of training and ballooned to 220 pounds (from 185).

"It's the Uniform that Does it!"

John suggested that I start with Rocky's boxing tools—light punching bag, heavy bag, headgear, jump rope, ring bell—and how they preyed on him. I turned them into monsters, and the resulting cartoon is later in this book in my take on Rocky.

I began to introduce an editorial slant into my cartoons, the way the editorial page cartoonists did in the political arena. This certainly required headwork as well as good draftsmanship. As an example, to depict the popular conception of Yankee supremacy—veteran players such as Johnny Mize would come over from other teams and revive their careers—I did a simple drawing of the team's unique vertical stripe uniform and inserted the familiar interlocked NY logo. But the end of each stripe was fashioned into a noose. And from those nooses dangled characters representing the other American League teams (eight altogether in those days), with an appropriate caption.

I delved into controversial subjects such as the threatened boycott of the 1960 U.S. Olympic team by black athletes. For one year, I contributed cartoons weekly for the editorial page of *The Sporting News*.

On the side, I created a cottage industry by doing full-page cartoons of star players for football programs at Ohio State, Wisconsin, Northwestern, Michigan State, Minnesota, Pennsylvania, Pittsburgh, Duke, Clemson, Louisiana State, Wyoming, College of the Pacific, California, and the Army-Navy game. Hey, anything to make a buck with a wife and three growing kids.

Through my travels—I was also writing sports features as befitted someone with a journalism degree—I knew the sports information directors at all these universities, and they were familiar with my cartoon work in newspapers in their areas. Among the pros, I sold program art to the Baltimore Colts and the San Francisco 49ers.

Because my usual regular work drawings were black and white, I relished the chance to experiment in color and did game program and brochure covers for Yale, the New York Jets, the Golden State Warriors, and the San Francisco Giants. I was also commissioned to do the program cover art for the golden anniversary of the PGA Championship at Firestone Country Club in Akron, Ohio.

After I heard Pat Summerall and Kyle Rote telecasting a New York Giant game, using the arcane lingo of football, I wondered, "Did the growing audience for the increasingly popular pro game—this was circa 1970—really know what they meant by a 'blitz,' 'swing pass,' 'clothesline tackle,' or 'fly pattern'?" So I called up my friend, the late Chet Simmons, who headed NBC Sports, and suggested I do cartoons to be run as on-air visuals during games to enlighten TV viewers. He bought it. And I produced a series of color illustrations which were interspersed on the TV screen for a few seconds during commentary. For major-league baseball telecasts the next summer, a batch of drawings was also commissioned to illustrate diamond idioms—"foot in the bucket," "bean ball," "hot corner," "pulling the string," etc. Hey, anything to make a buck, with those three growing kids needing higher education.

In the mid-1950s, Topps Chewing Gum commissioned me to do the little action cartoons on the backs of their baseball bubble gum cards. I received only a few bucks for each, but when you put together an assembly line of several hundred cards, you've got a payday. I also did the same back-of-the-card art for NFL player cards. In addition to a check, I would get full sets of cards. My daughters gave them away to kids in the neighborhood. A full set today is worth a few thousand bucks.

Half a century later, Topps called me again with a unique idea. They wanted me to do 195 original drawings of baseball players that would be inserted individually in random packs of baseball cards, so that the lucky purchaser would have an original piece of art as well as the cards. I would be paid a modest fee for each ink-and-wash drawing. I hesitated, however, because a baseball card measures only 2x3 inches, which meant minute, painstaking artwork. The multiplication factor won out, and you can still find some of the drawings floating around the internet.

I perfected different drawing techniques, mindful of an interview with Ted Williams. The Red Sox slugger was supposed to have a flawless, natural swing and eyesight that let him discern the stitches of a pitch as it approached home plate. That explained his .406

batting average in 1941, right? "Bullshit!" exploded Williams. "It takes practice, practice, practice." I did a portrait in wash (diluting black ink for shades of gray) as the frontispiece for a book on Williams, one of a series on the greatest year of great sports personalities—Joe DiMaggio, Arnold Palmer, Jim Brown, Frank Gifford—for which I procured writers and edited for Prentice-Hall Publishing. Concurrent with my sports work, for more than a year I produced a weekly television cartoon for NEA, using both realism and stylized caricatures, that appeared in our New York outlet, the *World-Telegram,* a sop to my vanity and a plug for the small screen's shows.

My drawing styles varied. I did black pen sketches. I mixed crayon and black brush. I applied chemicals on special duo-tone draw-

Olderman with Rocky Marciano, c. 1955.

ing board that brought out shading effects. I would break off a Conté crayon and, using the flat side, get edged shading to mold the contours of a person's face, as in this drawing of veteran comedian Ed Wynn that was one of my syndicated TV cartoons. In short, any success I had as an artist was the end result of application.

Now fast-forward to the advent of the twenty-first century. Venerable Bill Gallo was still doing sports cartoons for the *New York Daily News.* Drew Litton drew an editorial-page type of cartoon with a sports motif for the *Rocky Mountain News* (also distributed by my old syndicate, NEA). Peb, short for Pierre Bellocq, concentrated on horse racing cartoons for the *Daily Racing Form,* a specialized newspaper. Otherwise, the presence of the sports cartoon was practically non-existent on a regular basis in newspapers nationally. Since then, Gallo passed away and wasn't replaced. Litton's paper folded, and he went to his own website on the internet. Peb's drawings were discontinued. And newspapers were completely bereft of full-time sports cartoonists.

What happened? In the age of pervasive television, metropolitan afternoon newspapers with their feature slants, a logical display case for sports cartoons, virtually disappeared. News holes shrank. You were competing for space with breaking stories. The editorial cartoonist had a slot reserved for him; the sports cartoonist didn't. A new breed of editor came in, with emphasis on glitzy photo layouts and a penchant for downsizing. The cartoonists themselves retired or died or, like Hubenthal, turned to the editorial page; some went over to magazine illustration. And they weren't replaced. Even the National Cartoonists Society abandoned sports cartooning as a category in its annual awards (Litton and Peb were among

the last winners) more than a decade ago because, in reality, there remained too few of the breed.

And yet at a time when sports increasingly plays a bigger role in our culture, there are developments that virtually beg for cartoon

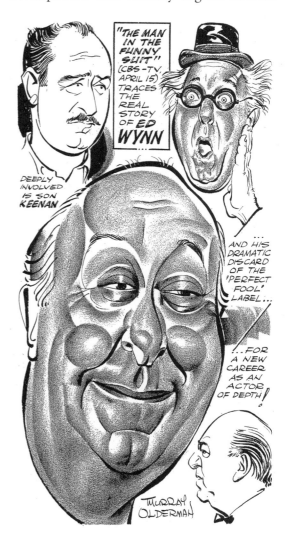

"TV in Sight"

reaction and comment—Olympic doping scandals, the steroids era, salary caps, the Alex Rodriguez suspension, franchise moves, just to name an obvious few—sports pages are bare of comment through expressive editorial art. I keep thinking some talented young cartoonist is going to come along and carve a print niche for himself in sports. Although such prize-winning editorial page cartoonists as Mike Luckovich and the late Jeff MacNelly occasionally commented on the world of fun and games, and comic strips (i.e. *Tank McNamara*) have dipped into the same area, the sports cartoon as we knew it is virtually extinct.

In its place is that cliché half-tone photograph of a runner sliding into second base.

(Above:) Olderman with Hank Greenberg, c. late 70s.
(Opposite:) Olderman in his home studio, 2012.

BECAUSE I WAS a working journalist as well as a sports cartoonist, I often enjoyed a different perspective in my relations with athletes. Cartooning is a lonely profession. You're tethered to a drawing board. I could tear myself away and have direct contact with those who played the game. In the growing chasm between high-salaried sports stars and working media, intensified by the 24-hour news cycle of radio and TV that emphasizes the scandalous, athletes tend to be wary of writers. Mickey Mantle and Roger Maris happened to think of me as a sports artist, not someone who was going to poke into their private sanctum. I had social involvement with other athletes away from their sports milieu because I liked them as people and spent time with them off the field. It was a different era. I didn't have to go through a cordon of agents and spokespersons to get to them. And even if we weren't always buddy-buddy, there was still a comradeship. If some of them didn't like me . . . well, that could be a story, too.

There are some notable omissions in my pantheon of the sports greats I have known and drawn. Michael Jordan came along when my work on the national scene was dwindling, and although I first saw him play as a member of the Olympic Dream Team, I never did a drawing of him. Similarly, I haven't been around Peyton Manning, although I did know and draw his father, Archie, when he broke in with the New Orleans Saints, and I did include Peyton in a Super Bowl color layout. I have basically limited myself in this volume to those I had some interaction with; that comprises a personal, meaningful collection of those who had a profound impact on the sports world since I embarked on my quest as a cartoonist-journalist more than half a century ago. The following pages reveal, alphabetically, how I saw and portrayed them.

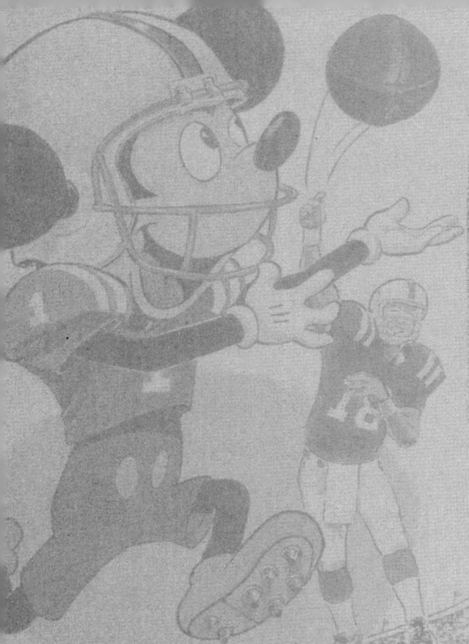

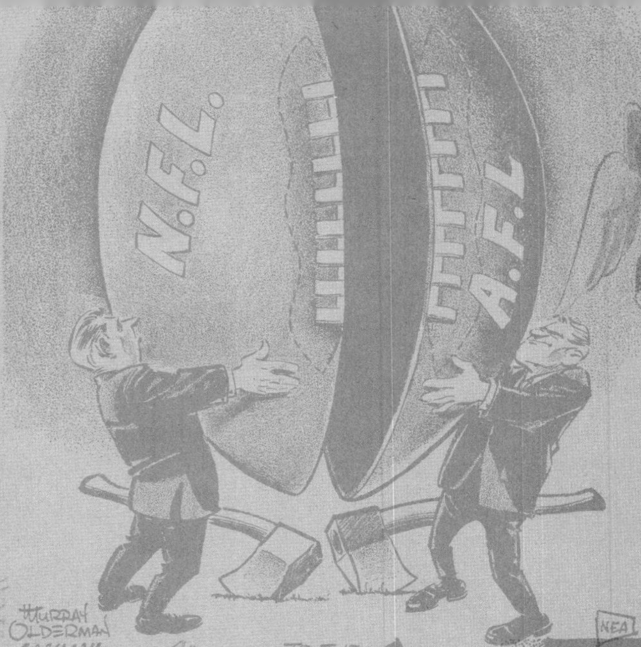
N.F.L.
A.F.L.
MURRAY OLDERMAN

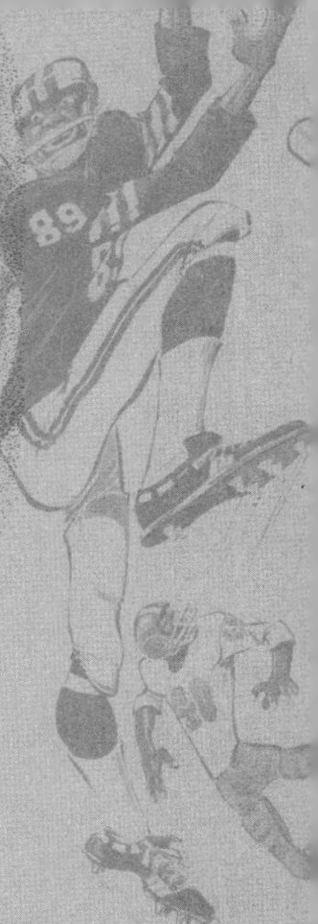

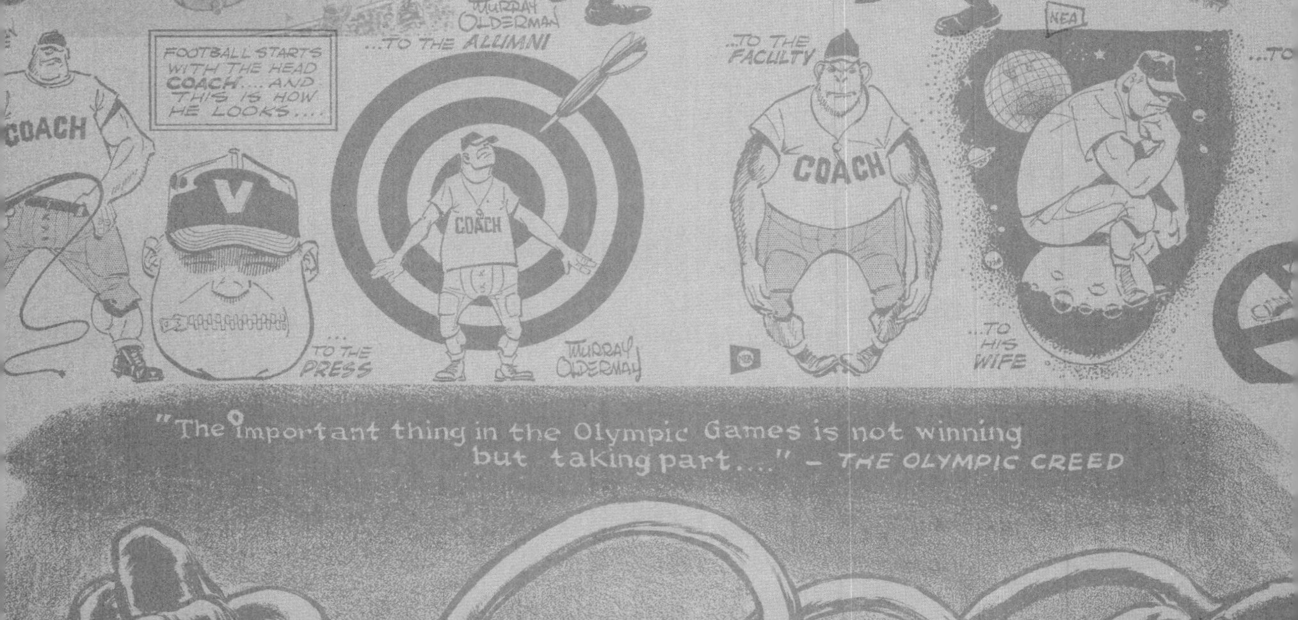
FOOTBALL STARTS WITH THE HEAD COACH ... AND THIS IS HOW HE LOOKS....
COACH
...TO THE ALUMNI
V
... TO THE PRESS
COACH
MURRAY OLDERMAN
...TO THE FACULTY
COACH
NEA
...TO HIS WIFE
...TO

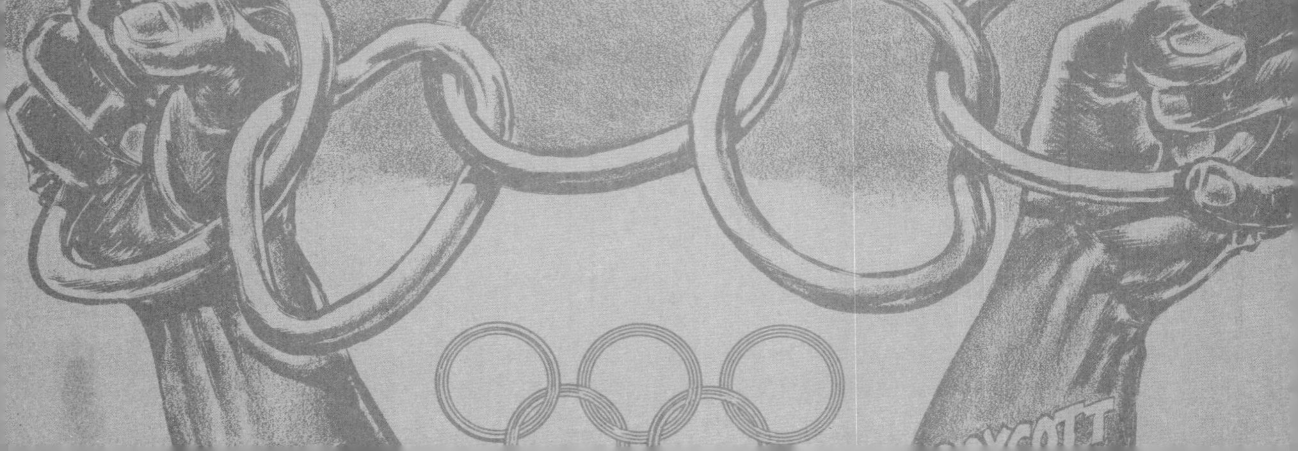
"The important thing in the Olympic Games is not winning but taking part...." - THE OLYMPIC CREED

From
A *to* Z

Henry Aaron

BASEBALL WASN'T A complicated pastime for Henry "Hank" Aaron. A guy some sixty feet away threw a ball toward him, and he lashed at it with a tapered stick that had a knob at the end. Running the bases or running down a ball from right field, he relied on his natural athletic instincts. As an 18-year-old kid in the Negro Leagues, he even batted cross-handed. In the minor leagues, he was asked why he brandished his bat with the label facing the pitch—you were supposed to hit it with the other side of the bat. "It's all wood, ain't it?" he responded. He looked so languid in the batter's box that pitcher Curt Simmons observed, "He was the only ballplayer I've ever seen who goes to sleep at the plate." Then added, "But trying to sneak a fastball by him is like trying to sneak the sunrise past a rooster." In twenty-three seasons with the Milwaukee and Atlanta Braves, he hit 755 home runs, surpassing Babe Ruth's hallowed record of 714 on April 8, 1973, and drove in an all-time high 2,297 runs. Yet playing in relatively small-market cities, he never received the acclaim of a Ruth or a contemporary Willie Mays. He was called Hammerin' Hank, but he was more rat-a-tat-tat. He never hit 50 home runs in a season. The phlegmatic star wasn't flashy but had depth as a person. He admired Jackie Robinson for his racial pioneering and was critical of Mays for his non-activism. He felt keenly slights suffered from being black. On his way to meet a writer for lunch in New York, it bothered him that going through a department store he was followed all the way by a suspicious employee. Since retiring as a player, he has served the Atlanta Braves with dignity in various management roles and received many honors, locally and nationally, including the Presidential Medal of Freedom, for his work supporting affirmative action for minorities.

"It's that Southern Cooking"

Kareem Abdul-Jabbar

KAREEM WOULDN'T LOOK ME in the eyes. We sat on the backless wooden stands of the basketball court at Loyola University near LAX, where the '70s Lakers practiced between games. He was stone-faced as I tried to engage the team's long-time center in conversation. His body was turned ninety degrees away from me, staring impassively ahead. But then I reached into my bag and pulled out his recently published biography and asked him to sign it for my son, who had played high school basketball, but was now in a psychiatric facility. "Really?" he said and wheeled around, suddenly expressive. "Tell me about him." That opened the door for the interview that had been arranged. Kareem's world embraced far more than throwing skyhooks through a basket. He abhorred the attention that his size (7'2") attracted and preferred to absorb himself in social and cultural issues.

But it also gave him a reputation of being aloof and surly that damaged his post-basketball endeavors. I was first aware of him when the buzz in New York basketball circles was about this elongated phenom at Power Memorial High School who was agile enough to dribble behind his back. His name then was Lew Alcindor. He came from a solid family background; his father was a transit authority police officer. He was recruited West by UCLA and led John Wooden's Bruins to three consecutive national championships, also converting to Sunni Islam. He played for twenty years in the NBA and scored 38,387 points, still the all-time record. Although he's stayed on the NBA fringes as an assistant and consultant, he is smart enough to be a head coach. But few people ever get behind that forbidding personality.

Bud Adams

TWO YOUNG OIL scions from Texas, Lamar Hunt of Dallas and Kenneth Stanley "Bud" Adams of Houston, changed the map of pro football in 1960, when, thwarted in their efforts to purchase existing NFL franchises, decided to form their own league. Rounding up other moneyed men, they organized the American Football League that ultimately merged into the greater NFL. Hunt generally gets credit as the founder of the AFL, but without the tangible support of Adams, the new venture would have never gotten off the ground. His father was Boots Adams, the head of Phillips Petroleum and the legendary Phillips Oilers who dominated amateur basketball. Bud had dabbled in sports before as a backup player on the University of Kansas football team, as a boxing promoter, and as the owner of a prime AAU basketball team, the Ada Oilers, over which we clashed because I derided their "amateurism." Now he had a football toy, the new Houston Oilers, who won the first two AFL championships as Adams spent lavishly for talent. In 1962, the third year of play, the Oilers and Hunt's team, the Dallas Texans, topped the young league's two divisions and were to meet in the title game, which prompted this syndicated cartoon of the two young pioneer owners squaring off. The Texans toppled the defending champion Oilers in overtime, but Hunt, discouraged by competing for attendance against "America's team," the NFL's Dallas Cowboys, moved his champs to Kansas City in 1963. Adams stayed in Houston thirty-three more years until he moved his team to Nashville in 1997 to become the Tennessee Titans. He was the senior owner in the NFL when he died at the age of ninety in October 2013.

Adams was by far the more gregarious of the two Texans, a man-about-town surrounded by the likes of Aristotle Onassis and astronaut Alan Shepard at a restaurant gathering I attended when the Oilers played in New York. On a reporting trip to Houston, I was once cajoled by Bud into joining him at a private party where the main focus was to fix up a kindly old judge from West Texas with one of the comely ladies in attendance. He was also a man who spoke his mind, and acted on it, once engaging a Houston sports columnist in a brawl at a league meeting that ended up with both of them sprawling on the floor.

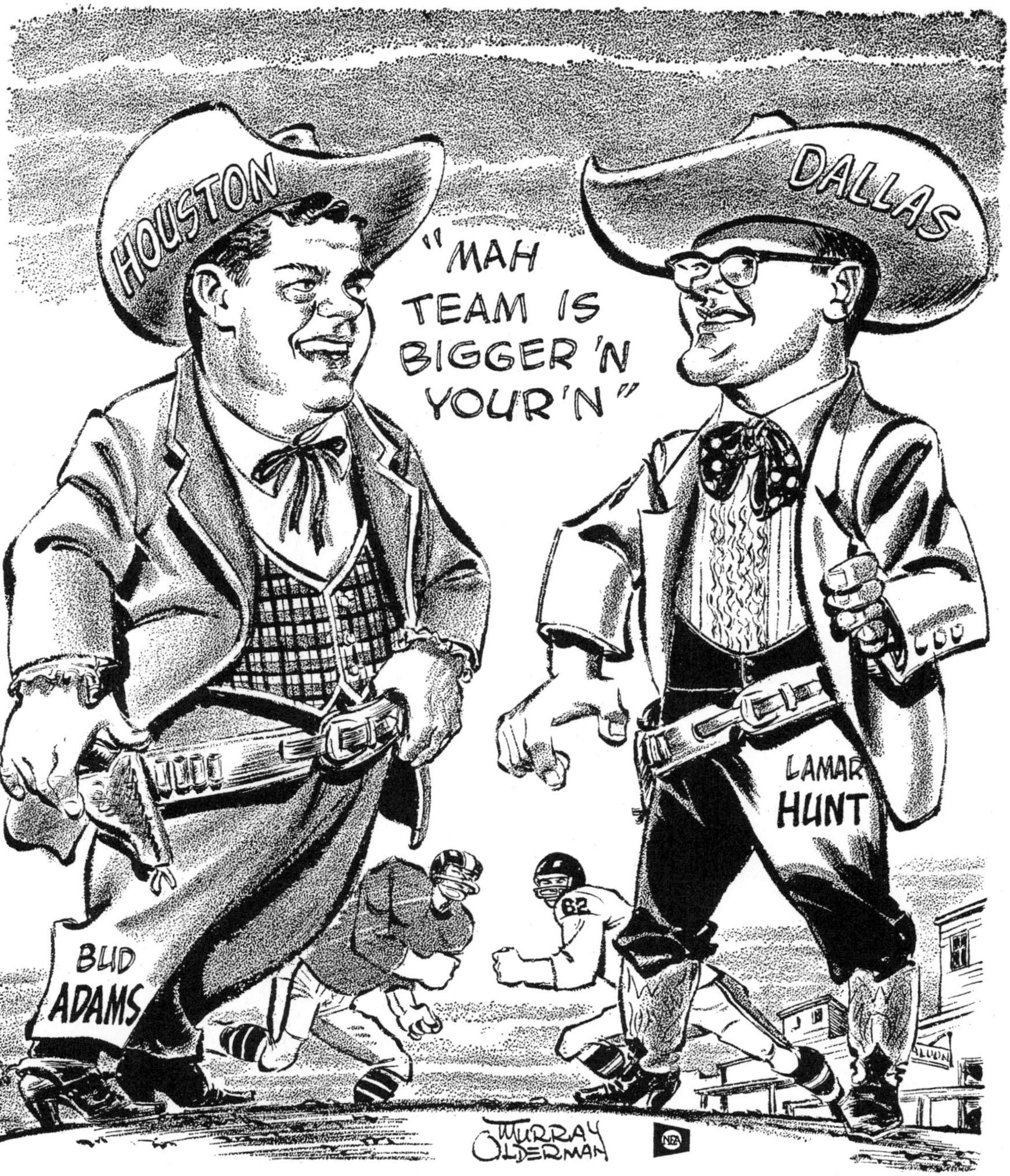
HOUSTON
DALLAS
"MAH TEAM IS BIGGER 'N YOUR'N"
LAMAR HUNT
BUD ADAMS
62
MURRAY OLDERMAN
NEA

Frank Albert

COMING OUT OF anesthesiology on the morning after I had open-heart surgery in 1995, I looked up at the foot of my bed at Eisenhower General Hospital in Rancho Mirage, California, and there stood Frankie Albert. I had no idea how he got there or how he even knew about my medical procedure. Frankie came to check on me from across the street at the Springs Country Club, where he had a home appropriately addressed 2 Stanford Court—he was an all-time Stanford football great. We had become friendly and played tennis together—Frankie even got me in a game with former Vice President Spiro Agnew. He was prominent in his own right as the pioneering college T Formation quarterback. Frankie was a slight guy for a football player, 5'9" and 166 pounds, but quick and gutsy. In 1939, Stanford won only one game with Albert as the tailback in the old Pop Warner Double Wing Formation. Clark Shaughnessy came in the next year and installed the T Formation with the adroit little lefthander under the center. He introduced the bootleg play, hiding the ball on his hip as he faked a handoff and sprinted around the end. Stanford went from 1-7-1 to 9-0 and defeated Nebraska in the Rose Bowl. Frankie was so prominent that he starred in a Hollywood movie, *The Spirit of Stanford*, opposite Marguerite Chapman, with such actors as Lloyd Bridges and Forrest Tucker. He lent me an old video of it stashed in his garage. But he was the most unassuming noted athlete that I ever met, albeit feisty when he had a couple of brews. I did this cartoon and a story for the *Los Angeles Times* on the fiftieth anniversary of that team, which also had Norm Standlee, Hugh Gallarneau, and Pete Kmetovic—all future pro stars—in the same backfield. After Navy service, Albert became the original quarterback of the San Francisco 49ers in the All-America Conference—I saw him lead a huge upset of the dominant Cleveland Browns—and ultimately their head coach. The Morabito brothers who owned the 49ers were so fond of Albert that they gave him five percent of the team, a nice annuity. I first used to see Frankie when he was Lindsey Nelson's partner as a TV analyst, doing Baltimore Colts games. We remained good friends until he succumbed to Alzheimer's disease in 2002.

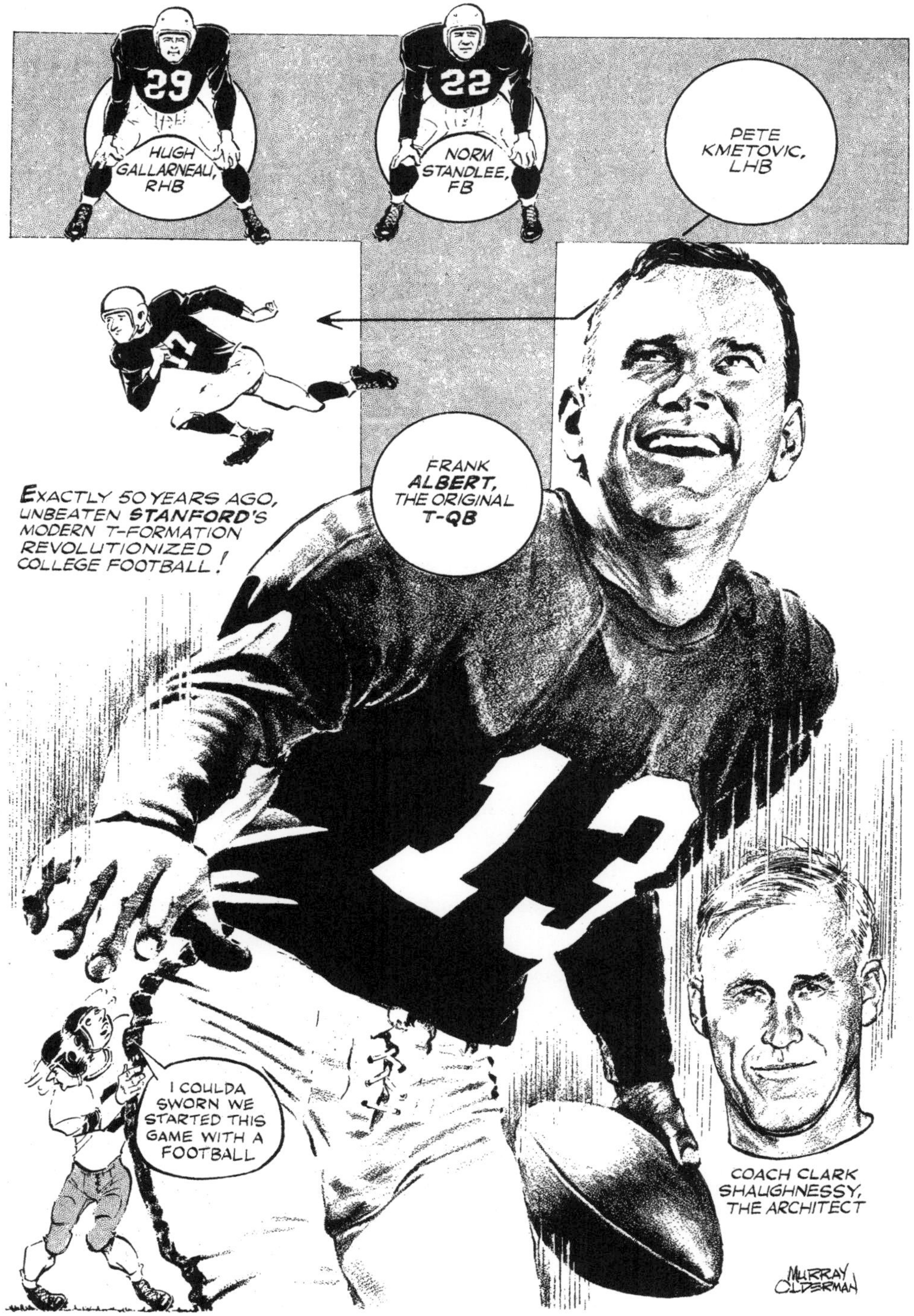
HUGH GALLARNEAU, RHB
NORM STANDLEE, FB
PETE KMETOVIC, LHB
FRANK ALBERT, THE ORIGINAL T-QB
EXACTLY 50 YEARS AGO, UNBEATEN STANFORD'S MODERN T-FORMATION REVOLUTIONIZED COLLEGE FOOTBALL!
I COULDA SWORN WE STARTED THIS GAME WITH A FOOTBALL
COACH CLARK SHAUGHNESSY, THE ARCHITECT
MURRAY OLDERMAN

Alan Alda

A LONG, LONELY weekend was looming as Alan Alda sat on the set of *Paper Lion*, being filmed on location at a small prep academy north of Miami, Florida. There was a break in the shooting for a couple of days. "I miss my wife and kids," he moaned over lunch. "Hey," I said to the young actor in his second film, "you're a big movie star now. Why don't you just get on a plane and go home? You can afford it." And he did and came back refreshed. At the time in 1968, Alan and I both lived in Leonia, a small New Jersey town on the reverse side of the Palisades near the George Washington Bridge to New York. Like me, he played tennis on the town courts and came to a party at my house. He borrowed a coffee-table book I had authored, *The Pro Quarterback*, to help prepare for his role as dilettante author George Plimpton, who as a lark briefly played for the Detroit Lions in training camp and wrote the book on which the movie was based. I was visiting the Florida location because I knew the unit publicist, Mort Engelberg, who enlisted me to draw this cover for the movie's promotional brochure. (Mort later became a successful Hollywood producer, starting with *Smokey and the Bandit*.) There were actual Lions players in the cast, among them Alex Karras and John Gordy, an all-pro guard and president of the NFL Players Association, with whom I was friendly and whose father was Poppa John Gordy, an iconic ragtime pianist in his native Nashville. Alda, who went on to achieve great success in the TV series *M*A*S*H* and was nominated for an Academy Award, amazed me because off-stage he had a genetic stammer and credited his wife, Arlene, a musician, with helping him mask it in his thespian chores. His father, Robert Alda, had been a movie star, and Alan, growing up, cringed at the way complete strangers mauled his dad in public. Alan kept his off-stage life private. He is a delightful, thoughtful man whose creative energies make him more than a mere actor. He has been a screenwriter, director, author, visiting university professor, and social activist. Unlike me, he never left small town Leonia.

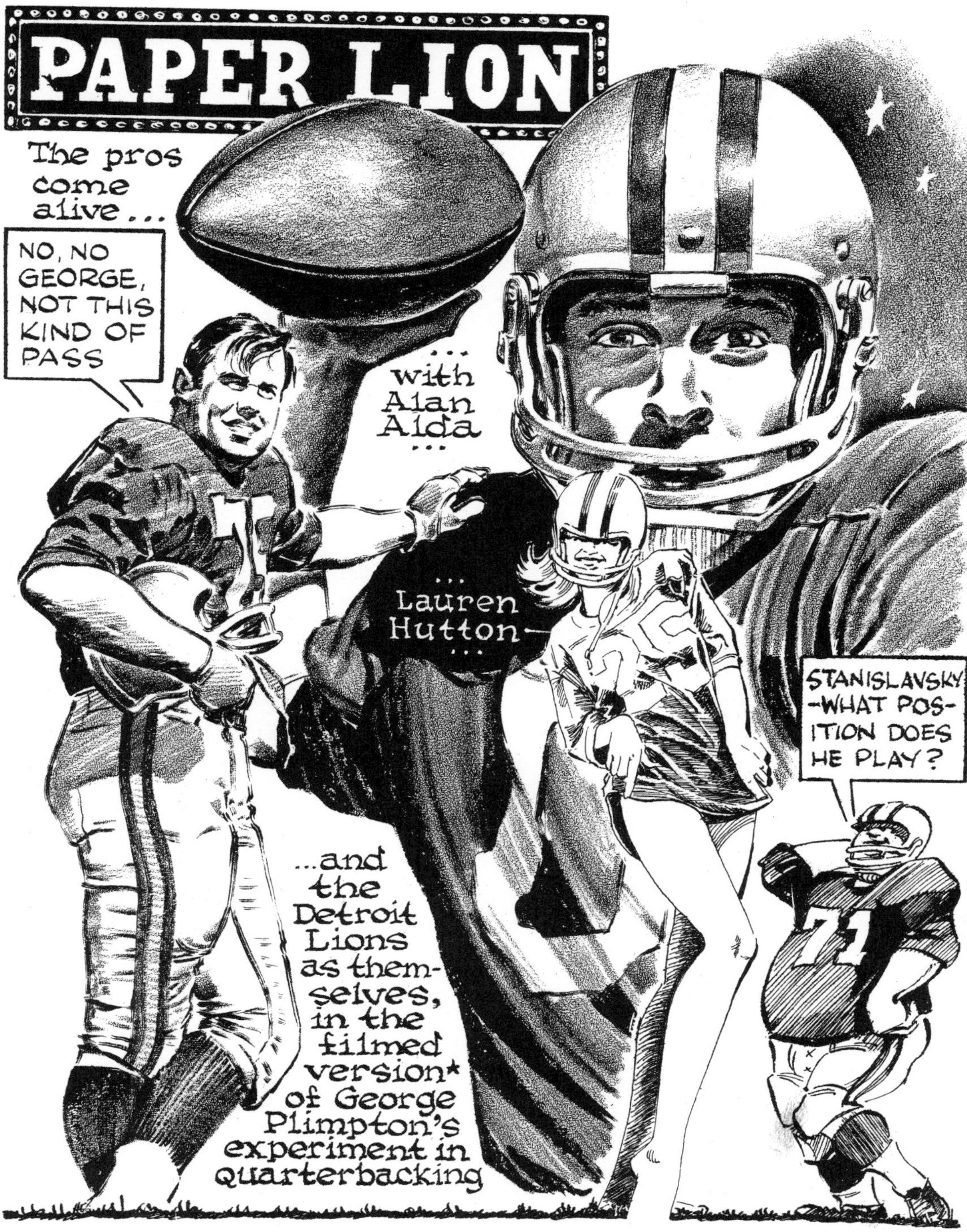
PAPER LION
The pros come alive ...
NO, NO GEORGE, NOT THIS KIND OF PASS
... with Alan Alda ...
... Lauren Hutton ...
STANISLAVSKY -WHAT POSITION DOES HE PLAY?
...and the Detroit Lions as themselves, in the filmed version* of George Plimpton's experiment in quarterbacking

Muhammad Ali

BEFORE HE CHANGED his name to Muhammad Ali and became an American icon, a young fighter from Louisville, Kentucky, was known as Cassius Marcellus Clay and made outrageous statements about his prowess and physiognomy. He came back from the 1960 Rome Olympics as an 18-year-old gold-medalist light heavyweight, paraded around New York by Dick Schaap, an enterprising journalist, charming cynical writers with doggerel poems and loud boasts. He emerged that fall as a legitimate professional heavyweight to revive a sport moribund since the retirement of Rocky Marciano. But there was also an edge to his bragging and disparagement of opposing fighters, which is when I drew this syndicated cartoon, trying to capture some of the frenetic anguish as he sought recognition. In England to fight Henry Cooper in 1966, he and trainer Angelo Dundee were holed up in a suburban rooming house that I visited. A pensive Muhammad Ali—he took on the new name after beating Sonny Liston to become heavyweight champ—sat reclined against a wall near a big punching bag rigged up in a hallway that he'd get up to swat peri-odically. He was tired of boxing, the 24-year-old confided to me, and wanted to quit the ring and devote his life to preaching his new Muslim religion. Yet he fought fifteen more turbulent, episodic years, including historic bouts with Joe Frazier ("Thrilla in Manila") and George Foreman ("The Rumble in the Jungle"). He was generally idolized by young people for his overtly iconoclastic stances on social issues, but I was turned off when he'd look at a crowd of newsmen and derisively call us "white devils." But Ali was also a magnificent athlete with great size and speed and ring craftiness until the punches he took over more than two decades of boxing left him with a diagnosis of Parkinson's disease, a way of masking pugilistic dementia, or what once was called bluntly being "punch drunk." I never saw a man absorb more punishment without throwing a retaliatory punch than Ali, against Larry Holmes in Las Vegas in his next-to-last fight, stopped after 10 excruciating rounds. Careful handling by the people around him shielded Muhammad Ali in his later years and kept his personal decline private.

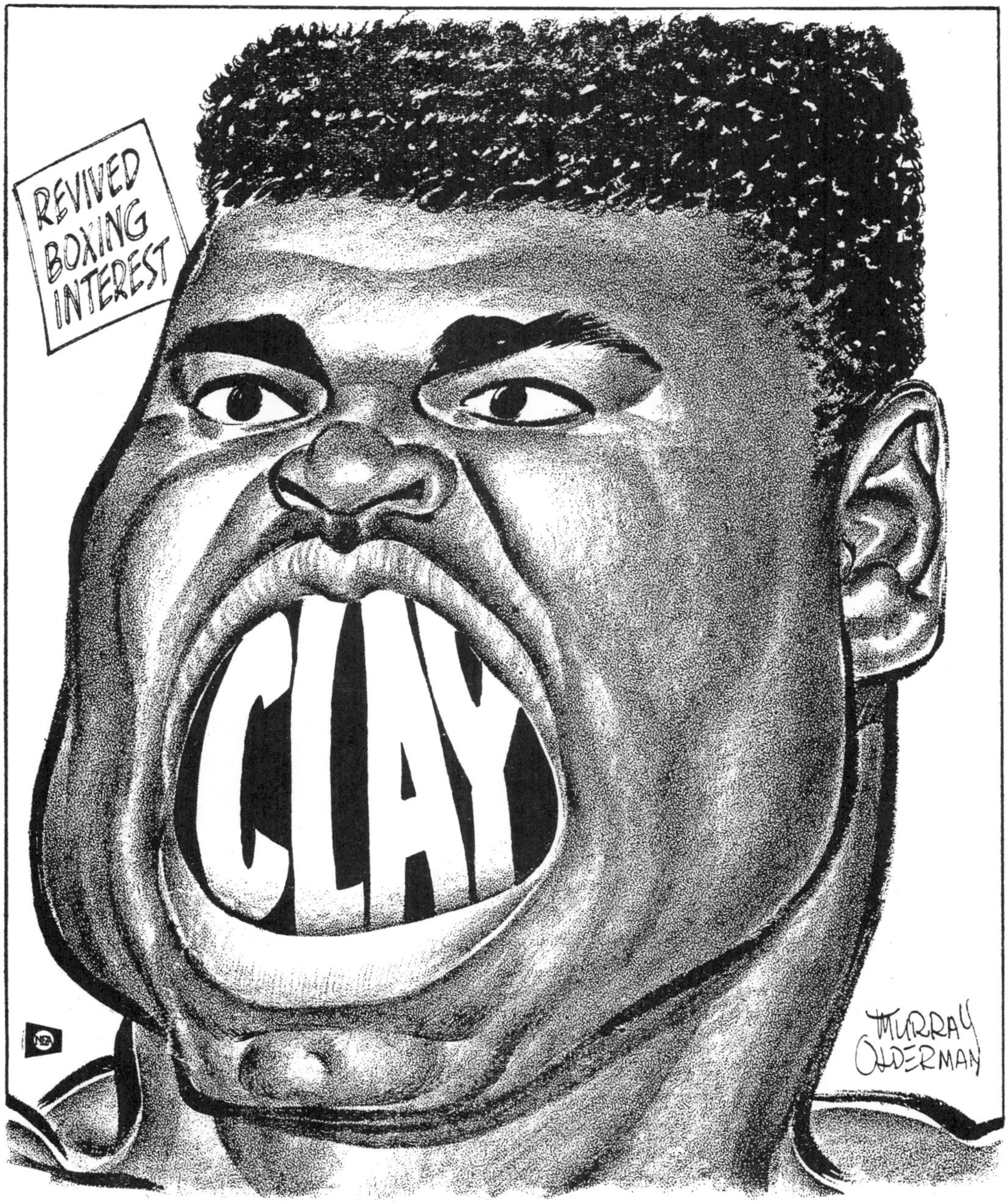
REVIVED BOXING INTEREST
CLAY
NEA
MURRAY OLDERMAN

"Him and His Big Mouth"

Arthur Ashe

ARTHUR ASHE WAS soft-spoken, reserved, and had a quiet demeanor. Hardly the earth-shaking type who would have a profound impact in shaping tennis. He came from the South, with roots in Virginia, but I never detected a Southern accent in his speech. Tennis wasn't the sport of choice for a black kid growing up in Richmond, but Arthur was too slender for football. Growing up on the one court in his "blacks only" playground, his skills were quickly apparent. A benefactor moved him to St. Louis for broader competition, and he earned a scholarship to UCLA, where he roomed with Charlie Pasarell—both future number one players in the U.S. In 1968, he won the first U.S. Open title in the Open era and defied apartheid by playing before a mixed audience in South Africa. At age thirty-two, he upset Jimmy Connors to win Wimbledon in 1975 and become number one in the world. He wrote me a note thanking me for this cartoon. We were in Stockholm at the Masters to close that season when Arthur lost his temper for the first time in ten years, by his count, as zany Romanian Ilie Năstase forfeited their match with his disruptive antics. The next day on the veranda of the hotel where we were staying, Arthur was reading the *International Herald-Tribune* when Năstase swept in and, from behind his back, pulled a bouquet of flowers and said to Arthur, "You beat the shit out of me." To me, Arthur whispered an aside, "He's nuts," and coolly went back to his crossword puzzle. Arthur tragically contracted AIDs from a faulty blood transfusion during his second heart surgery and died at the age of forty-nine.

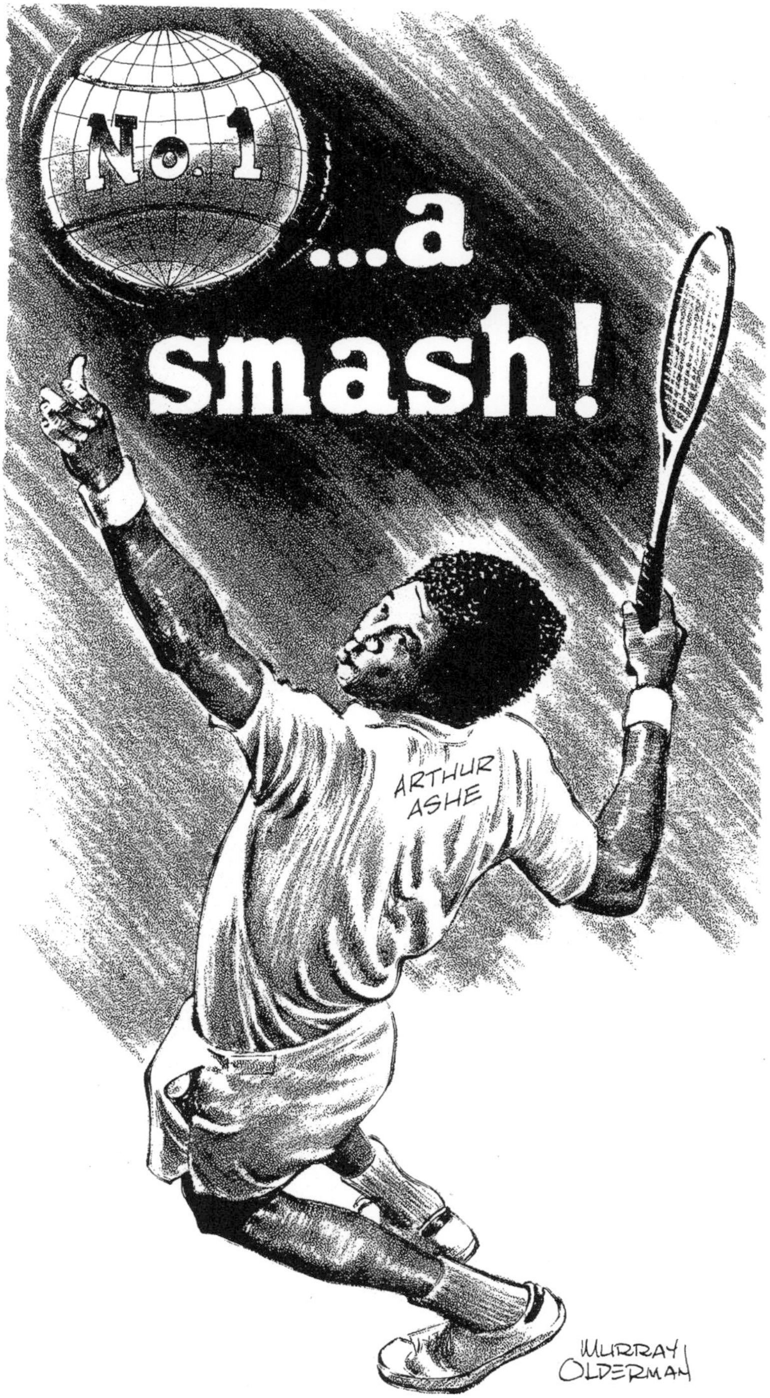
No. 1
...a smash!
ARTHUR ASHE
MURRAY OLDERMAN

Red Auerbach

ARNOLD AUERBACH NEVER liked to lose at anything, even a friendly tennis match at Kutsher's hotel in the Catskills, a hotbed of basketball where he spent some of his summers away from his regular job guiding the Boston Celtics dynasty. He wasn't really redheaded by the time I knew him. Mostly bald, in fact. And he had that gravelly voice and grumpy manner that put people off. But there's no denying the effectiveness of the court leader who won more championships (nine within ten seasons) than any coach in the history of the National Basketball Association until he was eclipsed by Phil Jackson of the Chicago Bulls and Los Angeles Lakers. Despite fifty-six years as coach, general manager, and president of the storied Celtics, right until his death at eighty-nine in 2006, Red was never a Bostonian. He came off the streets in the Williamsburg section of Brooklyn, played basketball at George Washington University in Washington, D.C., where he called home the rest of his life. A hotel room was his domicile all those years with the Celtics. That led to his publicized addiction to Chinese take-out food. His basketball strength was recognizing talent. The title run started in 1956 when he traded "Easy Ed" Macauley and Cliff Hagan to St. Louis for all-time great center Bill Russell. He pioneered the fast break with Bob Cousy, the "Hardwood Houdini," at point guard. He was egalitarian, making Chuck Cooper the first black player drafted in the NBA. The league office sent him a note that it didn't look good for him to be smoking cigars during a game. He responded that he'd stop when other coaches stopped smoking cigarettes (a prevalent habit half a century ago), but amended his habit to light up a stogie only in the final seconds of a game to signify a Celtics victory. I liked bantering with Red. I suggested to him that when Doc Naismith, the game's originator, put up the first peach basket at ten feet high, the average man stood 5'7" tall, and in the modern era, point guards were a foot taller; ergo, raise the basket to eleven or twelve feet. Red dismissed me as an ignoramus. He was a traditionalist. He liked the game the way it was. Which in his case was very good.

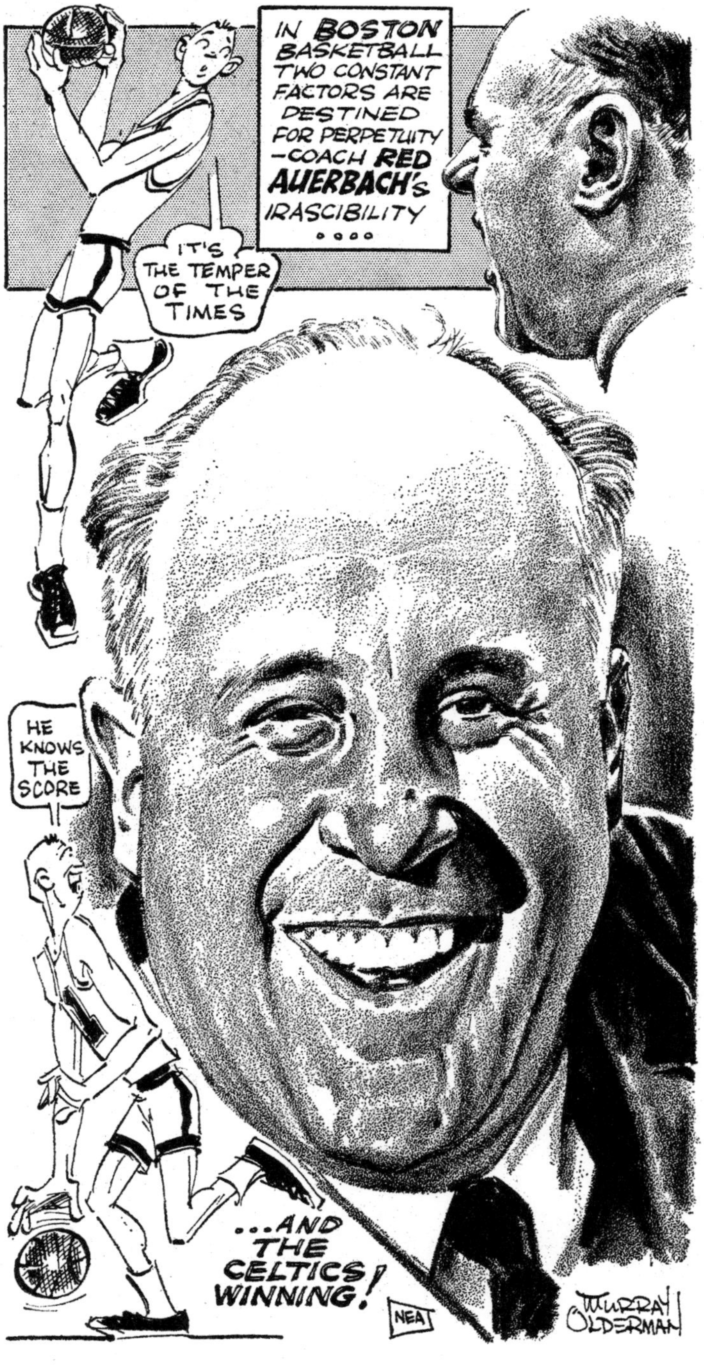
IN BOSTON BASKETBALL TWO CONSTANT FACTORS ARE DESTINED FOR PERPETUITY -COACH RED AUERBACH'S IRASCIBILITY ....
IT'S THE TEMPER OF THE TIMES
HE KNOWS THE SCORE
...AND THE CELTICS WINNING!
NEA
MURRAY OLDERMAN

"Seeing 'Red'"

Rick Barry

IN HIS POST-BASKETBALL career, he was a gifted broadcaster—gabby, bright, glib, good-looking. But Rick Barry, who loved the spotlight, made an unfortunate remark. During a 1981 NBA finals on CBS, a photo of smiling colleague Bill Russell flashed on the TV screen. Barry, working as an analyst, alluded to " . . . that watermelon grin." All hell broke loose and his contract was not renewed. Though he continued as a broadcaster, he slipped into obscurity. That fade-out dims an extremely talented basketball player who ranks with the best of any era. Two sons, Jon and Brent, also had NBA careers, now work as basketball TV analysts, and are more recognizable than the old man—but not in his league as a player. Rick was a 6'7" small forward with great speed and agility and finesse. "His mind," said Phil Jackson, "runs as fast as his feet." With an old-style underhand scoop, he was probably the best foul shooter ever. In his second NBA season, he averaged thirty-five points a game. At age thirty-one he drove the mediocre Golden State Warriors to an NBA title. After the upset of Washington in the final game, he spent the long night flight home to San Francisco writing an epic poem about it and recited it to a victory party assembled at 2:30 a.m., then got me to letter and illustrate it with drawings of the Warriors, distributed as a poster by the team's beer sponsor. Rick could be both likeable and petulant. We were at an airlines celebrity golf tournament, and Rick wanted to play tennis. He had skills, but was rusty from inaction. Losing the first set, he smashed his racket to pieces. He wanted to dominate in anything, and his abrasive personality alienated people. I saw him lose a tennis doubles tournament when Hank Greenberg advised his partner, Bob Klein of the Los Angeles Rams, to move up on Rick's second serve. Macho Rick wouldn't take anything off it and double-faulted for the match. Years later, the now penitent former star offered a *mea culpa*: "I acted like a jerk. Did a lot of stupid things . . . I was an easy person to hate." Rick was intelligent and cognizant enough to accept his failings and added ruefully, "It bothers me that I'm not even liked."

Speech bubble in inset panel: HE'S SUPER AT ANY STAGE

Caption box: RICK BARRY OF THE WARRIORS HAS MADE A QUICK JUMP FROM 'SUPER ROOK' TO ...

Logo: NEA

Title: SUPER SOPH

Signature: MURRAY OLDERMAN

"That Word 'Super' Again"

Johnny Bench

HE CAME OVER to my place to record a video for a sports journalism class I was teaching at the University of Oregon. We reside in the same complex in Rancho Mirage, California, though he keeps ties to Cincinnati, where he played his entire seventeen-year baseball career. Johnny Lee Bench had the credentials to proffer advice to aspiring young journalists. He was, first of all, the greatest catcher in the history of baseball, both offensively and defensively. Not just my opinion—ESPN labeled him so, and a bronze statue of Bench adorns the Reds' Great American Ball Park. He twice led the National League in home runs, three times in runs-batted-in, was twice league MVP, and was an All-Star fourteen times. The only glitch in his active tenure was that he never batted .300. He had a great arm and was agile enough at a compact 6'1" and 200 pounds to dunk a basketball as a high school center in Binger, Oklahoma. He was the natural leader of the "Big Red Machine" that dominated the 1970s, and then segued into a broadcast career. In that videotape, he used words such as "innuendo," "double entendre," and "infallible" in their proper context. "Sports became different with the advent of cable TV," he said. "Everybody became a sports writer. It became a zoo." He felt it personally: "When I went through a divorce, they started writing gossip." He was particularly upset with Dick Young, a New York columnist who insinuated, " . . . either I was gay or I was beating my wife." He never talked to Young again. Bench was outspoken about his teammate Pete Rose's exclusion from the Baseball Hall of Fame for gambling: "He played with the best credentials one could have. But the Hall of Fame is sacred. There are rules, and you don't break them." Bench has maintained an active life, raised a second family, even tried the Senior circuit as a professional golfer (he hits the ball a mile, but not always straight), and has strayed into diverse ventures. He gave me a rubber wristband that he was promoting and promised it would cure whatever ailed me. Oh, my aching back.

Reggie Jackson (OF)

Henry Aaron (OF)

Frank Howard (OF)

Ron Santo (3B)

Rod Carew (2B)

Rico Petrocelli (SS)

Denny McLain (P)

Willie McCovey (1B)

Ron Perranoski (RP)

Johnny Bench (C)

LEADER IN PLAYER VOTES CAST FOR NEA'S THIRD ANNUAL ALL-MAJOR LEAGUE TEAM WAS THE YOUNG CINCINNATI CATCHER!

MURRAY OLDERMAN

"Autographed Ball"

Yogi Berra

CREDIT JOE GARAGIOLA for a good part of the legend of Lawrence Peter "Yogi" Berra. They came out of The Hill section of St. Louis and played the same position: catcher. Garagiola was the smooth, slick talker. Yogi never knowingly said a funny thing in his life. Whatever malapropisms he inadvertently dropped—"nobody goes to that restaurant any more; it's too crowded"—were generally embellished by his buddy Joe. So "it ain't over 'til it's over" became part of the American sports lexicon. Yogi looked funny with his gargoyle-like squat body, knock-knees, toes pointed out, cockeyed grin. But he was a superb athlete, surprisingly quick, hit with power, and was adaptable enough to play the outfield during his Hall of Fame career with the New York Yankees. He was also "baseball smart" enough to manage both the Yankees and the Mets into the World Series. There is a Yogi Berra Museum in New Jersey, where he always lived. Accessible and genial, Yogi and his wife Carmen used to come out my way for celebrity golf tournaments. I did this verbose spoof of Yogi for the program of an annual New York baseball writers' dinner, a winter sports highlight in Gotham when he became the Yankees' skipper.

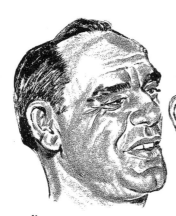

"In assaying the potentiality of our Yankee ensemble, I am neither self-delusive nor obtuse...."

"We have, in the aggregate, a pride of deservedly lionized baseball practitioners...."

"...and while I am a neophyte in the intricacies of managerial strategems...

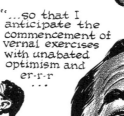

"I feel we shall be sustained by our legacy of a winning heritage, carefully nurtured by my able predecessors...

"...so that I anticipate the commencement of vernal exercises with unabated optimism and er-r-r...

(AND DAN)

"...AW HELL, FELLAS, YEZ KNOW WHAT I MEAN!"

("...DON'TCHA?")

MURRAY OLDERMAN

—NEWSPAPER ENTERPRISE ASSOCIATION—

George Blanda

EVERY QUADRAGENARIAN SHOULD have a year like George Blanda had in 1970. He was forty-three years old and comfortably settled into a niche as a placekicker with the Oakland Raiders, occasionally stepping into the lineup to relieve Daryle Lamonica at quarterback. In one five-week period, beginning October 25, he astounded pro football with a series of clutch performances. First, he entered the game with the score tied 7-7 and threw three touchdown passes and kicked a field goal to beat the Pittsburgh Steelers, 31-14. A week later, his 48-yard field goal with three seconds to play salvaged a 17-17 tie with Kansas City. The third week he came off the bench and threw a scoring pass that tied Cleveland with 1:34 remaining, then kicked a field goal as time expired for a 23-20 win. The following Sunday he took over for Lamonica again in the fourth quarter and hit Fred Biletnikoff for a touchdown with 2:28 left to beat Denver 24-19. The incredible streak ended with a Blanda field goal—he was among the last of the straight-ahead booters until soccer-style kicking prevailed—in the closing seconds to beat San Diego 20-17.

George was tough and gritty and sometimes hostile. You didn't have a conversation with him. You bantered with him. He spent his first pro decade with the Chicago Bears— Sid Luckman, their iconic leader, derided him to me as anti-Semitic—and signed with the fledgling American Football League in 1960 to lead the Houston Oilers to two titles, setting numerous passing records. Al Davis picked him up at the age of 39 for the Raiders and prolonged his career to an NFL record 26 seasons. Blanda became Davis's confidant for life. George traveled with the team almost until his death in 2010. Davis dedicated a Raider weekend to him and brought in Blanda's old teammates from all over the country to honor his memory. George, a Pennsylvania coal miner's son who made Chicago his home, wintered near me. I got along fine with crusty George, who was an invaluable source of football history for his period of play covering four different decades.

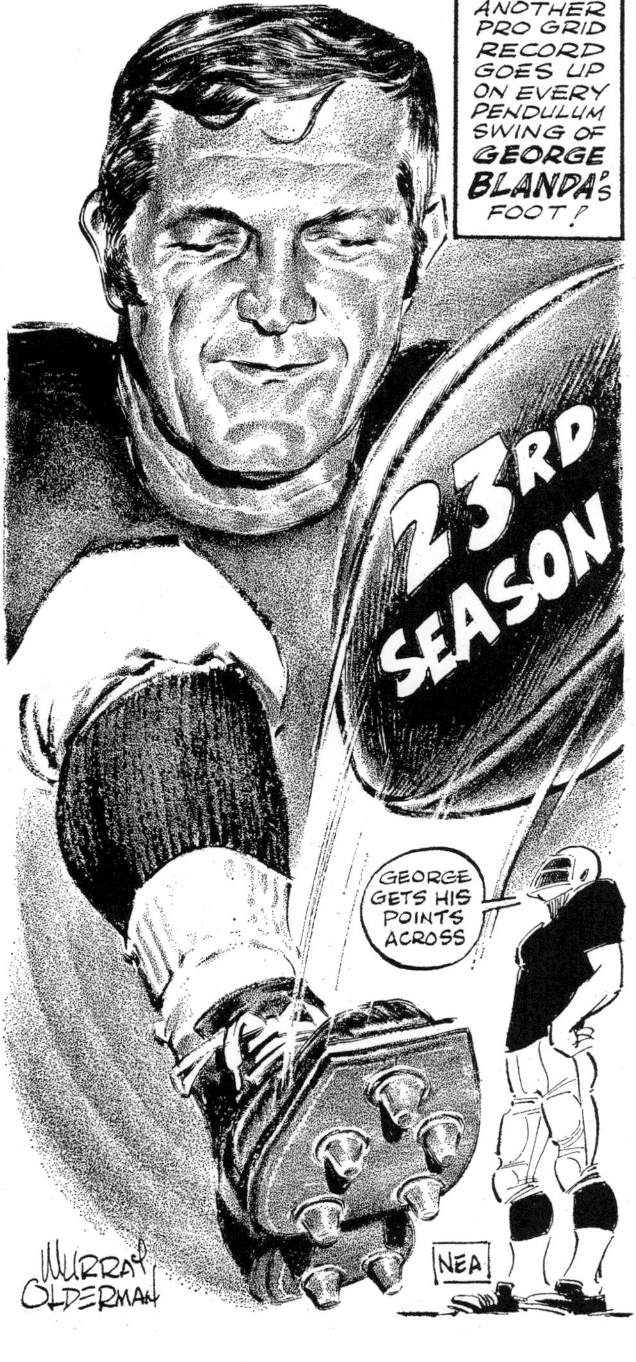
ANOTHER PRO GRID RECORD GOES UP ON EVERY PENDULUM SWING OF GEORGE BLANDA'S FOOT!
23RD SEASON
GEORGE GETS HIS POINTS ACROSS
MURRAY OLDERMAN
NEA

"...and Still Kicking"

Jim Bouton

IN THE PAGES of *Ball Four*, Jim Bouton's notably irreverent book about baseball, built around the diary of a season, the old Yankee pitcher recounts the following episode earlier in his career: "In September 1966, when the Yankees were in ninth place, twenty-six-and-a-half games out of first place, Murray Olderman of Newspaper Enterprise Association asked me what I thought was wrong with the Yankees. After carefully examining our statistics and lofty place in the standings I said, 'I guess we just stink.' The distortion was only minute.

"[Manager Ralph] Houk called me into his office. 'Olderman made you look bad,' he said. 'The players are all upset. I'm sure he misquoted you. You've got to be careful when you talk to these guys.'

"'Well, he didn't misquote me,' I said.

"Houk didn't think that was enough. He thought I should say more. I asked him like what. And he said I should apologize to the players. I said I would. And I did. I'm not sure what for, though. I mean, boy, did we stink."

As a writer, you learned to gravitate toward players with whom you felt a mental kinship. Bouton was one of these. Besides, early in his major league tenure, he was a helluva pitcher. And good copy besides. Jim (nicknamed "Bulldog") spoke his mind. He backed it with twenty-one wins in 1963 and eighteen in '64, when he pitched two World Series victories over the Cardinals. But arm troubles shortened the hard-throwing pitcher's big league span. Baseball people—both players and front office—considered his inside baseball revelations in *Ball Four* a betrayal of privacy, and he was ostracized socially. Bouton slipped to the minors and developed a knuckleball that got him stints with Seattle and Houston as a relief pitcher. When that petered out, tenacious Bulldog pitched for semi-pro teams in Bergen County, New Jersey, where we both lived. After a seven-year absence he caught on for a final short fling with the Atlanta Braves, did some TV work and acting, and wrote a couple more books. I saw him again at a Topps baseball cards luncheon in Greenwich Village, where he was the featured guest. By then he had become immersed in ballroom dancing.

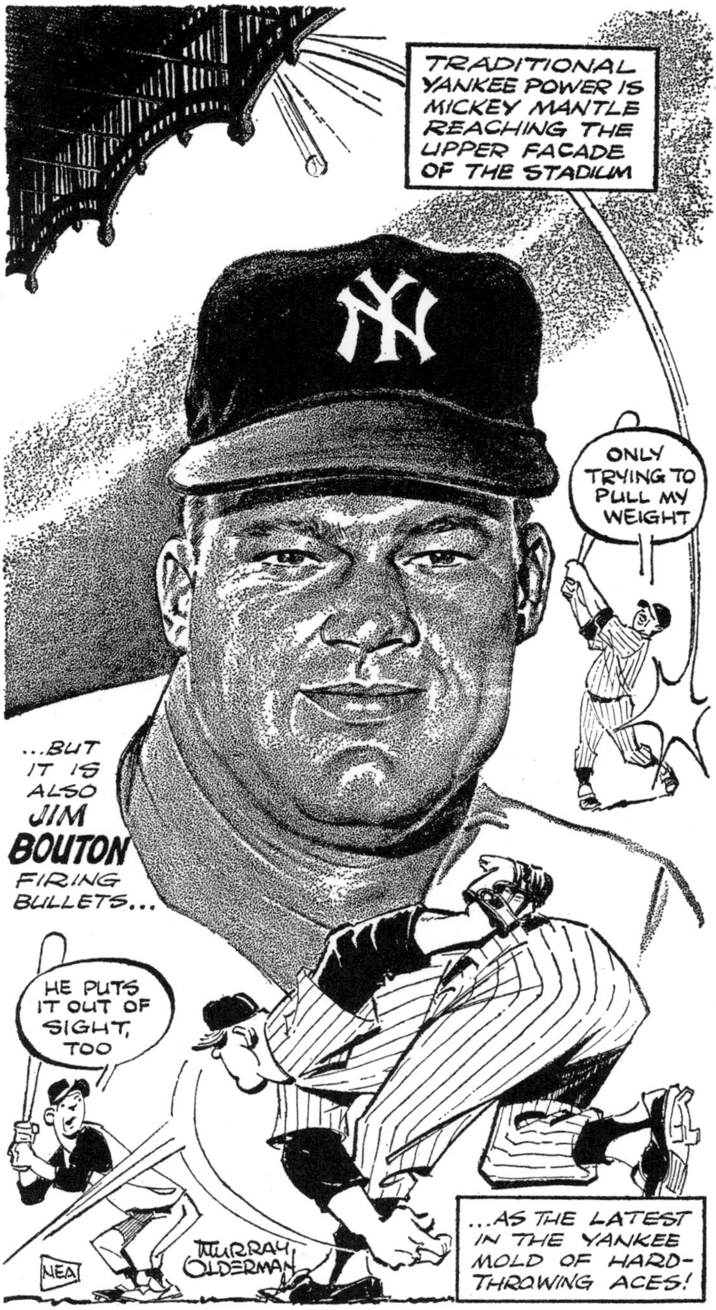

TRADITIONAL YANKEE POWER IS MICKEY MANTLE REACHING THE UPPER FACADE OF THE STADIUM
ONLY TRYING TO PULL MY WEIGHT
...BUT IT IS ALSO JIM BOUTON FIRING BULLETS...
HE PUTS IT OUT OF SIGHT, TOO
...AS THE LATEST IN THE YANKEE MOLD OF HARD-THROWING ACES!
NEA
MURRAY OLDERMAN

"Fire Power"

Bill Bradley

A TALL YOUNG man hung around the golf press tent for the U.S. Open at Bellerive, outside St. Louis, in 1965, performing odd errands. He was from nearby Crystal City, Missouri, where his father was president of the bank. He said he went to Princeton and played basketball there. That's like Pavarotti saying, "I sing." Bill Bradley was merely the greatest basketball player in the history of the Ivy League schools, but unassuming about his exploits. He scored more than 2,500 points; still the Ivy League record, averaged thirty per game, and won the James E. Sullivan Award as the nation's top amateur athlete in 1965 (the same year as that U.S. Open near St. Louis). Instead of capitalizing on his cagey talent, he went off to Oxford University on a Rhodes scholarship for two years and then played ten productive seasons with the New York Knicks, a vital cog on two NBA championship teams. He was almost under-sized as a forward at 6'5", couldn't jump, and had moderate speed. He made only one All-Star game appearance. But he was heady and steady. When he retired, he used his smarts to run successfully for the U.S. Senate from his adopted state of New Jersey. He served two additional terms as a Senator, gained some national prominence, and in 2000 made an unsuccessful bid for the Democratic Presidential nomination.

The tight-jawed athlete that I first met matured into a jowly politician, but one thing never changed—the upraised left eyebrow that lent him a perpetually quizzical look. He also remained unfailingly polite and accessible. In addition to his politics, Bill was a thoughtful, inquisitive elder statesman of basketball—he wrote a brilliant memoir, *Life on the Run*, that is among the finest sports books ever produced by an athlete. He had five other books published, delving into subject significantly more serious than basketball. When I ran across him again some years later in San Francisco—I have a vague recollection that it might have been in connection with a charitable penny-pitching contest that a local restaurateur ran and attracted such political figures as Governor Mario Cuomo of New York—Bill Bradley was still cordial and whimsical.

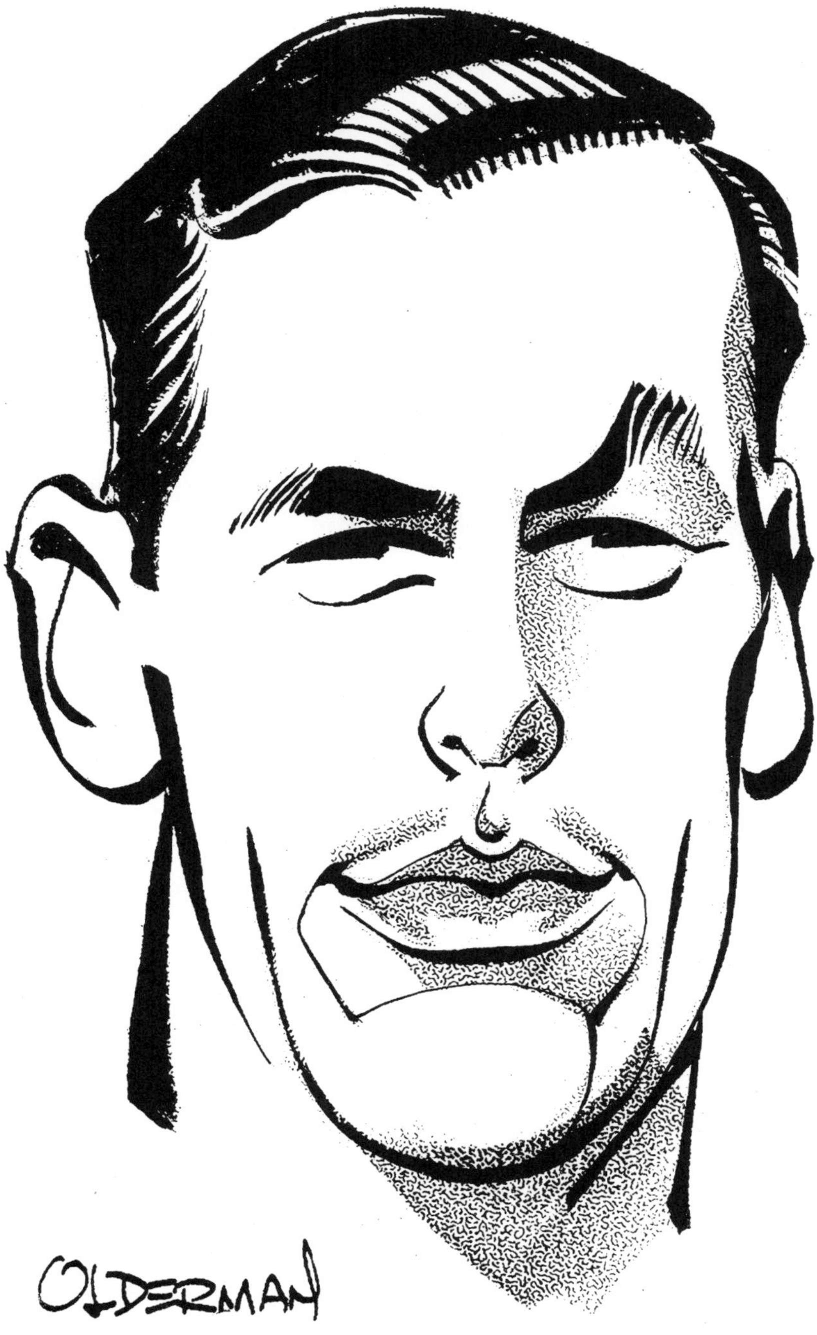
OLDERMAN

John Brodie

THE TROPHY THAT John Brodie is gazing at signified ultimate approval by his peers. In the 1950s, I suddenly realized that pro football, exploding in popularity, never chose a most valuable player. Through my NEA syndicate, and with the cooperation of the teams (and later the NFL Players Association), I sent ballots to every player in the league. The inaugural choice to receive the symbolic first Jim Thorpe Trophy in 1955 was wide receiver Harland Hill of the Chicago Bears. He was followed by such other Hall of Fame notables as Jim Brown, Frank Gifford, and Johnny Unitas. Brodie, a geriatric quarterback for the San Francisco 49ers, was the players' choice for MVP in 1970, with George Blanda the runner-up. I made the trophy presentation at an award special televised nationally by CBS, hosted by Glen Campbell, before the Pro Bowl game. At thirty-five, Brodie, whose development had chased venerable Y.A. Tittle from San Francisco to ultimate greater fame with the New York Giants, threw a league-leading twenty-four touchdown passes and was still agile enough to incur only eight sacks. In 1966, he had dickered with the Houston Oilers to jump to the rival AFL, kept the restaurant napkin on which a million-dollar offer was written, and collected a cool $900,000 after the leagues merged.

Brodie spent sixteen seasons with the 49ers, trailing only Unitas and Fran Tarkenton in passing productivity. Retiring after '73 and switching to TV golf commentary, the athletically versatile Brodie went on the PGA Senior golf tour, and actually won a tournament, but suffered a stroke in 2000 that has limited his physical activity. Innately cocky, he also had an edge to his personality, honed from all those years, despite his individual recognition, of not winning an NFL title. We remained in friendly contact, with Brodie based in La Quinta, California, until recent years, a fixture at Palm Springs area sports gatherings. I kept my association with the Jim Thorpe Trophy until I left NEA in 1987—it is still awarded by the Jim Thorpe Association in Oklahoma City. In 1957, two years after I devised the honor, the Associated Press took my cue and instituted a Most Valuable Player award of its own that is now, with the AP's broad newspaper reach, accepted as the NFL's recognition of its top player.

WITH A NOD
TO GEORGE
BLANDA,
OAKLAND

to
JOHN BRODIE,
Quarterback,
San Francisco
The
Jim Thorpe
Trophy
1970

NEA

MURRAY
OLDERMAN

Jim Brown

IT WAS CHILLING to sit across from Jim Brown on the set of *The Dirty Dozen*, a movie being filmed in a suburb of London. We were discussing truth. "I speak the truth," he said bluntly. "If you deny me, you're my enemy." He added reflectively, "Maybe it's what Cassius Clay says when he calls all white men the devil." He looked at me balefully and pointed a finger in my face. "You're 'Charlie,' baby. I'm fighting you." I flew across the Atlantic that summer of 1966 to see Brown because there were rumors the great Cleveland running back was going to quit football and become an actor. Which he did after an unsurpassed reign of nine years as the best football player I ever saw, regardless of position. Brown's attitude was motivated by a critical review I had written of his autobiography. My story about our meeting appeared in the *Cleveland Press* as the Browns started training camp without their fullback. Perversely, the white players started calling the black players "Charlie." I next saw Brown that fall in Houston, ringside at the Muhammad Ali-Cleveland Williams fight. He was now part of the Ali entourage. He looked at me, stuck out his right arm, and with his typical half-smile said, "You shot me down, baby, but I'll still shake your hand." Brown was no stranger to me. I saw him at a Cotton Bowl score three touchdowns for Syracuse in a 28-27 loss to TCU. After his second season as a pro, my syndicate flew him to New York to receive the Jim Thorpe Trophy as the NFL MVP, presented on the Ed Sullivan Show. We took him to dinner at Toots Shor's, and he was a daunting presence in an immaculately tailored dark suit with vest, completely filled out by his 6'2" frame and 228 pounds of rippling muscle. We talked about Jackie Robinson and his activism for black athletes, and Brown noted softly, "I admire Jackie Robinson for what he says, but I couldn't say those things myself—it's not my way." Later, speaking out had become his way when his remarkable athletic feats gave him a forum. After no one has matched his record of leading the NFL in rushing for eight (of the nine) seasons he played, his acting career kept him occupied for more than a decade, and in recent years he has worked with inner city children and has done consulting work for the Browns.

With his famed "Green Bay sweep" in which the running back follows pulling linemen and a fullback and then veers off to find the open space, Vince Lombardi introduced the "run to daylight" concept to professional football. In Cleveland, Jim Brown felt Paul Brown's precise running routes had constricted him. This cartoon was one of a series on football jargon drawn for NBC and inserted into game telecasts.

RUN TO
DAYLIGHT

MURRAY
OLDERMAN

Paul Brown

DURING THE EARLY 1950's domination of pro football by his team—they won six straight Eastern Conference titles and three NFL championships—I went to Cleveland to do a series on the Browns. I met Paul Brown in his office and asked if I could watch practice and talk to some players. "You can't do that," he said brusquely. Why not?

"You're from New York," he answered. "How do I know you're not working for the Giants?" He finally relented, and I watched the Browns and talked to Otto Graham, Dante Lavelli, and others. A year later, I was in Philadelphia to see the Browns lose their opener to the Eagles, 28-10. I approached their locker room with trepidation because I'd heard what a terror Brown was after a defeat. I hadn't seen him since my Cleveland episode. He stood in a hall off the entrance, tight-lipped with a snap-brimmed brown hat. Before I could identify myself or blurt a question, he said, with a flicker of a smile, "Say, that was a very nice, professional series you did about us."

Talk about being won over. Nobody could convince me the martinet leader of the Browns—named for him, of course—was a bad guy. Eight years later, I went to Cleveland again and asked why, at fifty-four, in his thirty-third coaching year, he continued the stressful tension. He smiled: "This is my fun, my life. What else would I do?" What he did, after clashing with new Browns owner Art Modell, was head a new expansion franchise in Cincinnati as chief owner and head coach and brought it to Super Bowl status. I was writing a book called *The Running Backs* and wrote a letter asking him about the origins of "the draw play," which he devised. A couple of weeks later, there was an answer, written longhand in pencil on the reverse side of my letter, beginning with this explanation: "My wife suffered a heart attack—she is still critical. I am writing this as I wait and stand by—sorry not written sooner." And then he detailed, adding a diagram, how the play evolved through a practice mistake, a delayed handoff to fullback Marion Motley. At sixty-seven, he finally stepped from the sidelines and into owner/elder statesman. At NFL functions he always greeted me with a warm, shy smile and a chuckle. Paul Brown was really the architect of modern, post-World War II football with his intensive attention to detail and such innovations as individual playbooks that were more valuable than the Bible, plus calling offensive plays through guards shuttling in from the sidelines.

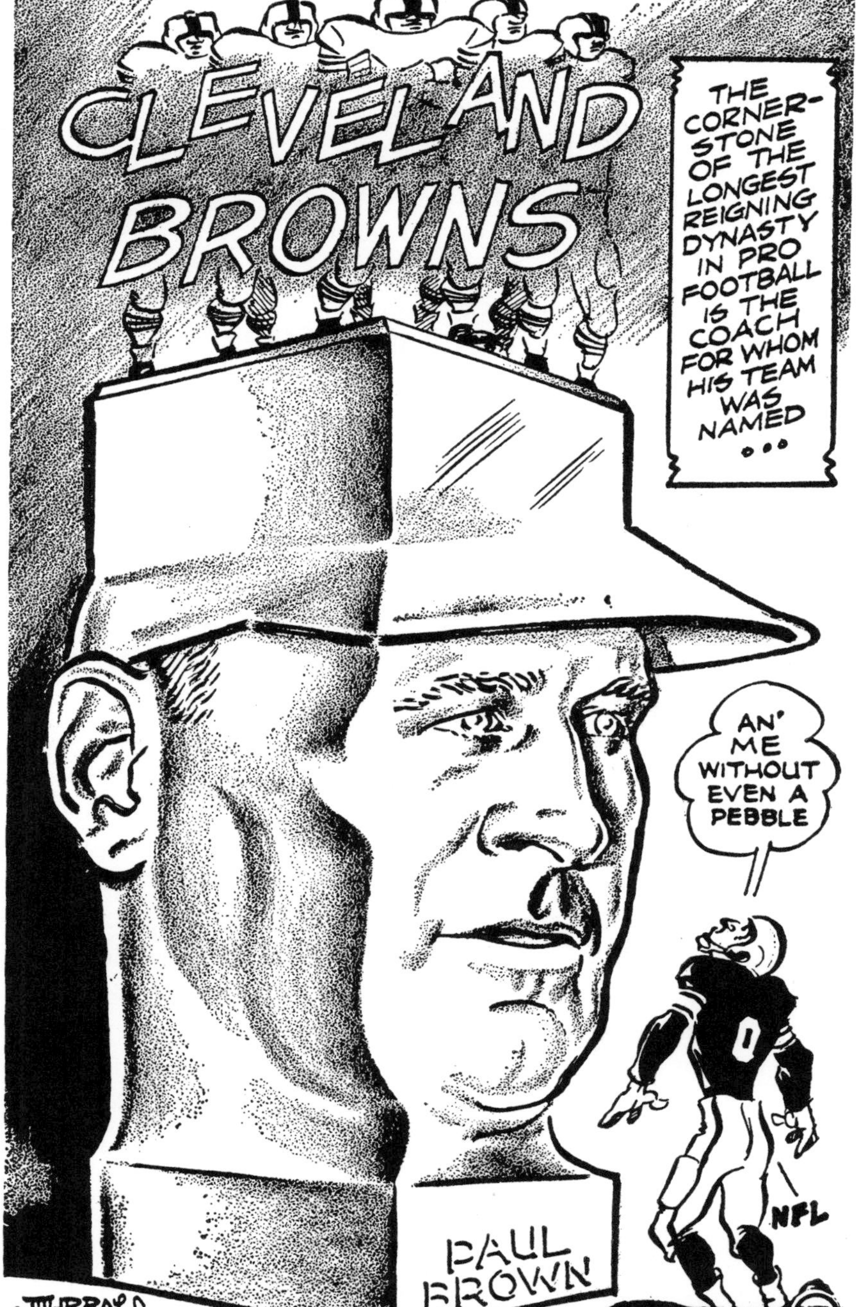
CLEVELAND BROWNS
THE CORNER-STONE OF THE LONGEST REIGNING DYNASTY IN PRO FOOTBALL IS THE COACH FOR WHOM HIS TEAM WAS NAMED ...
AN' ME WITHOUT EVEN A PEBBLE
PAUL BROWN
NFL
MURRAY OLDERMAN
NEA

Bear Bryant

A LADY CALLED from Atlanta to tell me she had purchased online a signed letter from Paul Bryant to me as a birthday gift for her husband, a huge Alabama football fan. Could I tell her more about Bryant's reference to a story we were doing? It was a simpler time in sports when "Bear," as he was known, ruled the Crimson Tide as it won the 1961 national championship, and he was named Coach of the Year. I mailed him a note suggesting that we collaborate on a series for my syndicate. He replied that he would be delighted. No mention of remuneration, which will shock today's sports agents. We met in Harrisburg, Pennsylvania, where he was doing a coach's clinic, and that fall NEA ran my three-part series "by Paul Bryant as told to Murray Olderman," illustrated with this cartoon. I dredged up a copy of the series and sent it to the lady in Atlanta. Bryant's teams in his twenty-five seasons at Alabama went on to claim five more national titles. One winter, Darrell Royal, of Texas, and Bryant came to New York for a coaches' meeting and called me to escort them for a night on the town. I took them to Harlem and the famed Apollo Theater, where comedian Nipsey Russell was the featured performer. They sat us right

down in the front row, the only white audience members. Nipsey looked down and asked Bear's companion, "Where are you from, honey?" She replied, "Buhm-in-ham, Alabama." Nipsey smiled broadly, "Why, you one of us." Bear could only handle it for a few minutes. He got up and strode out to a cab back to mid-Manhattan.

In 1970, after USC shredded Alabama, 42-21, with Sam Cunningham of the Trojans running wild, Bryant became the first to integrate football in the South. His strength as a coach was a disciplined, tough program and prompting talent like a whip-armed quarterback from Beaver Falls, Pennsylvania, to come down and ignore the stench of the paper mill in Tuscaloosa. That was Joe Namath's start. Often overlooked is Bryant's own athletic background. He got his nickname when a sideshow came to his native Fordyce, Arkansas, and the strapping 12-year-old Bryant was induced to wrestle a muzzled bear for a dollar a minute. He matriculated as a 6'4" end at Alabama, playing on a winning Rose Bowl team. The other end, All-American Don Hutson, became a legendary receiver for the Green Bay Packers. Together, they later ran a dry-cleaning business in Tuscaloosa.

IN THE WAKE OF BEAR BRYANT's 1958 RETURN TO ALABAMA ...
...THE CRIMSON TIDE HAS EMERGED AGAIN AS A NATIONAL POWER!
MURRAY OLDERMAN
NEA

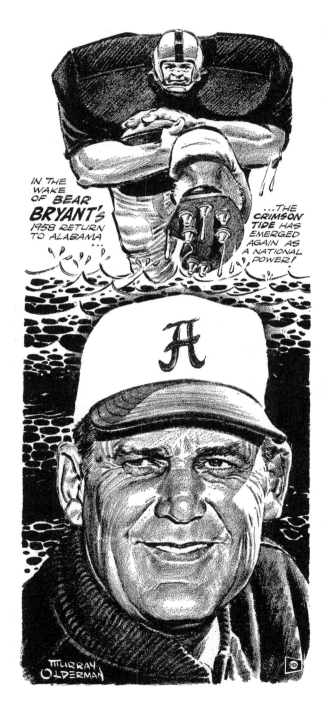

"High Tide"

Dick Butkus

THE CHICAGO BEARS were spending a week at Rickey's Hyatt in Palo Alto before a game with the San Francisco 49ers, and I went there to check out their storied middle linebacker, Dick Butkus. He had already won the George Halas Trophy, an award I instituted for the NFL's top defensive player. Over a hulking body, more than prototypical for this glamorous defensive position, there was this dichotomous baby face. I'd been around Butkus before when he emerged as the nation's top defensive collegian at Illinois and embodied the animalism of the sport, a player who wallowed in its physicality. In a coffee table book I wrote, *The Defenders*, Russ Thomas, the Detroit general manager, was quoted: "He's an annihilating sonuvabitch." Off the field, however, he was pacifistic and taciturn, one of nine kids in a Lithuanian immigrant family from a tough, hard-hat Chicago neighborhood, converted by football into moder-

ate affluence with enough polish to spout Shakespeare publicly and appreciate what the game did for him. "Football was something I could make a living at," he said, "so I'm the luckiest guy around. A lot of guys can't say that." Abe Gibron, then the coach of the Bears, said, "When he doesn't think something's important, he's shy and withdrawn. But then the whistle blows, and he goes sort of crazy." Butkus was once accused of biting a referee on the arm. He retorted, "If I'da been dumb enough to do that, I'd have bitten his arm off." He played nine ferocious years in the NFL to merit consideration as the best ever at his position. "My goal was to be recognized as the best," he said candidly. "When they say middle linebacker, I want them to mean Butkus." He later gravitated into a broadcasting and acting career in which he played self-deprecating roles, but always with dignity.

DICK
BUTKUS,
LINEBACKER,
CHICAGO BEARS
NFL DEFENSIVE
PLAYER OF YEAR,
1970

MURRAY
OLDERMAN

NEA

Roy Campanella

THE LIBRARY OF Congress, publishing a book on Italian-American athletes, included my cartoon of the Hall of Fame catcher, Roy Campanella, and his hitting exploits. I had noticed a unique pattern in his playing days with the Brooklyn Dodgers. Starting in 1951, when he won the first of his three MVP awards and achieved a career best .325 batting average, he fluctuated between high and low seasons through 1956. Thus, "Alternating Current." He hit with power (forty-one homers in 1953) and productivity. His 142 runs-batted-in that same season was the record for a catcher. His father was the son of an Italian immigrant; his mother was African-American. "Campy" was the second man to break the color line in major league baseball, following Jackie Robinson, after playing in the Negro Leagues and Mexico. He was a great receiver, too, with a cannon arm that picked off two Yankee runners in a World Series. Campy had completed a decade in Brooklyn and was preparing to move with the Dodgers to Los Angeles when, going home on an icy road on the north shore of Long Island, his car skidded into a utility pole and overturned, leaving him paralyzed from the chest down the rest of his life. The stocky Campanella was the opposite of Robinson in personality—genial, even-tempered—and a natural leader. My lingering recollection of Roy Campanella is a gab session in the Dodgers dugout, with the garrulous catcher telling me stories and giggling. I think he would have been the first black manager in the majors.

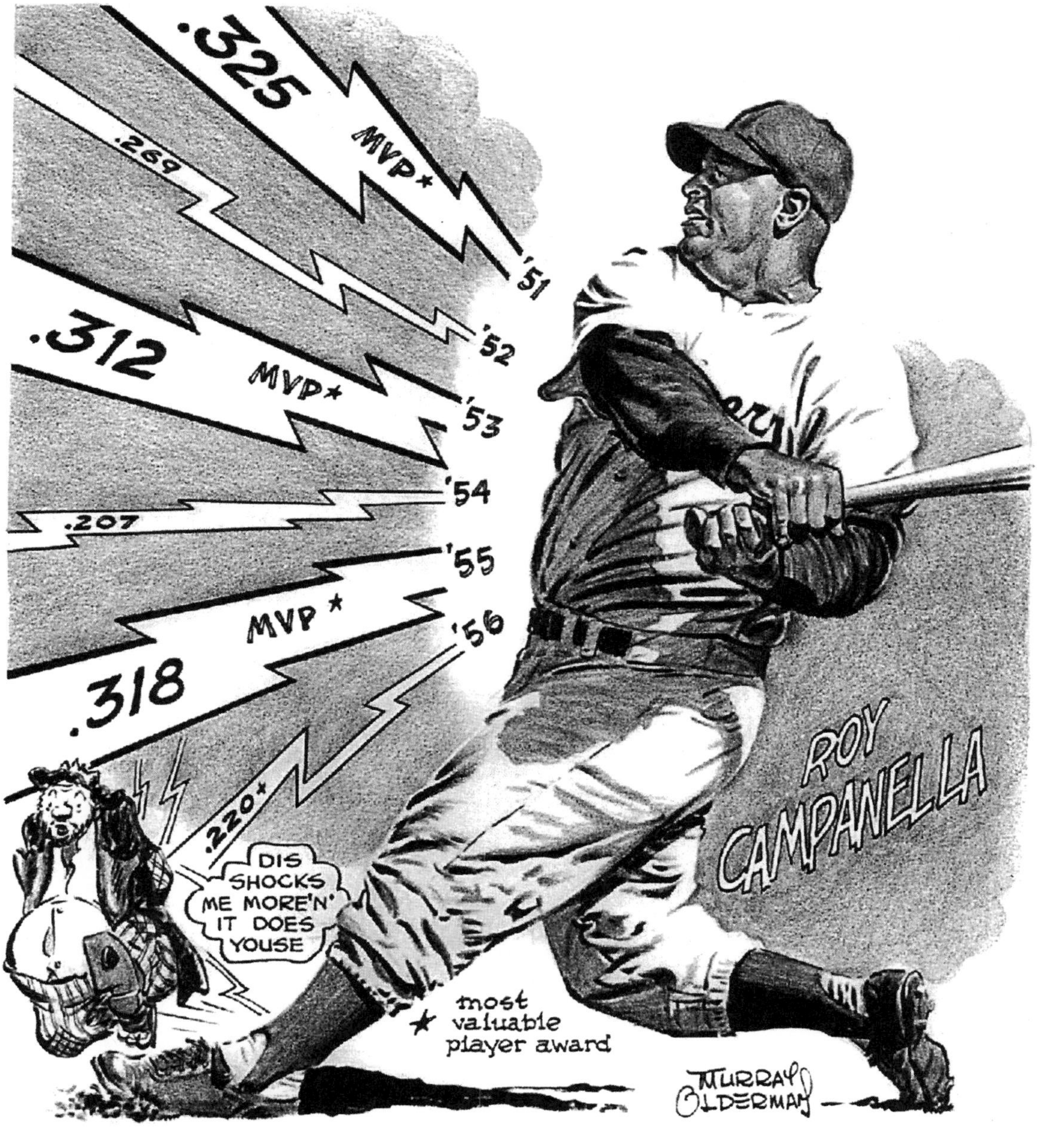
.325
MVP*
.269
'51
'52
.312
MVP*
'53
'54
.207
'55
MVP*
'56
.318
.220+
DIS SHOCKS ME MORE'N' IT DOES YOUSE
ROY CAMPANELLA
★ most valuable player award
MURRAY OLDERMAN

"Alternating Current"

Billy Cannon

IN NEW ORLEANS to help select the Football Writers Association of America All-American team, I decided to detour on a Friday night in 1959 to Baton Rouge to watch the nation's most exciting running back in action. Undefeated LSU was trailing #3 ranked Ole Miss late in the fourth quarter in a slanting rainstorm as Billy Cannon retreated to his 11-yard line to catch a punt and head upfield. He eluded seven tacklers to complete an historical eighty-nine yard touchdown run for the 7-3 victory by the Bayou Bengals. Cannon, one of the most enigmatic characters ever in sports, had it all: 6'1" tall, a muscular 216 pounds, ran one hundred yards in 9.4 seconds, could have been a national shot-putting champ. Billy won the Heisman Trophy that year. Pete Rozelle, NFL commissioner-to-be, signed him secretly to a Los Angeles Rams contract. Bud Adams of the new AFL Houston Oilers also signed him for $100,000 (a huge sum at that time) under the goal posts of the Sugar Bowl and won the legal battle for his services. As a rookie, Billy rebuffed me in a post-game interview. The next week, I got a letter from him, a first ever for me by any athlete, on Oiler stationery, with the following, in his handwriting:

Dear Mr. Olderman,

I'm sure that this letter will come as a big surprise to you. The reason I'm writing is to apologize for the rude way I acted in the dressing room after the game Sunday.

Cannon led the Oilers to the first two AFL titles, leading the league in rushing. In 1962, he was pancaked on a tackle when a San Diego linebacker landed on him, and tore muscles in his back. He was never the same runner. Al Davis of Oakland traded for him, converted and bulked him up to tight end, and he made All-AFL in 1967. Meanwhile, he studied dentistry and post-football became a highly successful orthodontist in home town Baton Rouge, raised a thriving family, yet strangely was involved in a millions-of-dollars counterfeiting scam in 1980 that sent him to federal prison for two-and-a-half years. Since release, he retrieved his dental license, was hired by the Louisiana penitentiary system, and re-formed its medical services. A strange life saga of one of the most inexplicable athletes ever.

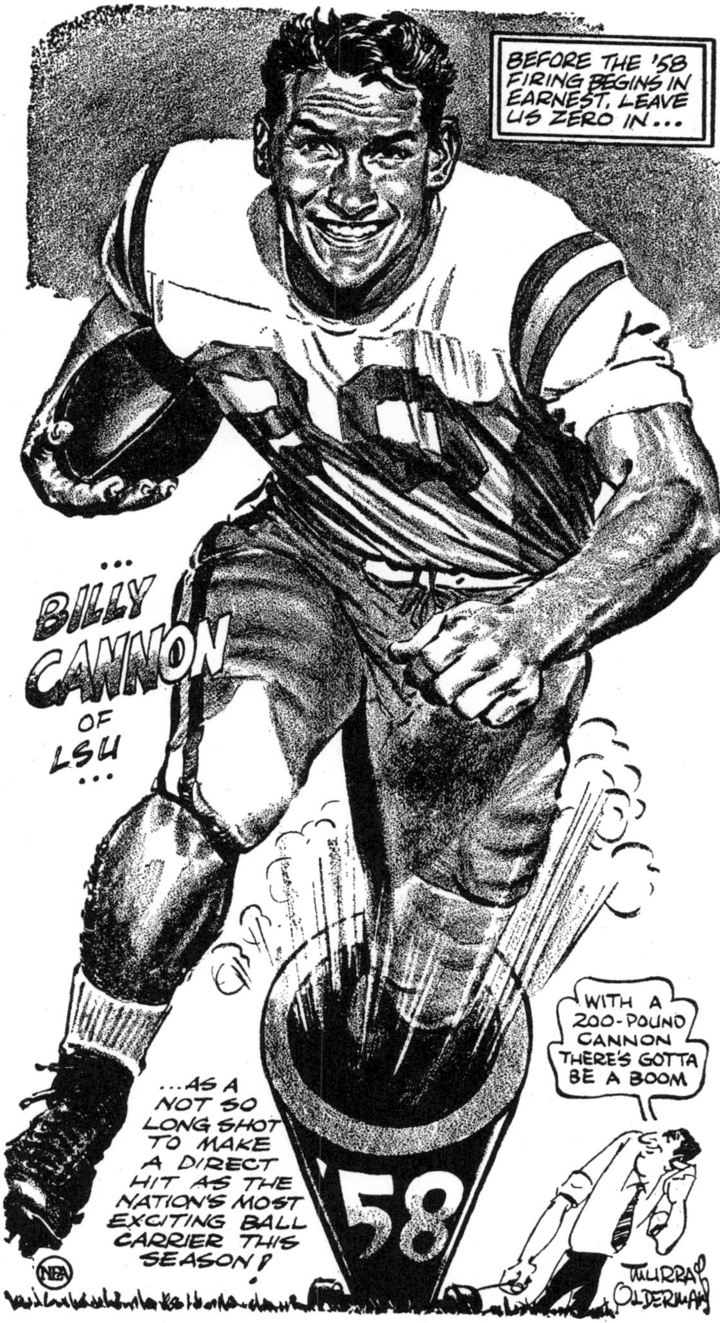

BEFORE THE '58 FIRING BEGINS IN EARNEST, LEAVE US ZERO IN...
...BILLY CANNON OF LSU...
...AS A NOT SO LONG SHOT TO MAKE A DIRECT HIT AS THE NATION'S MOST EXCITING BALL CARRIER THIS SEASON!
WITH A 200-POUND CANNON THERE'S GOTTA BE A BOOM
'58
NEA
MURRAY OLDERMAN

"Opening Shot"

Wilt Chamberlain

ONE OF THE most embarrassing moments for me in sports was my first glimpse of Wilt Chamberlain. Already a high school basketball legend in Philadelphia, he was spending the summer at a New York Catskills resort, Kutsher's Country Club, as a busboy. Harry Grayson, the NEA sports editor, was with me to watch summer basketball in that hotbed of the Borscht Circuit. Pulling on a cigar, Grayson saw this immensely tall seventeen year old sitting placidly in a veranda chair, bent knees almost at a normal man's height. He slowly walked around Wilt's chair, completing a full circle, peering at the youngster as if he was from outer space, then flicked ashes from the cigar and walked off without a word, completely insensitive to the kid's feelings. So unbelievably rude that I wince recalling it. Wilt shrugged it off. He was comfortable in his height (7'1"), desensitized to comments tall people draw: "How's the air up there? Is it snowing?" He had only one hang-up. He despised being called "Wilt the Stilt". He wanted to be "The Big Dipper." Wilt was agile enough to double as a track star at Kansas. He had a good repertoire of shots and was a strong defender. He dominated the NBA the moment he joined the Philadelphia Warriors in 1959 and was league MVP that rookie season. Wilt lived life extravagantly, embellished by such claims as having slept with 20,000 women. His greeting was a big smile and a cheery, "My man!" Yet I sensed a lonely searching in him. One Sunday morning he showed up at my tennis club. He had driven 125 miles just to practice his serve with our pro. And then he drove back 125 miles to his palatial home in Los Angeles. Over fourteen NBA years, Chamberlain averaged thirty points per game, including an astounding fifty point average for the entire 1961–62 season, scoring one hundred points on a memorable night against the New York Knicks in Hershey, Pennsylvania. The knock on Wilt was that in the decade they competed directly against each other, the Boston Celtics, Bill Russell's team, won nine NBA titles to one for Wilt. I thought it was unfair because Russell was always surrounded by better players. The Big Dipper did produce championships for the Philadelphia 76ers and Los Angeles Lakers. And he was a nice, genial guy to be around. Without circling his chair.

President's
Cup
· · ·

Wilt Chamberlain

"Endorsement"

63.

Roberto Clemente

THE TRAGIC NATURE of the death of Roberto Clemente tends to obscure the extraordinary talent he exhibited as an athlete. On the eve of December 31, 1972, he took off in a plane from San Juan International Airport, in his native Puerto Rico, on a mercy mission to Nicaragua. The community-minded Clemente, a renowned eighteen-year major league star, the foremost Latino in the game at the time, had sent three planeloads of food and supplies to beleaguered Managua, hit with a devastating earthquake, but corrupt officials diverted the contents. Clemente chartered a fourth plane and decided to go along on this New Year's Eve to make sure the cargo got to the right hands. The plane barely got off the ground, banked sharply, and plunged into the Atlantic Ocean. His body was never recovered. Posthumously, he was inducted into the Baseball Hall of Fame a year later. He grew up, the youngest of seven children, working alongside his father in the sugar cane fields of rural Carolina, Puerto Rico. Baseball was his ticket out. The Brooklyn Dodgers signed him to a minor league contract for Montreal. This was one talent Branch Rickey let get away as the Pittsburgh Pirates grabbed him in the rookie draft a year later. He spent his entire major league career there, leading the small market Pirates to two World Series titles, getting a hit in all fourteen games—in 1971 he hit the deciding homer in a 2-1 seventh game victory over the Baltimore Orioles. He amassed a career .317 batting average, topping the National League four times, hitting with power, and establishing himself among the greatest defensive right fielders ever (twelve Gold Gloves), with a cannon throwing arm. He didn't have the pizazz of a Willie Mays personality because language barrier difficulties limited him at first. When announcers tried to call him Bobby, he insisted on Roberto. In our dugout conversations, he was sensitive about the slights endured by being a black Latino in baseball. He was a guy who believed in giving back—he served in the U.S. Marine Corps reserve, where he overcame a back injury. His off-seasons were largely devoted to charity work. A Roberto Clemente Award was instituted annually for a player of outstanding skills who excels in community services and is presented during the World Series. Before his death, he capped his playing career by getting his 3,000th major league hit in his last at-bat.

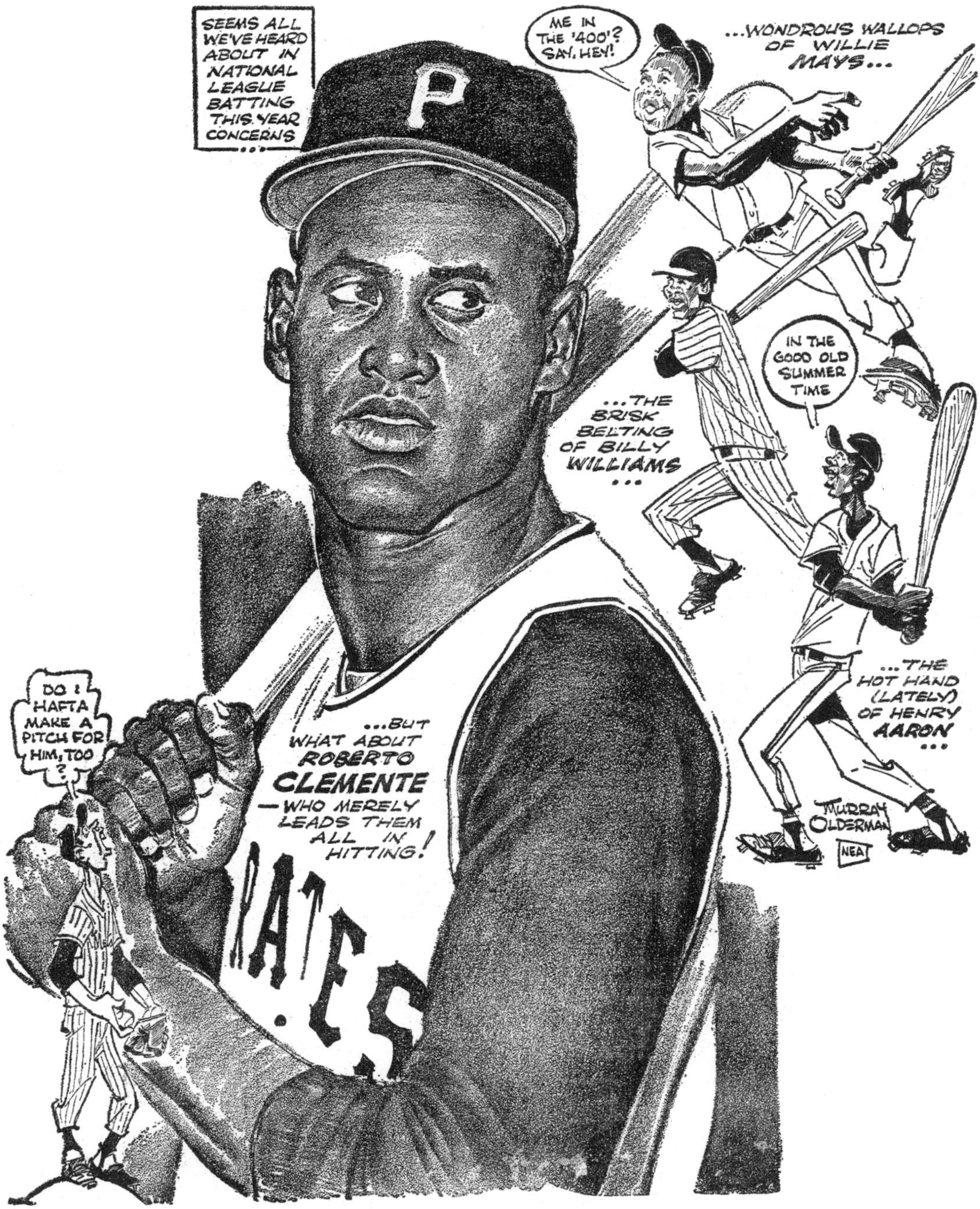
SEEMS ALL WE'VE HEARD ABOUT IN NATIONAL LEAGUE BATTING THIS YEAR CONCERNS ...
ME IN THE '400'? SAY, HEY!
...WONDROUS WALLOPS OF WILLIE MAYS...
...THE BRISK BELTING OF BILLY WILLIAMS ...
IN THE GOOD OLD SUMMER TIME
...THE HOT HAND (LATELY) OF HENRY AARON ...
DO I HAFTA MAKE A PITCH FOR HIM, TOO ?
...BUT WHAT ABOUT ROBERTO CLEMENTE —WHO MERELY LEADS THEM ALL IN HITTING!
P
RATES
MURRAY OLDERMAN
NEA

Charlie Conerly

THE MARLBORO SIGN in Times Square showed off this leathery guy in cowboy duds with dents in his nose and gray at the temples, a tattoo on the forearm, a lit cigarette dangling from his thin lips. Hardly the look you'd associate with a virile pro football player. But there was no mistaking Charlie Conerly, the venerable quarterback of the New York Giants, once the hottest topic in the five boroughs. Charlie was a World War II Marine corporal who fought in the bloody invasion of Guam and had a carbine rifle shot out of his hands. The native Mississippian returned to college at Ole Miss and led the nation in passing as an All-American single-wing tailback. As a twenty-seven-year-old rookie for the Giants, he was the tailback in Steve Owens's A-formation until Jim Lee Howell, who once caught his passes, converted him to a quarterback. Charlie led the Giants to an NFL championship in 1956, played 14 NFL seasons, threw almost 3,000 passes, and at 40 was the oldest man at the time to play his position. Charlie, a taciturn man, was underappreciated for his role in making the Giants the showcase team as pro football boomed in popularity. He and his buddy, Frank Gifford, would sit in the back of the plane returning from a road trip, sipping furtively from flasks, exercising the perks of old guard warriors. They helped new offensive coach Vince Lombardi master the complexities of a pro offense. He had a special forte of being able to pass in dismal weather conditions. Charlie was one of the grittiest players ever, absorbing considerable punishment over the years as the Giants went through yo-yo up-and-down periods, never complaining when his pass protection broke down and he became the butt of public criticism. I had only one negative moment with him. The Giants had drafted a young quarterback, Lee Grosscup, as his eventual successor, and I collaborated with Grosscup on a big article for *Sports Illustrated*. The Giants were training at the Bear Mountain Inn up the Hudson. Charlie came up to me on the sidelines and said, "That was a horseshit story." That was it—typically laconic. Charlie and his wife Perian, a pro football author, were part of the Manhattan social scene right through the Marlboro days, then faded gracefully back to Clarksdale, Mississippi, where he was known as "Roach," and ran a string of shoe stores.

JIM THORPE TROPHY

Professional football's most coveted award has come of age this year...

...IN THAT THE MEN OF THE NATIONAL FOOTBALL LEAGUE HAVE HONORED THEIR ELDEST...

Charley Conerly!

MURRAY OLDERMAN

Jimmy Connors

WHILE ACKNOWLEDGING HIS greatness as a tennis player, I regarded Jimmy Connors as among the most churlish athletes I have encountered. At thirty-nine, he reached the U.S. Open semi-finals in a memorable match against twenty-four-year-old Aaron Krickstein in which he trailed 2-5 in the fifth set and milked the Flushing Meadows crowd with pump fists and leering tactics to demoralize his young opponent. His on-court demeanor was mean-spirited, arrogant, self-centered, callous, and insensitive in dealing with both his fellow players and fans. He was blatantly vulgar in some of his gestures. He was consistently abrasive and contentious. I brushed up against him and his Prince Valiant hairdo at a tennis press conference in which he chastised me for daring to ask a follow-up question to a brusque comment he made. I saw enough of him from a measured distance to know I didn't want to get any closer. Yet no one ever got more out of himself physically. At 5'10" and 150 pounds, he didn't measure up to most of his contemporaries. There were gaps in his game. He lacked a strong first serve, though he compensated with spin and wily placement. His forehand could be inconsistent. But he exerted himself brutally, hit out on every shot, ran every ball down, and had remarkable longevity. Raised in Belleville, Illinois, across the Mississippi from St. Louis, Connors was taught and coached to prominence by his mother, Gloria. At nine, he played in his first U.S. boys national tournament. Gloria took him to Southern California at sixteen to be mentored by Pancho Segura, and by nineteen he was playing doubles with Pancho Gonzales. He was among the first to abandon the traditional wooden racket for a taut steel frame that transformed modern tennis. The truth is, he merits inclusion with the all-time greats of the game, and after he was ranked number one in the world for five straight years, I wrote "Jimmy Connors deserves to be regarded as a national treasure in tennis." His record of 109 ATP tournament titles in tennis' open era might be as durable as Joe DiMaggio's fifty-six-game hitting streak in baseball, and it included eight Grand Slam triumphs. No one, however, will convince me he was a nice guy.

FIREMAN'S FUND PROGRAM, SAN FRANCISCO

MAY 1974

Howard Cosell

IN THE NEW York Giants' locker room, Howard Cosell confronted Frank Gifford at his cubicle, and said patronizingly to the all-pro running back who would one day share a broadcast booth with him, "Young man, your milieu is incontrovertibly unexcelled in the pantheon of the gridiron, but not in front of a microphone." I happened to be standing there and pointed out to Howard that he had mangled the use of "milieu." For all his flaunted erudition, Cosell would jumble syntax. That was not my first encounter with the polysyllabic broadcaster. I took my wife to a Giants' baseball game, seated directly behind home plate in the old Polo Grounds, and was explaining the nuances of the sport. On the other side of her sat this guy who countermanded everything I told her. He introduced himself as Howard Cosell, a lawyer representing Monte Irvin, the Giants outfielder, and new to broadcasting. He devised of a show for which he enlisted Chris Schenkel (I wrote Schenkel's radio show) and then got behind the mike himself. What followed was a meteoric rise in sportscasting. Besides being bombastic, Howard was truly brilliant in bringing a new dimension to describing sports. The

Brooklyn native changed his name from Cohen to Cosell, put on a hairpiece, and told it like it was. Occasionally, Howard would go overboard with self-importance, but he had a keen sense of justice, tremendous retention, and innate ability to talk off the cuff in his distinctive nasal New York style. Monday Night Football became an institution mostly because of him. I liked Howard, but did clash with him once or twice. He was producing a heavyweight championship broadcast in Las Vegas with Chris Schenkel as the voice, and in a restaurant encounter accused me of diverting Chris from the job at hand (believe me, bon vivant Schenkel needed no one to guide him astray). Howard's iconoclastic stands on sports issues—he was among the first to champion Muhammad Ali—didn't endear him to the establishment, and he wrote a couple of books that took potshots at the people with whom he worked and was virtually ostracized from the business. He spent his last couple of years in bitter seclusion. Yet he should be given credit for bringing a fresh tone and a strident, investigative approach to the coverage of major sports in America.

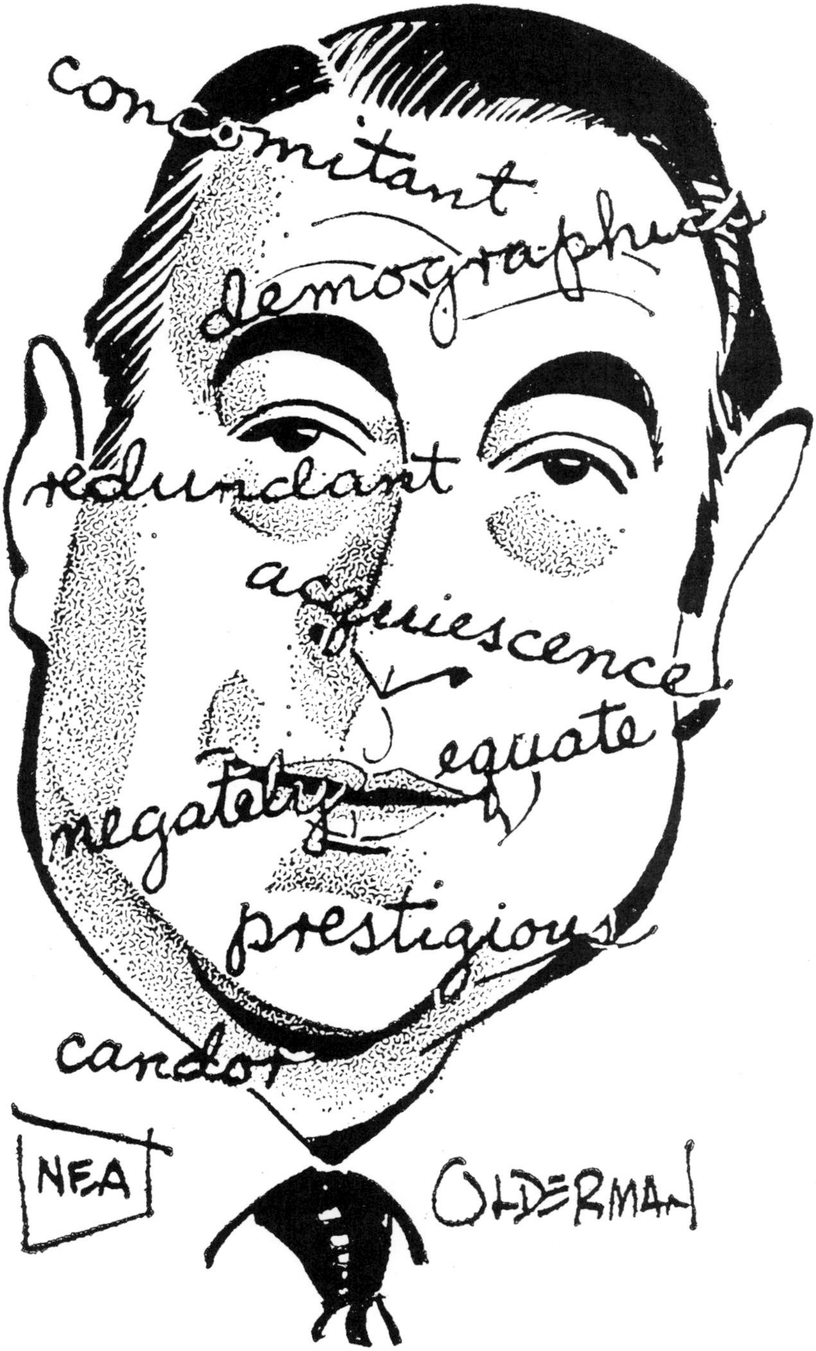
concomitant
demographics
redundant
acquiescence
equate
negatory
prestigious
candor
NEA
OLDERMAN

Bob Cousy

GROWING UP IN a French-speaking home on Long Island, Bob Cousy rolled his "r"s in a Gallic style that he never overcame, even when he went into broadcasting as a pro basketball analyst. I prompted his broadcast partner, Chris Schenkel, to roll the "r" Cousy style in his introduction of the former Boston Celtic great at a testimonial dinner. Cousy took the ribbing good-naturedly. He was low key off the court, but he was the most spectacular player in the early NBA, somewhat of an anomaly for a lean 6'1" point guard with a skinny neck and a pinch-cheeked face—twice cut from his high school team—and actually snubbed by the Celtics in the 1950 draft though he starred at nearby Holy Cross. He was picked by something called the Tri-cities Blackhawks, quickly passed on to the Chicago Stags, who immediately folded and put their three backcourt men up for grabs. The Celtics, picking third from names drawn out of a hat—the others were Max Zaslofsky and Andy Phillip—reluctantly settled for Cousy. He was an immediate sensation. He had unusually long arms, big hands, and dared in that prosaic period of basketball offense to pass the ball behind his back or through his legs. What I liked was his prima donna personality in action. If the player he was guarding beat him for a hoop, it was a cinch the next time the Celtic leader got the ball he was going to the basket no matter what. He averaged more than eighteen points a game for his career, floating graceful running hook shots with either hand. As shown in this cartoon, he was the NBA's most valuable player in 1957, collecting the award that I had devised for my syndicate two years earlier (it was then called the Maurice Podoloff Trophy). He pioneered a pell-mell, improvisational style of fast break offense that left the rest of the league behind for the thirteen years he played. The Celtics at one point won five straight NBA crowns. He reached a point of statesmanship that he was one of the few people allowed to address his coach, Red Auerbach, by his given name, Arnold. I admired Cousy the person, too, and sent my son to a summer camp he ran during the off-season in New England because he didn't just lend his name to the operation but was a hands-on, caring administrator for the kids entrusted to his care. I count him among the genuine, nice people in sports.

THE SHOWCASE OF BASKET-BALL IS THE **NBA** ALL-STAR GAME IN ST. LOUIS JAN. 21 . . . .

FEATURING AS ALWAYS *BOB* **COUSY,** WHO'LL GET FROM MAURICE PODOLOFF THE *PRESIDENT'S TROPHY...*

HE CATCHES THE AYE!

...THE **NEA** AWARD SYMBOLIC OF THE BEST IN THE GAME AS DETERMINED BY THE PLAYERS!

MURRAY OLDERMAN

Cus D'Amato

WITH ALL HIS accomplishments as a maverick trainer and manager of prize fighters, Constantine "Cus" D'Amato was most proud of the fact that he held the record for standing at attention without moving on guard duty in the service at Camp Shanks, New York, during World War II. Cus was a disciplined man dedicated to challenging the promoters (I was going to say thugs) who ran boxing. I found him at the Gramercy, a ratty fight gym up one flight of stairs on 14th Street in lower Manhattan, where he slept on a floor mattress, with a ferocious dog on a leash to ward off neighborhood gangs, and literally plucked kids off the street and converted them to champions. That's where he discovered Floyd Patterson, his ticket to the big time, the youngest at twenty-one to win the world's heavyweight crown. That's where he convinced Rocky Graziano to convert from street fighter to ring professional. He also steered a Puerto Rican émigré, Jose Torres, to the world's light heavyweight title. Cus taught the peek-a-boo style, both gloves up to the face protectively, that was Patterson's trademark. As a city kid, D'Amato aspired to

be a fighter, but was derailed by an eye injury suffered in a street fight. Beneath a tough Bronx veneer, he was a kindly man obsessed with his sport. We were driving to a New Jersey training camp once, and I mentioned the Giants' sensational new young outfielder. "Who," asked Cus, who read the sports pages religiously for boxing mentions, "is Willie Mays?" Combating the International Boxing Club that monopolized the sport, he rented a small apartment overlooking Times Square, where he said he could look out the window to track his nefarious enemies. It didn't have a bed. The grizzled fight handler became a bit of a dandy, sporting a black homburg. We collaborated on a big story for *True*, a leading general magazine, about Patterson's rise. Late in life, he moved to the Catskill Mountains to open a gym, under the auspices of Jimmy Jacobs, a boxing film collector, and discovered a young Mike Tyson at a nearby reform school. Under Cus's tutelage—he even formally adopted the boxer—Tyson developed into the dynamic knockout king who captured the heavyweight title at the age of twenty in 1986, a year after D'Amato's death.

There is only room for good (i.e.–Cus D'Amato)...

...and evil (the IBC and assorted allies)...

Strange ...IN
THE LITTLE
WORLD OF
CUS D'AMATO!

MURRAY OLDERMAN

Al Davis

HE WAS JUST an obscure assistant coach at little Adelphi College on Long Island when I met Al Davis at a New York football writers luncheon. "You're from Spring Valley?" he gushed with that big-toothed smile. "I used to go there and stay at Bauman's Hotel with my folks." That was in my little village northwest of the Big Apple. We began a long off-and-on association that lasted more than sixty years. Brooklyn-bred Davis's helter-skelter ride through all levels of football took him to head coach of an All-American-loaded loaded service team as a twenty-three-year-old private; scouting for the Baltimore Colts; assistant jobs at The Citadel, USC, and the Los Angeles/San Diego Chargers; head coach and general manager of the Oakland Raiders; commissioner of the American Football League, and finally controlling, controversial owner of the Raiders for forty-five years. I saw him try to recruit world-class shot-putter Dallas Long for football on the Trojan campus. I took him for his favorite stuffed clams at a northern New Jersey restaurant. I drew a logo for the AFL when he took over. A couple of years might pass without any word from him. The phone would ring. His sec-retary would say, "Mr. Davis will call you at 12:30." (He never functioned before noon.) "He wants something," He commissioned me to publish two Raider-funded books after Super Bowl triumphs. He overnighted a $3,000 expense check to start on a project that kept me on retainer almost four years for a Raider Hall of Fame that never materialized. The last two years of his life we collaborated on an autobiography that he decided not to have published. (Post mortem, I produced a third-person biography, *Just Win Baby: The Al Davis Story*, that Coach Tom Flores endorsed, "Finally a book that reveals the true Al Davis.") Al Davis was truly an enigma. He was a brilliant football strategist and built a winning dynasty in the poorest pro market. He shaped modern pro football by forcing the merger of the AFL and NFL. He defied the league by moving from Oakland to Los Angles and then back to Oakland. His personal idiosyncrasies—he wore only black and white because he was color blind—subjected him to ridicule. He was a maverick in every sense of the word. The drawing opposite was the mural that accompanied his merited induction into the Pro Football Hall of Fame.

COMMITMENT TO
EXCELLENCE

VINCE LOMBARDI
TROPHY

RAIDERS

RAIDERS

MURRAY
OLDERMAN

Jack Dempsey

THE MAN AT the bar, greeting all comers to his Broadway restaurant, loomed taller than I expected. The vision I had of Jack Dempsey was this lean, crouching prize fighter looping sledge-hammer blows on a flickering screen to the face of a ponderous giant named Jess Willard, sending him to the canvas seven times in the first round until he slumped prostrate. It made him the heavyweight champion of the world. This latter-day Jack Dempsey stood dignifiedly erect, just a trace jowly, hair on top still black, but going gray at the temples, and genial in demeanor. I was at the restaurant with Harry Grayson, NEA's iconic sports columnist of the 1940s and '50s who had been one of only two writers nationally to pick Gene Tunney to defeat Dempsey in their epic "Long Count" fight of 1927. Now the old champ ordered up drinks and playfully grabbed at the skittery Grayson—they had become pals—and kidded him about his sputtering cigar. I had difficulty identifying this Dempsey with the fierce, destructive "Manassa Mauler" of lore who was accused of having plaster in his gloves to destroy Willard.

Boxing legends like Dempsey were imbedded in American culture. My father, an immigrant who knew nothing about sports, called my little brother Dave and me "Dempsey" and "Tunney." Meeting the real thing was a riveting memory. Dempsey and Tunney, now friends, showed up together at a New York boxing writers dinner and joined Grayson and me at our table. It was more than flattering. I was awestruck in the presence of the two men who epitomized the Golden Era of Sports during the "Roaring Twenties." They personified living history. When the intellectualized Tunney, befriended by famous novelist George Bernard Shaw, got up to leave, I remember his signoff: "Cheerio, old chaps." Dempsey, who rose to fistic prominence after a young hobo existence riding the rails, was more a man of the people, albeit with his own checkered history. He was married to both a Hollywood star and a Broadway musical star; he even made a film with Myrna Loy. My lasting tableau, though, is of the man who presided over Jack Dempsey's Broadway Restaurant.

NEA
OLDERMAN

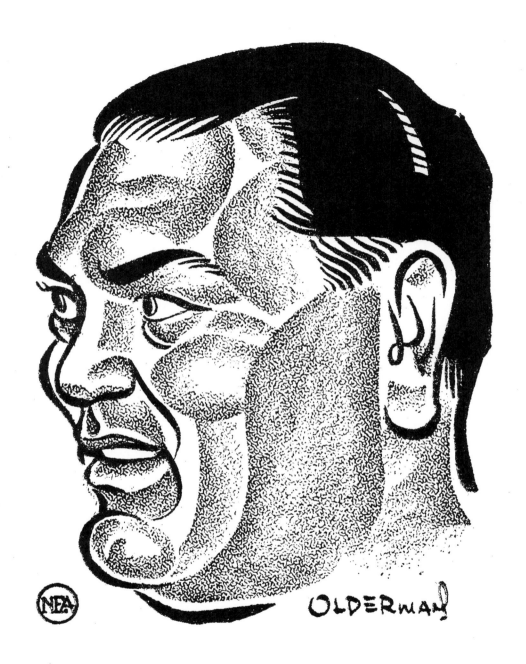

Dan Dierdorf

ENGROSSED IN A post-game locker room gab session with Dan Dierdorf, I completely forgot about the expensive Japanese single reflex zoom binoculars through which I had tracked the jocular offensive tackle of the St. Louis Cardinals that afternoon in San Francisco's Candlestick Park. When I got home, sans unmarked binoculars, Dierdorf and his Cardinal mates were already in the air to St. Louis. I figured my pricy gadget was gone. The next morning, on a chance, I called the Cardinal office in St. Louis. Yes, they had a pair of binoculars matching my description. Dierdorf had spotted them in the cubicle where we talked and turned them over to the Cardinals' equipment manager for safekeeping. Now figure the odds on that in the chaos of football dressing quarters. I first got to know Dan on off-season American Airlines golf junkets for prominent athletes. He was approachable, friendly, and laughed with gusto. But in grid gear, after an All-American collegiate career at Michigan, he launched his 285 pounds with the ferocity to be named the top offensive lineman by the NFL Players Association for three straight years. In 1979, he suffered a fearsome knee injury on the road against the New York Giants. It took three guys to load him on a stretcher and into an ambulance. On the plane trip home, his left leg stretched out on a row of seats, he joined teammates in their regular card games. "I was all sedated," he recalled wryly. "Those sharks fleeced me for $140." The real damage: knee cartilage frayed beyond repair and removed; medial collateral and anterior crucial ligaments torn ragged and in pieces; his joint capsule ripped all the way around. He was told by his operating surgeon he'd never play again. Instead, he lasted 13 seasons, through 1983, all with the Cardinals, had the flexibility to even do a turn at center late in his career, and was inducted into the Pro Football Hall of Fame in his native Canton, Ohio, a sentimental turn for him. "I have a body," he said without false modesty, "that was built to play the game of football." Then he took his effusive personality into the broadcast booth, first with ABC Monday Night Football, followed by longtime service as a color analyst with CBS and other diverse broadcasting chores, for the next thirty years. I reminded him of the binoculars every time I saw him.

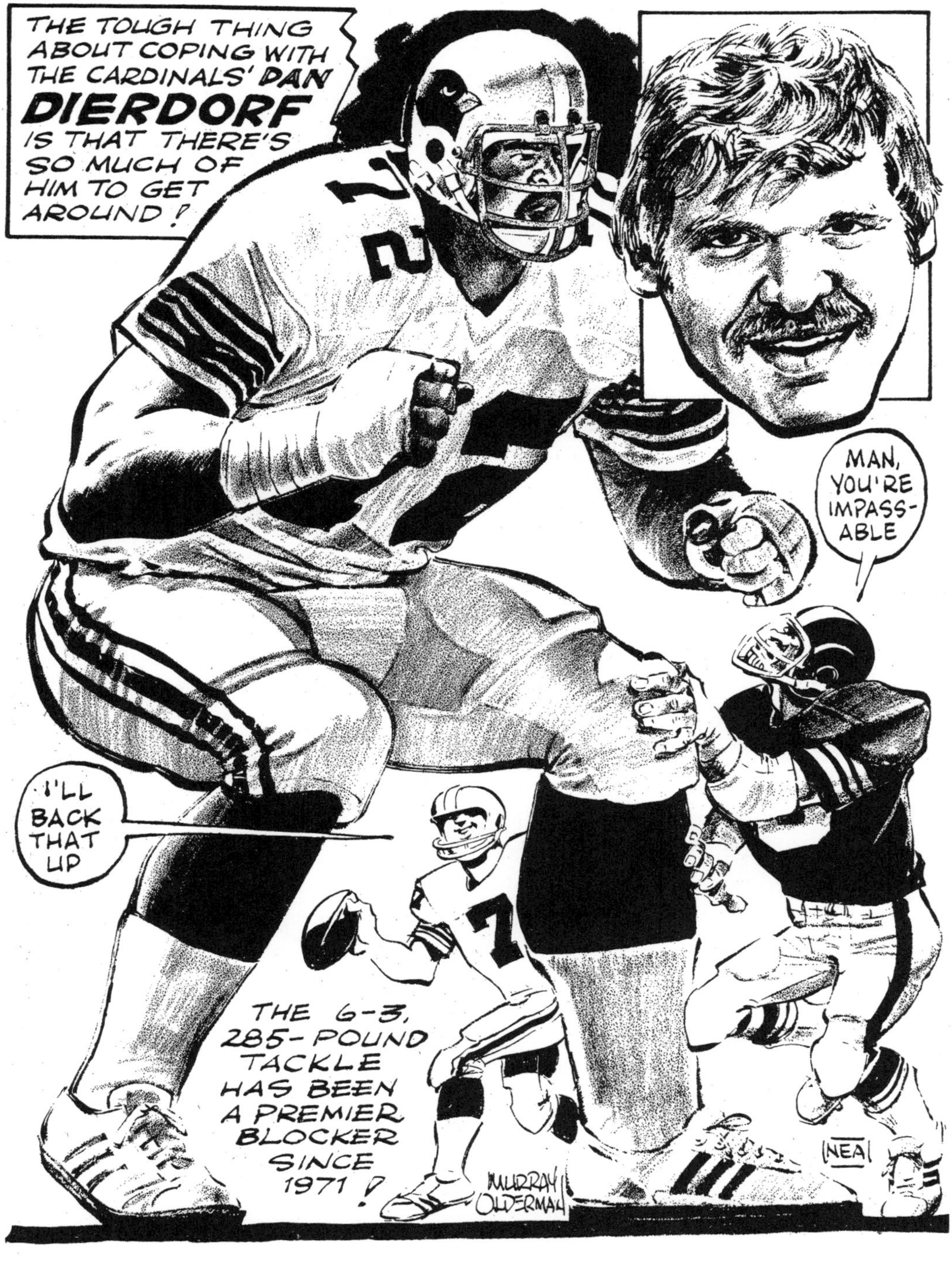
THE TOUGH THING ABOUT COPING WITH THE CARDINALS' DAN DIERDORF IS THAT THERE'S SO MUCH OF HIM TO GET AROUND!
MAN, YOU'RE IMPASS-ABLE
I'LL BACK THAT UP
THE 6-3, 285-POUND TACKLE HAS BEEN A PREMIER BLOCKER SINCE 1971!
MURRAY OLDERMAN
NEA

Joe DiMaggio

THE GOLF CART veered off the 13th green at Mission Hills Country Club in Rancho Mirage, Calif., and headed to my back patio. My wife Nancy had a meat loaf sandwich ready for the gray-haired man with the familiar aquiline face. Joe DiMaggio needed his customary fix during a pro-am round at the Dinah Shore golf tournament, the women's version of the Masters. We had penetrated the sullen veneer of the Yankee Clipper's public persona. I had seen DiMag play centerfield for the Yankees—the last time I paid for a sports ticket—but he retired the year I came to New York as a syndicated cartoonist and feature writer, so I never covered him professionally. But the legendary Yankee centerfielder—it's unlikely his 56-game hitting streak in 1941 will ever be broken—was the honorary umpire at celebrity tennis tournaments that I managed to play in. Joe wasn't very quick in mastering the love-15-30-40 scoring of tennis, but by this time in his life he had shed some of his reclusiveness and relished company. Over coffee, I would listen raptly to his stories about the old playing days, and he was a surprisingly good raconteur. I recall particularly his tales of the eccentricities of teammate Johnny Broaca, a pitcher from Yale. Only one subject was verboten. No mention of Marilyn Monroe, the great love of his life, to whom he'd been married briefly and on whose grave he ordered flowers every day. DiMag identified me as "the tennis player" so I swasn't a writer-interloper. Although he was increasingly white-haired and stooped, the old slugger remained a competitor. His playing partner in American Airlines celebrity golf tournaments in Hawaii or Puerto Rico was Otto Graham, the great Cleveland quarterback. When Otto would get off the links, he'd seek me out for a set of tennis. DiMag groused that Otto was wasting his energy and thereby affecting their golf scores. The old Yankee was also notoriously penurious. I edited a series of books for Prentice-Hall on the greatest year of famous athletes and assigned colleague Al Silverman to write *Joe DiMaggio: The Golden Year, 1941*. Before he would cooperate, DiMag insisted that Al pay him $500 (half the author's advance) just to talk to him. The wash portrait I did, opposite, was the illustration for that book.

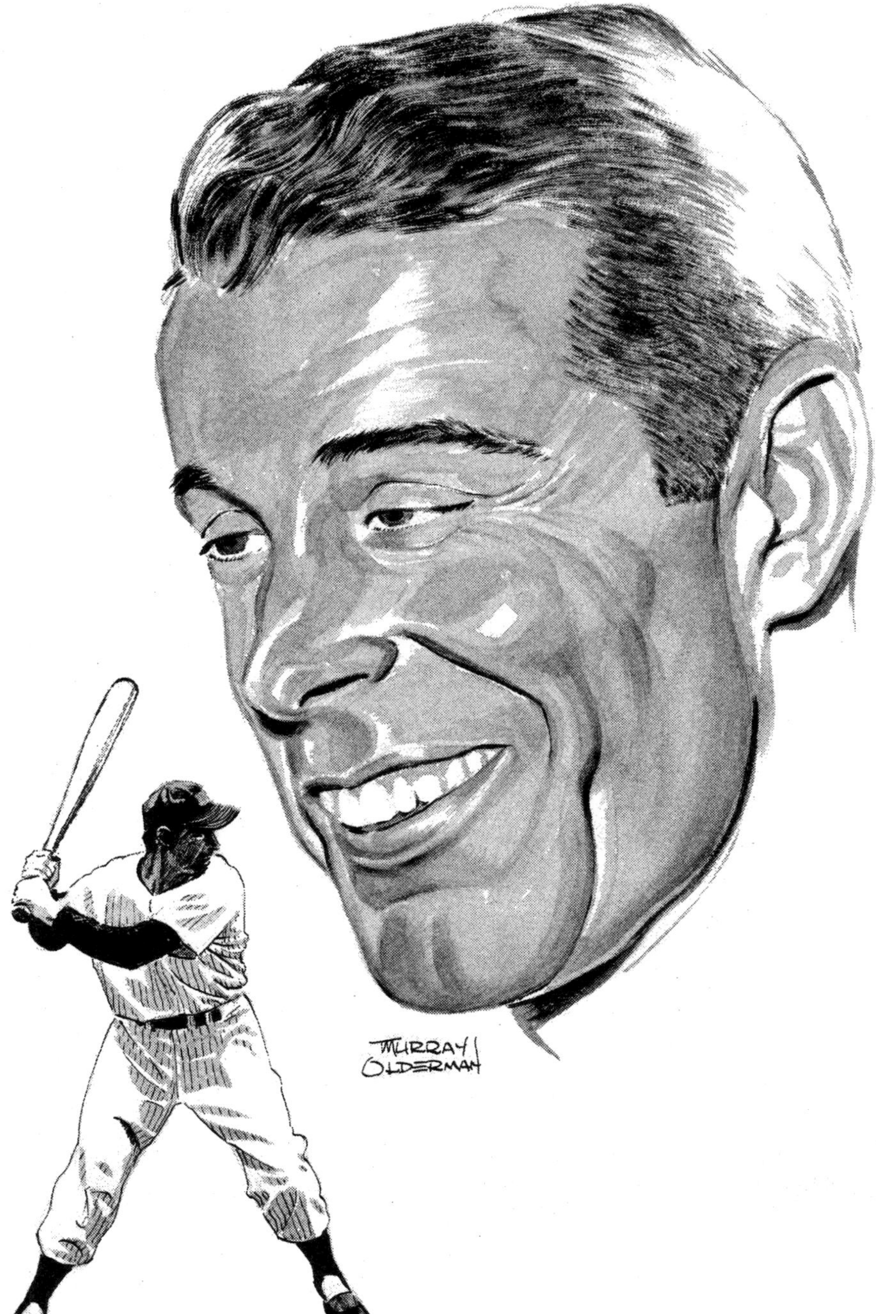
MURRAY
OLDERMAN

Mike Ditka

CARROLL "BEANO" COOK, an unflagging advocate for the glories of college football, first put me on to Mike Ditka. Beano was the sports publicist for a decade at the University of Pittsburgh, a bastion of gridiron toughness, and in early 1958 wanted the world to know about a young sophomore tight end coming up to varsity who not only caught passes, but served as the team's punter and doubled as a linebacker on defense. So he got me to do a drawing of Ditka that he distributed to newspapers through western Pennsylvania. Many cartoons of Ditka followed over the years because he became an All-American at Pitt, was drafted number one by the Chicago Bears in 1961, voted NFL Rookie of the Year, and played twelve seasons (with the Bears, Eagles, and Cowboys) that earned him the designation of being the first tight end elected to the Pro Football Hall of Fame. And that ain't all. Because "Iron Mike," the tough scion of Ukrainian stock (the original family name was Dyczko, changed to the relief of headline writers) in the coal and steel mining area of Pennsylvania, was then introduced to coaching by Tom Landry in Dallas. "Papa Bear" George Halas, with whom Ditka feuded over salary—he actually had signed with the Houston Oilers of the AFL before the leagues merged—brought Ditka back to run the Bears for eleven seasons. He won Super Bowl XX and shares the honor with Tom Flores of being the only men to experience Super Bowl victories as players, assistant coaches, and head coaches. After another three years as head coach of the New Orleans Saints, Ditka shifted to broadcasting and a host of other business ventures, including his own brand of wine. Uniform number eighty-nine was retired by the Bears, the last numeral the franchise will shelf. As player or coach, Mike was entertaining to deal with because he always spoke his mind, bluntly and irreverently and occasionally with a touch of humor.

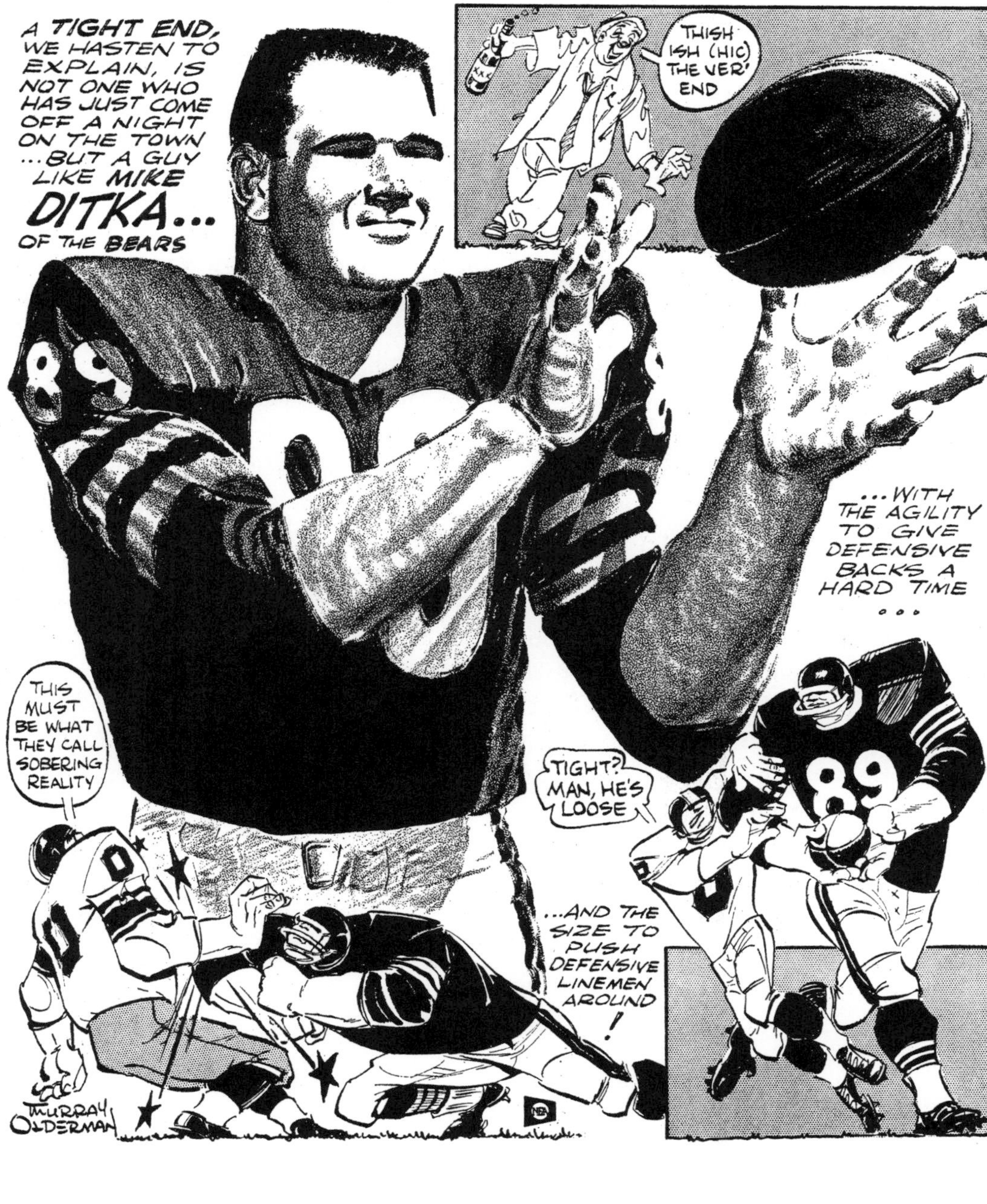
A TIGHT END, WE HASTEN TO EXPLAIN, IS NOT ONE WHO HAS JUST COME OFF A NIGHT ON THE TOWN ...BUT A GUY LIKE MIKE DITKA... OF THE BEARS
THISH ISH (HIC) THE VER' END
...WITH THE AGILITY TO GIVE DEFENSIVE BACKS A HARD TIME ...
THIS MUST BE WHAT THEY CALL SOBERING REALITY
TIGHT? MAN, HE'S LOOSE
...AND THE SIZE TO PUSH DEFENSIVE LINEMEN AROUND!
MURRAY OLDERMAN

"Man on the Wing"

Don Drysdale

NO FAMILY BLENDED athleticism more impressively than the Drysdales of Morningside Country Club in Rancho Mirage, California. When I entered their family room, on one wall hung the Cy Young Award from 1962, emblematic of the best pitcher in baseball. Under it was a plaque from the Baseball Hall of Fame, bearing a metallic likeness of Don Drysdale, elected in 1984. On the opposite wall, lucite supports held the Broderick Cup, awarded to Ann Meyer as the outstanding college female athlete of the year for 1979. And there was another silver bowl designating Ann as Women's Basketball Player of the Year (the only female ever signed to an NBA contract). Unfortunately, the idyll of Don and Ann Meyer-Drysdale, married just seven years, with three young children, ended on July 3, 1993, when the former pitching great, who became a prominent broadcaster, the partner of iconic Vince Scully airing Los Angeles Dodgers games, was found dead of a heart attack in a hotel room in Montreal at the age ·of fifty-six. He was an athlete to be remembered. No one worked up a case of overt hostility to hitters more than the big right-hander. His career with the Dodgers bridged both Brooklyn and Los Angeles and included a spring holdout when he and Sandy Koufax banded together to demand, unsuccessfully, $100,00 contracts. He won 209 games in fourteen seasons and once threw six consecutive shutouts. A frayed rotator cup in his shoulder ended his pitching career. "I got tired of taking all those pain killers," he told me. He once took his wife to a baseball fantasy camp that featured Dodger manager Tommy Lasorda. Ann was off on the side shooting baskets. Lasorda drifted over and challenged her to a game of one-on-one. "It almost gave him a heart attack," Drysdale recounted for me with a laugh. "She bounced the ball through his legs. She bounced it over his head. Tommy wouldn't give up. She destroyed that poor sucker. He was beet red when he came back to the baseball field." Don was smart. There was no backboard in the Drysdale driveway and not a basketball in sight.

Ann Meyer, top women's basketball player...

I'M SEEIN' STARS

THE DRYSDALES

Don Drysdale, Hall-of-Fame pitcher...

MURRAY OLDERMAN
FOR PALM SPRINGS LIFE

Leo Durocher

"THE LIP" ONCE sent a drink over to my table at a restaurant in Scottsdale, Arizona, during spring training in his extravagant period as manager of the Chicago Cubs. I also saw him as a wizened, sad old man hanging around the little ball park in Palm Springs, California, where the Angels once did their vernal exercises, mute and incommunicative until his last days. Those were only two of the many incarnations of Leo Durocher, one of baseball's most fascinating personalities. First there was the slick young shortstop for the New York Yankees in their "Murderers Row" phase, who palled around with Babe Ruth until the Bambino accused him of stealing his watch and called him "The All-American Out." (Light-hitting Durocher carried a .247 batting average for his seventeen playing seasons in the majors.) He moved on as captain and field leader of the fabled St. Louis Gashouse Gang, winners of the 1934 World Series. Next he took over as Brooklyn's playing manager and in 1941 produced the exciting Dodgers' first pennant in twenty-one years. Bon vivant Leo—he wed Hollywood star Laraine Day—also hung with gamblers and mobsters and was suspended for the entire 1947 season. A surprise shift across town to skipper the New York Giants led to a 1951 pennant (on Bobby Thomson's historic "Shot Heard 'Round the World" home run) and 1954 World Series sweep of the favored Cleveland Indians. Then on to the Cubs, where mouthy Leo the Lip briefly turned mute, talking publicly only through a coach and producing the cartoon opposite. His epitaph remains his most famous utterance: "Nice Guys Finish Last."

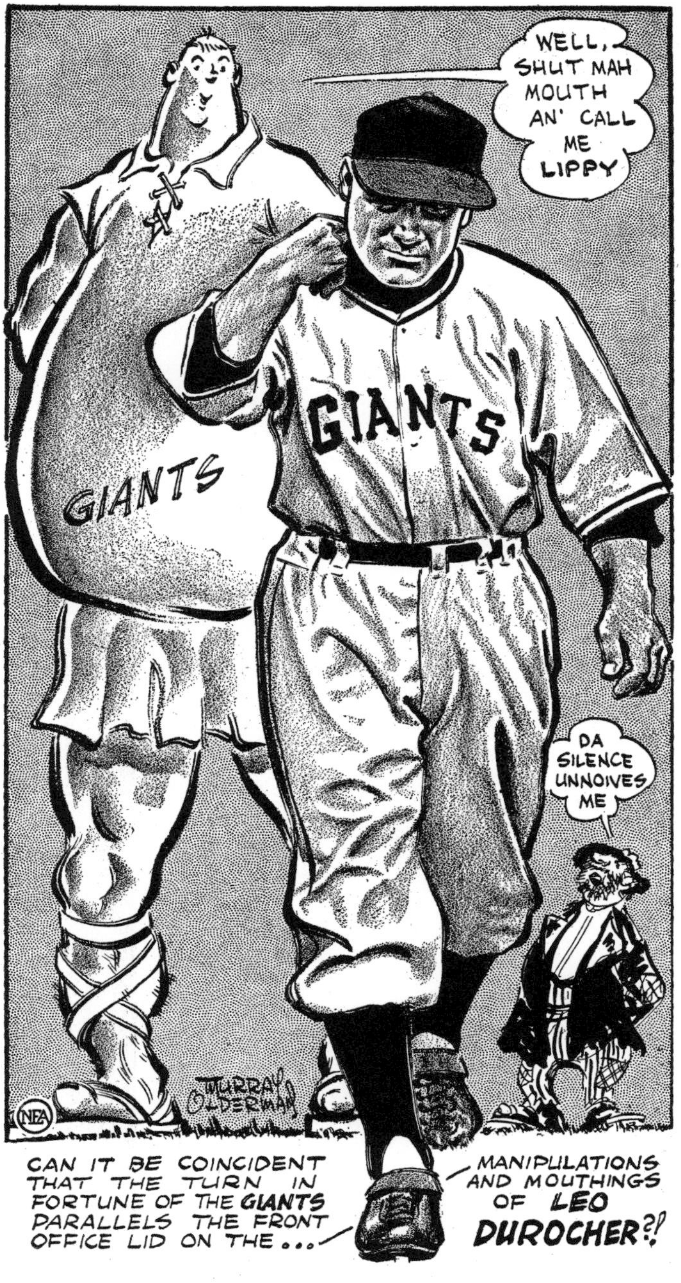
WELL, SHUT MAH MOUTH AN' CALL ME LIPPY
GIANTS
GIANTS
DA SILENCE UNNOIVES ME
MURRAY OLDERMAN
NEA
CAN IT BE COINCIDENT THAT THE TURN IN FORTUNE OF THE GIANTS PARALLELS THE FRONT OFFICE LID ON THE . . .
MANIPULATIONS AND MOUTHINGS OF LEO DUROCHER?!

"Stiff Upper 'Lip'"

Chris Evert

ONE SPRING IN Florida, my young son Mark was getting his first tennis lesson on Fort Lauderdale city courts by the resident pro, Jimmy Evert. But I couldn't help noticing on an adjoining court a pig-tailed little girl—she couldn't have been more than five years old, if that—whaling two-hand backhands across the net with intensity and ferocity. And accuracy. "Who," I asked Jimmy, "is that?" "Oh," he answered almost nonchalantly, "that's my daughter . . . Chrissy." That was my introductory view of one of the greats of women's tennis, for Chris Evert grew up to reach the finals of thirty-four Grand Slam tournaments and take the trophy in eighteen of them while winning 1,309 matches over a career that stretched from pre-teen to retirement at thirty-five in 1989. She was well grounded in the game since Jimmy had played tennis at Notre Dame before settling down as a teaching pro. At fifteen, Chris beat Margaret Court, then the number one player in the world. She won at least one Grand Slam event for thirteen straight years, and she competed in an era that featured such mar-velous contemporaries as Billie Jean King, Evonne Goolagong, Martina Navratilova. The blistering two-hand backhand remained the trademark of her game. That and an incomparable competitive streak with a steely demeanor that earned the cognomen of "Ice Maiden." All the while, Chris also managed to lead an intriguing personal life. When she first emerged as a champion, she was engaged to Jimmy Connors—they were both ranked number one in the world. Then she married top British tennis player John Lloyd and for a decade called herself Chris Evert-Lloyd. During that period, I had dinner with them one night in Los Angeles and she sighed that when she retired from the game, "my ambition is to travel." That was puzzling for someone who covered the five continents hitting tennis balls in every conceivable milieu. "But all I've seen," she lamented, "are the insides of hotel rooms." More recently, Chris Evert has remained visible running a tennis academy to develop young American talent and as an analyst for ESPN.

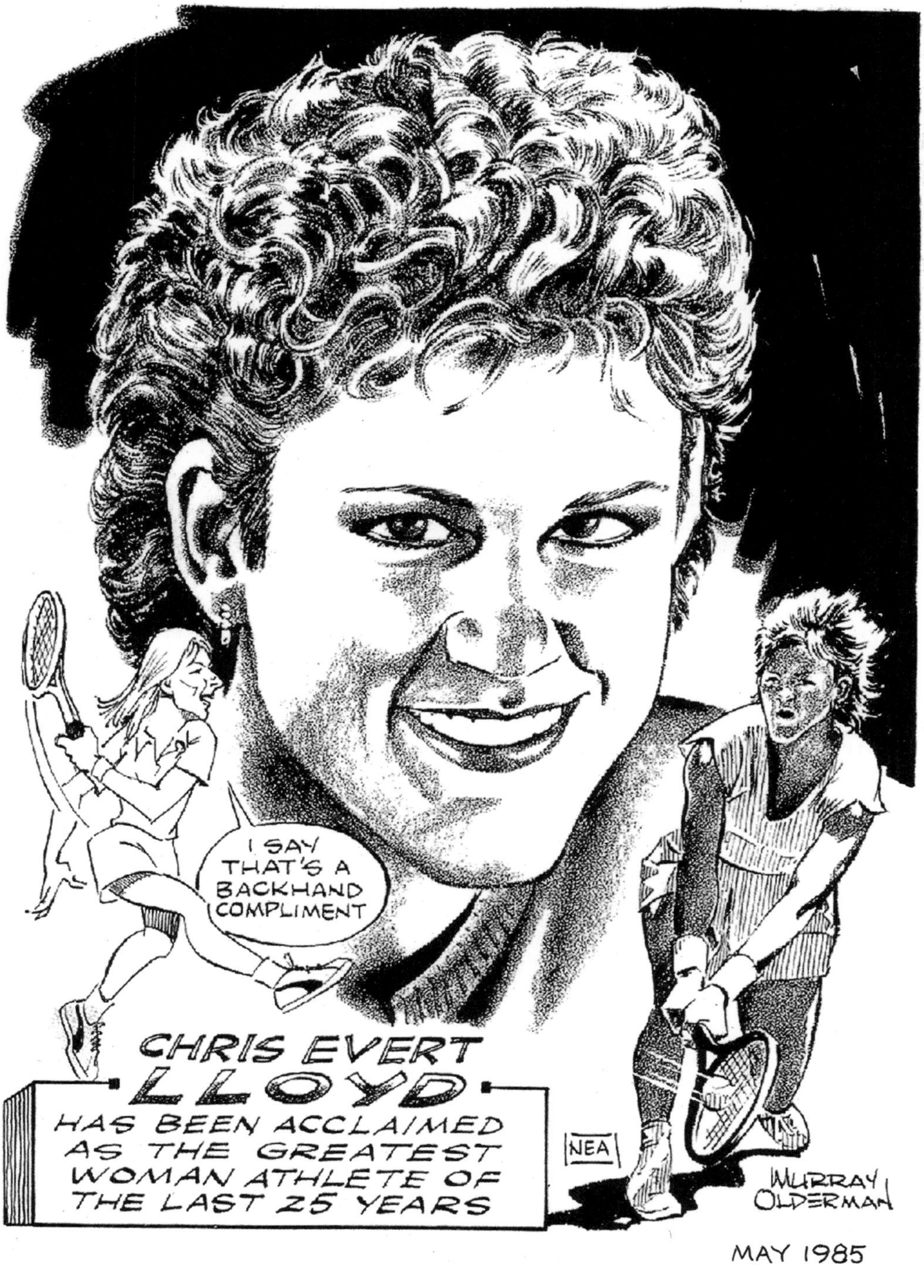
I SAY THAT'S A BACKHAND COMPLIMENT
CHRIS EVERT
LLOYD
HAS BEEN ACCLAIMED AS THE GREATEST WOMAN ATHLETE OF THE LAST 25 YEARS
NEA
MURRAY OLDERMAN

MAY 1985

Bob Feller

THE ACE OF the Cleveland Indians pitching staff was unique in that he commuted to games from his country home to the stadium on the Lake Erie waterfront in his own little single-engine plane. When three teammates—Bob Lemon, Al Rosen, and Early Wynn—were chosen, along with Feller, to play on the American League squad in the 1951 All-Star game in Cincinnati that summer, Feller offered them a lift to the southern Ohio city. As Rosen tells it six decades later, when burly Wynn clambered aboard Feller's plane, he had to step on a wing to reach the cabin, and the wing tip dipped all the way to the ground. The four Indian ballplayers barely squeezed into the tiny Piper Cub. Feller at the controls wheeled it onto the asphalt of Lake Front Airport and gunned the engine for takeoff. Rosen remembers that as the plane cruised down the runway, wheels struggling to lift off, pavement starting to run out, Feller was scrunched over the stick and exhorting, "C'mon, baby! C'mon, baby!" Not a note of encouragement for his neophyte flight passengers. Aerial dynamics kicked in, and they got aloft and flew serenely to Cincinnati, but ran into a severe rainstorm over the city as they descended to land. "We were bouncing around," recalls Rosen, "like ping pong balls." Feller made the return flight alone. He was a man apart from the moment he trudged off the family farm in Van Meter, Iowa, and into the national consciousness as a seventeen-year-old in 1936 by striking out eight St. Louis Cardinals Gashouse Gang batters in three innings in a spring training game. His signature pitch was a fastball that dipped and veered and hopped and always eschewed a straight line, and it was augmented by a curve that looked like it was looping off a table. Cy Slapnicka, a scout for the Cleveland Indians, signed him for one dollar and an autographed baseball. He never pitched a day in the minors. And over the next eighteen years, interrupted only by four years in the Navy as a Chief Petty Officer during World War II, Feller won 266 games and showed he belonged in any discussion of the greatest pitchers in baseball history. A little standoffish in personality, he could do a good turn, like letting my syndicate's sports editor, Harry Grayson, use his name on a three-part series distributed nationally to newspapers.

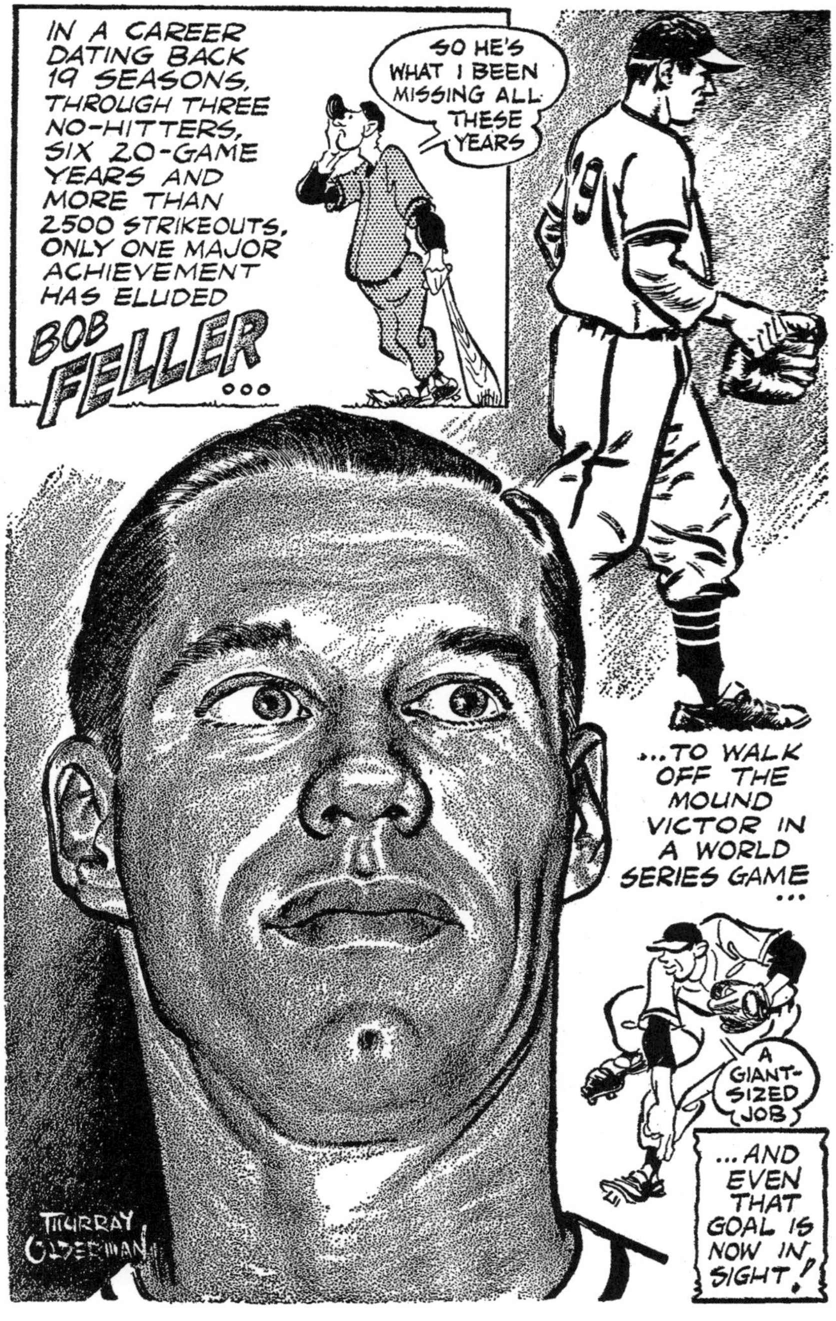
IN A CAREER DATING BACK 19 SEASONS, THROUGH THREE NO-HITTERS, SIX 20-GAME YEARS AND MORE THAN 2500 STRIKEOUTS, ONLY ONE MAJOR ACHIEVEMENT HAS ELUDED
BOB FELLER ...
SO HE'S WHAT I BEEN MISSING ALL THESE YEARS
...TO WALK OFF THE MOUND VICTOR IN A WORLD SERIES GAME ...
A GIANT-SIZED JOB
...AND EVEN THAT GOAL IS NOW IN SIGHT!
MURRAY OLDERMAN

"To Top it Off?"

Curt Flood

WAYNE ANDERSON, THE Cincinnati trainer, introduced me to Curt Flood on the steps of the Reds dugout when the aspiring young outfielder was a rookie. He was personable and articulate, and we shared a common interest. Curt was also an aspiring sports artist. Little did I know that Curt Flood would become one of the pivotal, historical figures in freeing baseball players from indentured serfdom. Jackie Robinson had broken the sport's color line a few years earlier, but Flood sacrificed his successful playing career to get all players their earned due. Curt had moved on to twelve distinguished years with the St. Louis Cardinals, a key player in two World Series victories, received the Gold Glove Award as the National League's top centerfielder seven straight seasons, elevated his hitting to accumulate a .293 lifetime batting average, but the Cardinals traded him after the 1969 season to the Philadelphia Phillies in a multi-player swap. "I'm not going to be treated like chattel," he said, and refused to report to his new team. At the time, all player contracts were subject to the "reserve clause" which bound them in perpetuity to the whims of the team. With the blessings of Marvin Miller, head of the players union, who warned him that he might be risking his baseball future, Flood filed suit against Commissioner Bowie Kuhn and Major League Baseball to negate the trade. He sat out the 1970 season while it was going through the judicial system, and ultimately it reached the U.S. Supreme Court, which ruled against him in 1972 in a divided decision, one justice abstaining because he had stock in Anheuser Busch, the corporation that owned the Cardinals. The Phillies traded his contract to the Washington Senators, for whom Curt played a few desultory games and then retired to Majorca, an island off the coast of Spain, and opened a bar while resuming his interest in painting. Meanwhile, buoyed by Flood's defiance, Miller and the players union negotiated a collective bargaining agreement with the owners under which pitchers Andy Messersmith and Dave McNally sought free agency and won, striking down the reserve clause and opening the floodgates for players to make millions. Curt hit hard times and never reaped a cent. His last job was as a baseball radio analyst in hometown Oakland, where we renewed our friendship.

"One Big Pitch Still Left"

Whitey Ford

HE WAS THE go-to pitcher of the New York Yankees when they were in their fun-loving phase and making the scene regularly in mid-Manhattan as Mickey Mantle, Billy Martin, Hank Bauer, Joe Pepitone, and all the gang did their post-prandial rounds of the Copacabana, Toots Shor's, and other boîtes. Whitey Ford, a wise-cracking Irishman who was more New Yorker than any of them since he was born in the mid-Manhattan tenement district and grew up across the East River in Astoria, Queens, liked his off-field fun as much as the rest, but never at the risk of affecting his performance on the pitcher's mound. Whitey wasn't as gifted physically as some of the pitching greats—he didn't overpower batters, but he threw with guile and reason. Ford carried the Yankee tradition of winning for sixteen seasons, making his debut as a rookie with nine straight victories. Called the "Chairman of the Board" because he was always in control of the situation on the mound, he was a favorite of Casey Stengel, a demanding curmudgeon, who scheduled Whitey's pitching turns to face the toughest teams because the lefthander excelled against the best, using every trick in his arsenal of pitches. If he could get away with it, he wasn't above doctoring the ball, as he admitted frankly after retiring from the Yankees. In the early years, he and Mantle and Martin were a social triumvirate, and when Billy left, it was just Whitey and Mickey on fun forays. Before he and Mantle played in the 1961 All-Star game in San Francisco, they were guests of Giants owner Horace Stoneham at the Olympic Golf Club and ran up a $400 tab. Stoneham bet him double or nothing on the premise Ford had to strike out Willie Mays in the All-Star game, which he did with a secretly-loaded spitter. No wonder one of his nicknames was "Slick," used as the title of his autobiography (for which Mickey Mantle wrote the preface). That same year, Whitey, at age thirty-three, reached a personal high record of 25-4 and was the MVP of the World Series. He and Mantle were later jointly inducted into the Baseball Hall of Fame.

"Pitching for Membership"

Bob Gibson

THE ONE MAN in the realm of sports that I wish I'd made more of an effort to spend time with, to get to know as a person, is Bob Gibson because I sensed that his interests and passions went beyond merely playing a game, though a surly veneer he used to fend off strangers might have been off-putting. His skills as a pitcher were obvious, and his intensity as a competitor made him a compelling figure on the mound, but there was intelligence behind all of that. He was the youngest of seven children raised in Omaha, Nebraska, overcame childhood pulmonary problems and rickets to excel in sports, and went to Creighton University on a basketball scholarship. Both the Harlem Globetrotters and Cardinals vied for his services, and though he got a bonus from the Cards, he delayed his baseball career for a year to tour with the Globetrotters. Once settled in with the Cardinals, who paid him $4,000 to quit dabbling in basketball during the off-season, he quickly established himself as one of the most intimidating pitchers of his era. Over seventeen seasons, he won 251 games, had a career ERA of 2.91, and struck out more than 3,000 batters. He twice won the Cy Young Award as the National League's outstanding pitcher. In the 1967 World Series, Gibson threw three complete victories to pace the Cardinals' 4-3 triumph over the Boston Red Sox. His '68 season, at the age of thirty-two, was incomparable. He had an ERA of 1.12, best ever in the live ball era. He threw twenty-eight complete games in thirty-four starts and was never pulled from the mound—in those other six, he was removed for a pinch hitter. Match that against current starters who are through after one hundred pitches, even if they're throwing a no-hitter. Against the Dodgers once, he struck out the side on nine pitches for an "immaculate inning." In the opening game of the '68 World Series, he struck out seventeen against Detroit, a Series record that still stands. I realize the foregoing is a mass of statistics, but it's the only way to document just how marvelous his pitching was. And when he wasn't scheduled for mound work, the Cardinals often used the versatile Gibson as a pinch hitter because the athlete was capable of hitting the ball out of the park, too.

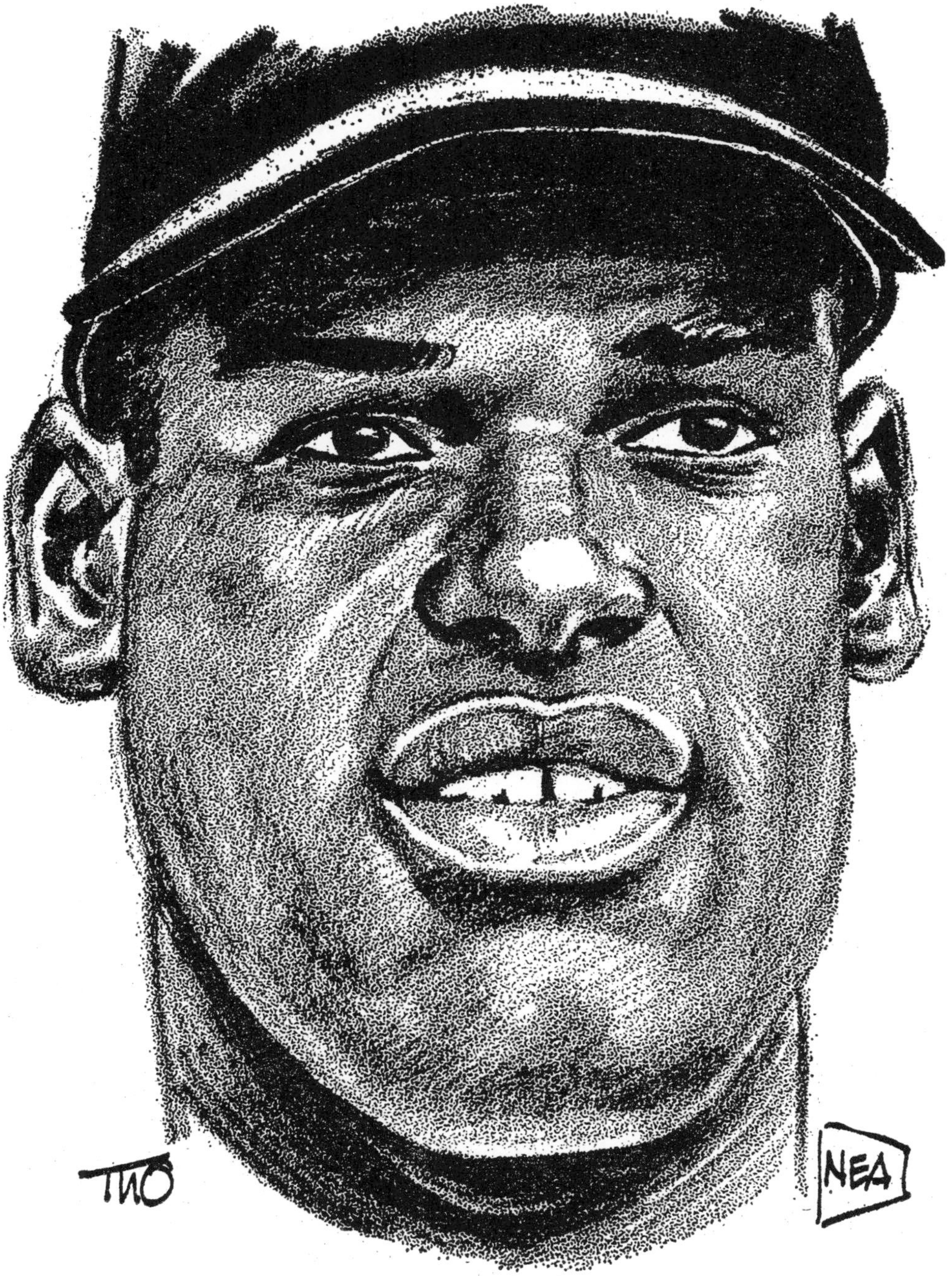
NEA

Frank Gifford

THE KID FROM the oil fields outside Bakersfield, Calif., considered me a hippy because I drove a red Austin-Healey 3000 and wore the long sideburns becoming fashionable in the 1960s. But I made points in his esteem the day Howard Cosell confronted him in the locker room of the New York Giants and spewed polysyllabic words at Frank Gifford to make him feel intellectually inferior. One was "milieu" and, standing by, I informed Howard that he had the meaning completely wrong. Howard hemmed and hawed in chagrin, and Frank giggled. Gifford, the star back of the Giants, became close enough to come to a dinner party at my house across the Hudson River in New Jersey with his first wife, Maxine, a beauty queen at USC, where Frank first gained national prominence as an All-American. To the Big City fans who embraced him, Frank epitomized California cool, and he had the veneer. Hollywood handsome—he actually worked in films during college—and outwardly poised. But his ticket was innate football ability under pressure. He wasn't big at 6 feet and 195 pounds; he wasn't particularly fast. At first, the Giants also played him in their defensive backfield. But Vince Lombardi, an obscure Army assistant brought in to take over the offense, built his attack on Gifford running the famed Lombardi sweep. I woke up Frank one December morning at the Excelsior Hotel in mid-Manhattan, where he and Maxine and their kids lived during the 1956 season, to tell him that he had been awarded the Jim Thorpe Trophy as the MVP in the NFL, then took him to Baltimore for a nationally televised game for presentation of the award at halftime. When he headquartered at the Concourse Plaza Hotel closer to Yankee Stadium, Frank used to invite me for post-game cocktail gatherings with other players and hangers-on. On a flight from Atlanta we both happened to be on, he got me bumped to first class because handsome Frank befriended the stewardess. He was smart enough to realize football wasn't going to last forever, so he began to train for work in burgeoning television. In 1960, a Chuck Bednarik hit gave him a season-ending concussion, and he was out all of the next year, too. But even in his 30s, he missed the game and came back as a receiver for three productive seasons before retiring and landing the ABC Monday Night Football gig that established him on TV.

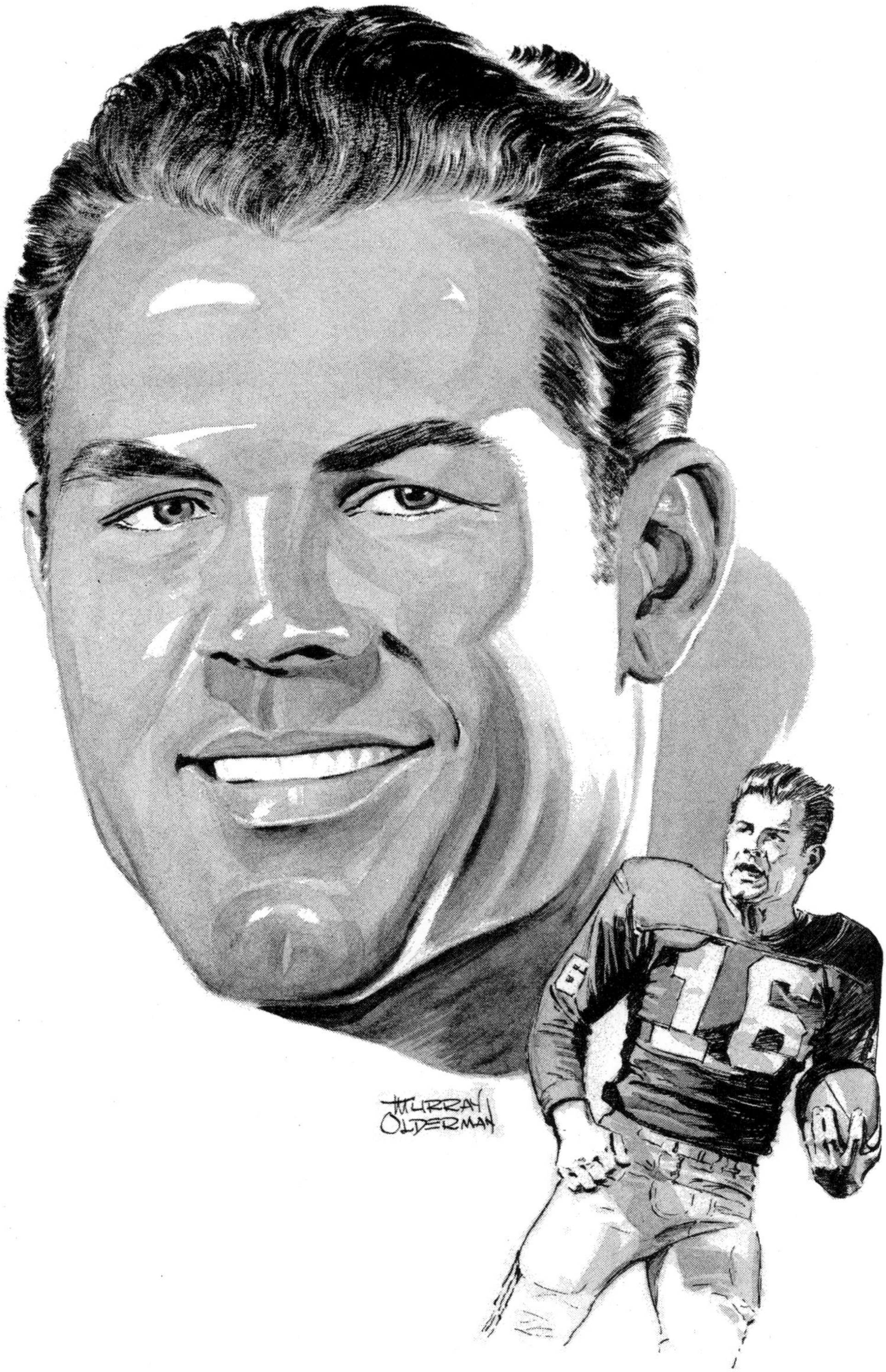
MURRAY
OLDERMAN

Pancho Gonzales

HE WAS A difficult man to know. You weren't sure if you were getting the tough kid from the barrio with emotionally stoked fires of anger or the acquired sophisticate who traveled the world playing tennis. Richard "Pancho" Gonzales was an enigma, shaped by his rise from the cracked, uneven concrete courts of east L.A., where he played ten self-taught hours a day, to dominate a sport once considered country-club effete. By twenty, he won the U.S. Championships at Forest Hills, but reportedly wasn't invited to the victory dinner—his delinquent truancy, a knife scar on his left check, and a bad conduct discharge from the Navy made him "socially unacceptable." He won again the next year and turned pro to tour with Jack Kramer, but wasn't ready for the old master and got creamed. A couple of years later, he was beating all the top players and started an unmatched eight-year run as number one in the world. Powerful, cat-quick, and remarkably fast for a guy 6'3" tall, Pancho established himself as one of the greatest ever. By the time of the Open era in 1968, Pancho was forty years old but still played memorable matches. At Wimbledon, he lost two grueling sets to Charlie Pasarell before darkness postponed play to the next day, when Pancho rallied to even it 16-14 (before tie-breakers), 6-3, and then fought off seven match points for the 11-9 win. At 41, he beat reigning world champ Rod Laver in a $10,000 winner-take-all five-set duel at Madison Square Garden. Pancho managed to get married six times, too, the last to Andre Agassi's sister, Rita, while he was the pro at Caesar's Palace in Las Vegas, but also maintained a home at my tennis complex in Rancho Mirage, California, where he amiably and graciously participated in clinics.

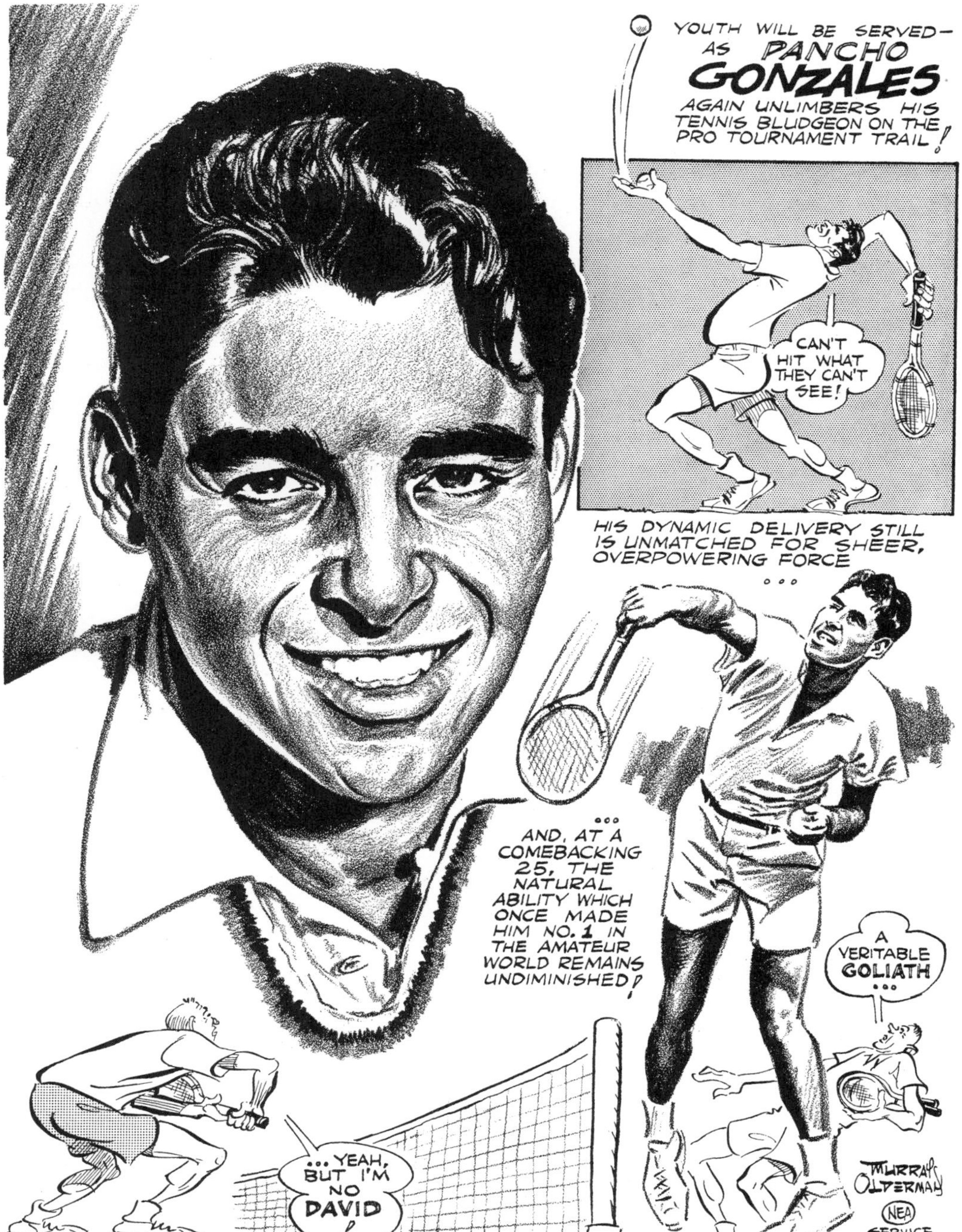
YOUTH WILL BE SERVED—AS PANCHO GONZALES AGAIN UNLIMBERS HIS TENNIS BLUDGEON ON THE PRO TOURNAMENT TRAIL!
CAN'T HIT WHAT THEY CAN'T SEE!
HIS DYNAMIC DELIVERY STILL IS UNMATCHED FOR SHEER, OVERPOWERING FORCE ...
... AND, AT A COMEBACKING 25, THE NATURAL ABILITY WHICH ONCE MADE HIM NO. 1 IN THE AMATEUR WORLD REMAINS UNDIMINISHED!
A VERITABLE GOLIATH ...
... YEAH, BUT I'M NO DAVID!
MURRAY OLDERMAN
NEA SERVICE

Otto Graham

IT ALWAYS INTRIGUED me that Otto Graham was involved, albeit peripherally, in the Dr. Sam Shepard murder case—the Cleveland osteopath was convicted of killing his wife in a celebrated trial half a century ago (later acquitted on re-trial). The Grahams and the Shepards moved in the same Bay View suburb social circle, and the cops even let Otto through tight security to view the murder scene. You see, Otto was a straight arrow, married all his adult life to Beverly, his college sweetheart. Also a straight talker. Beverly was studying singing at Northwestern, and Otto walked in at the end of a recital. "Your last note was sharp," commented Otto, a musician himself (his father led the band at Waukegan High; Otto played piano, cornet, French horn, and violin). It took some talking to get her to take back his ring and pin. We're also talking here about a man who, when I'm asked to rate the greatest quarterbacks, I put at number one. Otto played ten seasons with the original Cleveland Browns, and they reached the championship finals ten times, winning the All-America Conference all four years of its existence and three NFL titles. The year he retired, the Browns had their first los-ing season. And he came to them without any experience at the position. At Northwestern, which he attended on a basketball scholarship, Coach Pappy Waldorf saw him throwing spirals in an intramural touch football game and induced to come out for football. His senior year he was an All-American single wing tail-back and then enlisted in the Navy as an air cadet. Paul Brown, also in the Navy, signed him to join the Cleveland franchise starting up in 1946, as its quarterback. Otto was suc-cinct about his new role: "Hand the ball off to [fullback] Marion Motley and get the hell out of the way." Too modest: he was a brilliant passer who ran with agility and was imperturbable under pressure. We hit it off the minute I came into a Browns' dressing room. He was frank, funny, and relaxed, though he bridled at Coach Brown calling the plays. I kept close tabs on Otto later as a coach of the College All-Stars annually against the NFL champs, three years heading the Washington Redskins, and a long stretch as the Coast Guard Academy coach before he bought and ran a small country club in Sarasota, Florida, that I visited. Otto, as you might guess, was a scratch golfer.

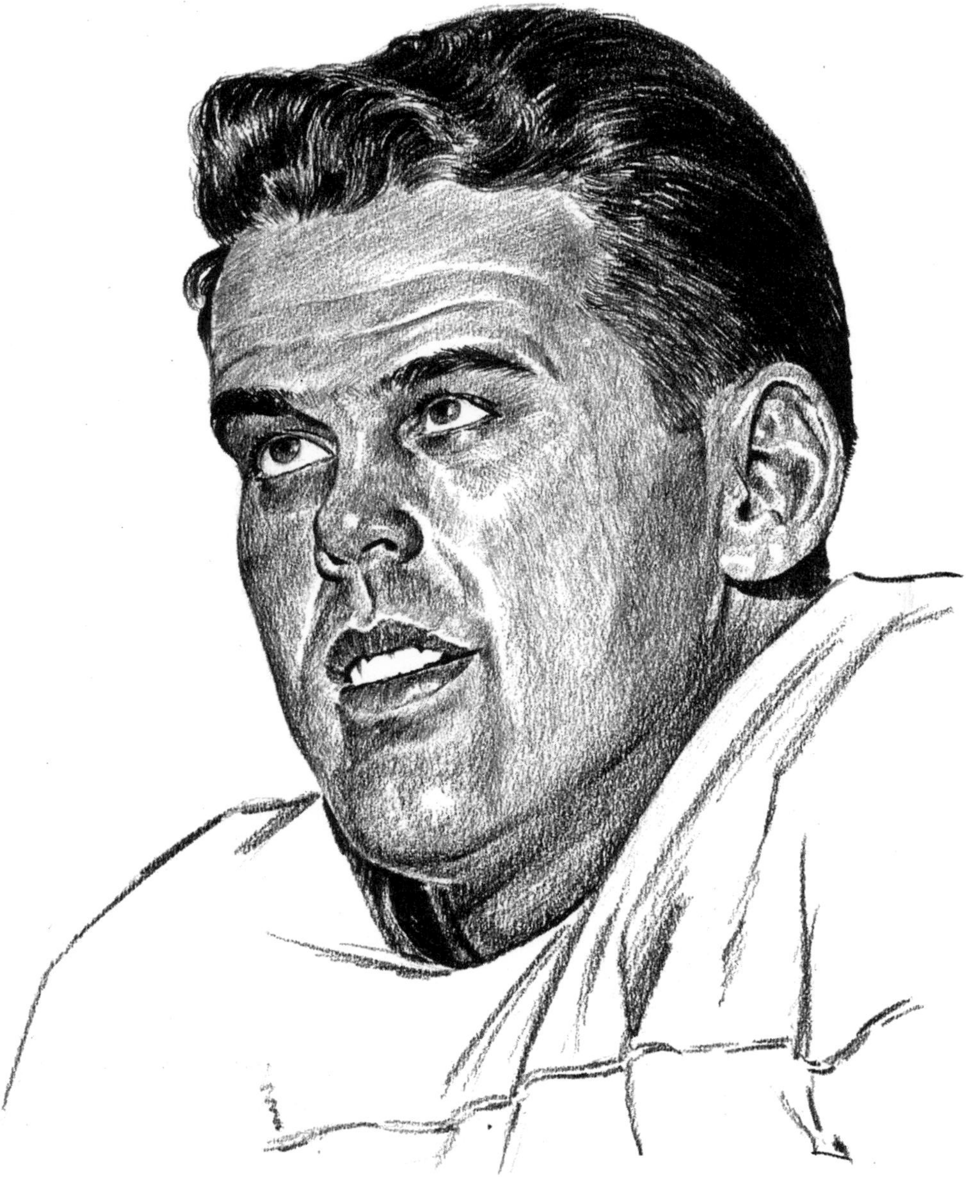

OTTO GRAHAM

Hank Greenberg

MY FAVORITE TEAM growing up was the Detroit Tigers, American League champs in the mid-1930s. I can still reel off their 1936 starting lineup, with one asterisk. Hank Greenberg, the first baseman who captivated every Jewish youngster in the country, was out with a broken wrist. As a teenager, I hopped a bus from my village to see the Tigers in Yankee Stadium and, before the game, snuck down to behind the Detroit dugout for a closer look at real major leaguers. Going back up through the reserved section, I saw a large young man with slick black hair sitting on the aisle. I gulped and squeaked, "Are you Hank Greenberg?" "No," he answered abruptly, and I went on my way. But it was Hank. I never told him this when we became friendly tennis adversaries years later. I faced Hank in the finals of a celebrity tennis tournament at the Concord in the Catskills, with Pancho Gonzales, the resident pro, as our ball boy. Hank won in straight sets, duly reported in the *New York Times*. As a tennis player, ironically, the slugger dinked the ball. We collaborated for a tongue-in-cheek *Tennis* magazine story on how to play younger guys. "Give 'em a bad call right off the bat," he said, "to upset them." Wily Hank. We played in Manhat-

tan, Montego Bay, the Beverly Hills Tennis Club (with Walter Matthau in attendance), wherever we encountered each other, and then I'd listen raptly to Hank ruminate about his life. "I was a macho athlete and had never been rejected," he said wistfully. "When my wife left me, it took me a year to get over it." Greenberg pooh-poohed the allegation that in 1938, the year he hit fifty-eight home runs, pitchers colluded not to give him anything to hit the last five games to protect Babe Ruth's hallowed record of sixty. "I had my chances," he said. "I was nervous and just didn't hit the ball." A Wall Street player the last half of his life, with his own ticker tape at home, Hank related how he averted losing his personal fortune by getting a tip ten minutes before a Friday stock market closing that Penn Central, in which he was heavily invested, was going under. He unloaded. His wife didn't and lost 1,000 shares. Hank's distinguished playing career—twice MVP, a still-standing American League record of 183 runs batted in (in 154 games)—was interrupted by four years in the service during World War II. After a short playing hitch with Pittsburgh, he was a crafty baseball front office executive, partnering with equally wily Bill Veeck.

Mean Joe Greene

HE CAME INTO the National Football League with a ready-made reputation. He was "Mean" Joe Greene, the smiling terror from Temple, Texas. And right from the start it was apparent he would be one of the great ones. Greene was Coach Chuck Noll's first draft choice when he took over the Pittsburgh Steelers in 1969—the team went 1-13, but Mean Joe was NFL Rookie of the Year and lived up to his name by getting ejected twice for slugging opposing players. After his fourth season, he was voted the winner of the George Halas Trophy as the outstanding defensive player in professional football. It wasn't even close. The runners-up, the Redskins' Chris Hanburger and the 49ers' Dave Wilcox, received one-fourth of Greene's tally in balloting I conducted for the NEA syndicate, polling all players in the NFL. He won it again two years later while the Steelers were in the dynastic midst of winning four Super Bowls in six years, powered on defense by the "Steel Curtain" featuring Greene at defensive tackle abetted by three other future Hall of Famers—linebackers Jack Lambert and Jack Ham, and safety Mel Blount. Mean Joe was big for his time, super quick off the ball, with a combative attitude that lasted all twelve seasons he played for Pittsburgh, making him one of the greatest defensive linemen in NFL history. But maybe his ultimate fame came from a prize-winning Coca-Cola commercial made in 1979 and aired at the Super Bowl that year. Shot over three days, it showed a scowling Mean Joe in football gear hobbling under the stands, where a little boy offered him the soft drink, which he guzzled in one swig as his donor slunk off. Mean Joe turned and said "Hey, kid," then graciously tossed the Steelers jersey slung over his shoulder pads to the eager youngster. It transformed his public persona into an amiable giant. Off the field, I found him personable and smiling, the antithesis of his gruff bad-boy image. "I don't hate anybody," he said to me. "I'm loose, easy going. But if a guy takes a shot at me, I might go back and get him." Especially if the other guy happened to be carrying a football. "Going after the quarterback," he added, "is like playing king of the mountain. When you get him, you're on top of the mountain."

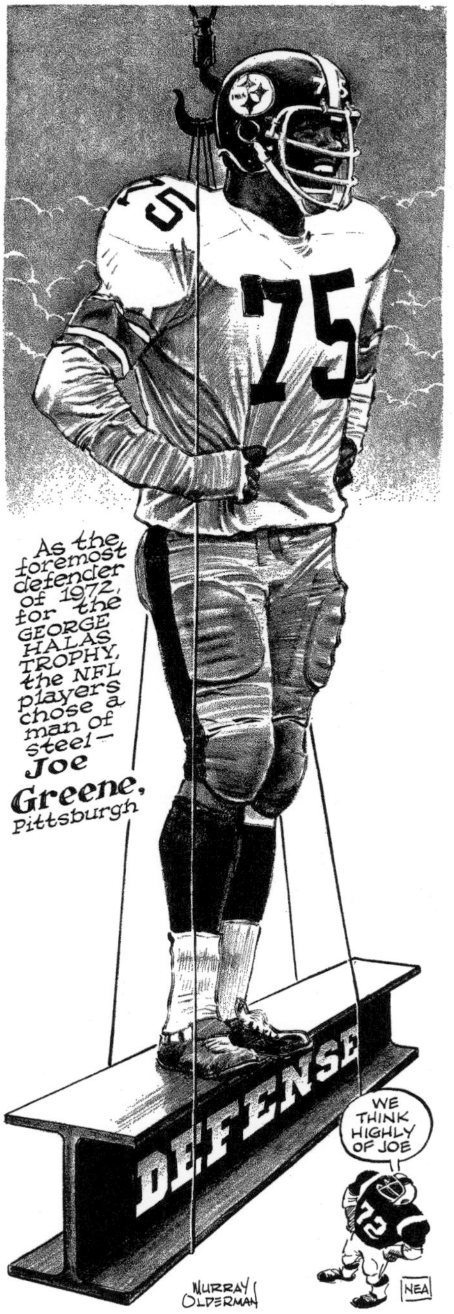
As the foremost defender of 1972, for the GEORGE HALAS TROPHY, the NFL players chose a man of steel— Joe Greene, Pittsburgh
75
75
75
DEFENSE
WE THINK HIGHLY OF JOE
72
MURRAY OLDERMAN
NEA

"Strong Support"

John Havlicek

"HONDO," AS HE was known, didn't invent the Sixth Man in basketball, but he embodied its personification. Frank Ramsey, his predecessor on the Boston Celtics, was the first Sixth Man, originated by Coach Red Auerbach because Hall of Famers Bob Cousy and Bill Sharman were already starters in the backcourt. Ramsey, a guard, too, was good enough to be in the regular lineup, so Auerbach used him as the first man off the bench, logging as much time as the starters. The strategy worked so well that it became basketball doctrine, and now the NBA gives out a Sixth Man Award annually. Havlicek, of Czech-Croatian descent, was a first round draft choice out of Ohio State, playing on a team led by Jerry Lucas, with Bobby Knight as a reserve. He was a 'tweener at 6'5" and could be used at shooting guard or small forward. The Celtics, in the early years, inserted Hondo in the backcourt as the sixth man, but over time he became so important to both their offense and defense that he played virtually full time, and as the cartoon opposite indicates was averaging more than forty-five minutes a game in the latter part of his sixteen-year pro career, during which the Celtics captured eight NBA

titles. In the 1965 championship series finale against the Philadelphia 76ers, he made one of the great plays in NBA lore. With five seconds left in the deciding game, Philadelphia down by a point, Hal Greer of the 76ers inbounded the ball. Hondo, standing with his back to the passer, suddenly leaped, spun, and tapped the ball to teammate Sam Jones to seal the win. He was also Boston's all-time leading scorer and ceaseless on the court, never letting up. Celtics great Bill Russell called him "the best all around player I ever saw." After his playing days, the popular Hondo became a regular at celebrity pro-ams for golf tournaments around the country, and when he came past where I lived at Mission Hills Country Club, site of the Dinah Shore, I'd come out and remind him archly that he could have been a pro football player. Knowing he had been a high school quarterback, the Cleveland Browns also drafted him coming out of college and brought him to training camp. He had a good shot at making the roster as a wide receiver, but decided, rightly, that his future was really in pro basketball and left to find his destiny with the Boston Celtics.

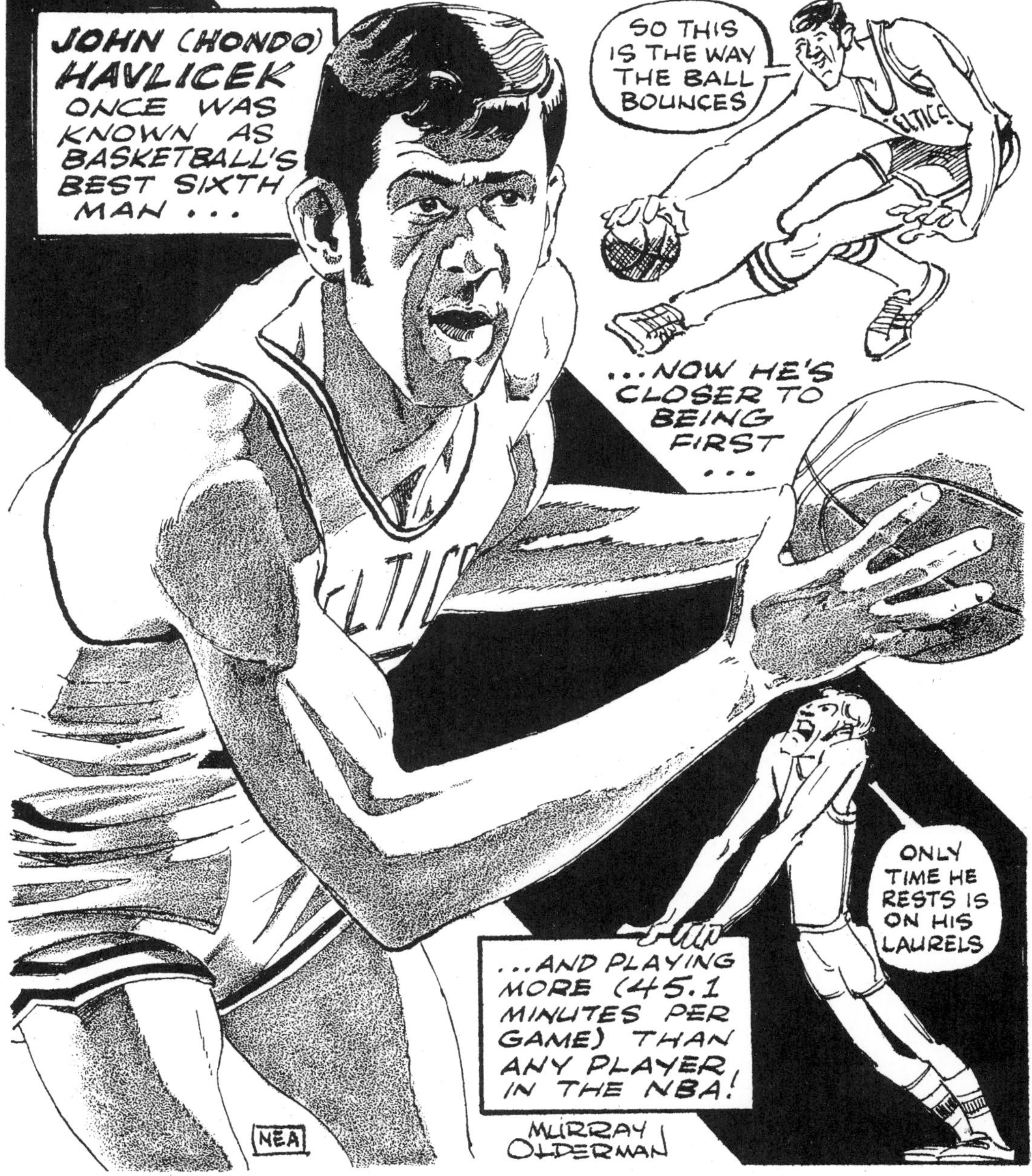
JOHN (HONDO) HAVLICEK ONCE WAS KNOWN AS BASKETBALL'S BEST SIXTH MAN ...
SO THIS IS THE WAY THE BALL BOUNCES
...NOW HE'S CLOSER TO BEING FIRST ...
ONLY TIME HE RESTS IS ON HIS LAURELS
...AND PLAYING MORE (45.1 MINUTES PER GAME) THAN ANY PLAYER IN THE NBA!
NEA
MURRAY OLDERMAN

"Playing More"

Woody Hayes

ON MY FIRST visit to Ohio State, the epicenter of college football frenzy, I was stiffed by Woody Hayes, making his debut in 1951 as the Buckeyes' head coach. On assignment for the *Minneapolis Star*, I was making a motor tour of Big Ten football camps with Dick Cullum of the sister *Minneapolis Tribune*. When we chugged into Columbus, Ohio, for the expected interview with the head coach, there was no Woody Hayes. He refused to see us. I gave it another shot a couple of decades later when Ohio State came out to play California on October 7, 1972, and the Buckeyes were quartered at the Mark Hopkins Hotel in San Francisco. I met Woody outside the hotel atop Nob Hill, overlooking the scenic bay on a crisp, beautiful day, and he was delightful. The martinet coach was wearing red, flaring, cuffless pants and told me the story of two guys meeting on the street and one says, "How's your wife?" And the other replies, "Compared to what?" Applying it to football, under criticism for its brutality—"the football guy is the anti-hero," he declaimed—Woody philosophically said, "Compared to other activities of young people, football is so far out front there's no contest. We put on a wholesome show, sincere enough because we want to win."

That Ohio State team, powered by freshman running back Archie Griffin, a two-time Heisman Award winner, went on to the Rose Bowl, one of eight Hayes-coached appearances in Pasadena. He also produced five national champions. "I'm a mean old walrus," he told me, "but I believe I've been a credit to the game of football." That assertion, however, came into doubt when his twenty-eight-year Ohio State tenure ended ignominiously on the sideline of the 1978 Gator Bowl after he punched an opposing Clemson player who had intercepted a pass. The tempestuous Buckeye coach was almost sixty-five at the time. He was a controlling figure with a conservative style that was dubbed "three yards and a cloud of dust," but he was an influential force—eleven future college head coaches served on his staffs at Denison, Miami of Ohio, and Ohio State.

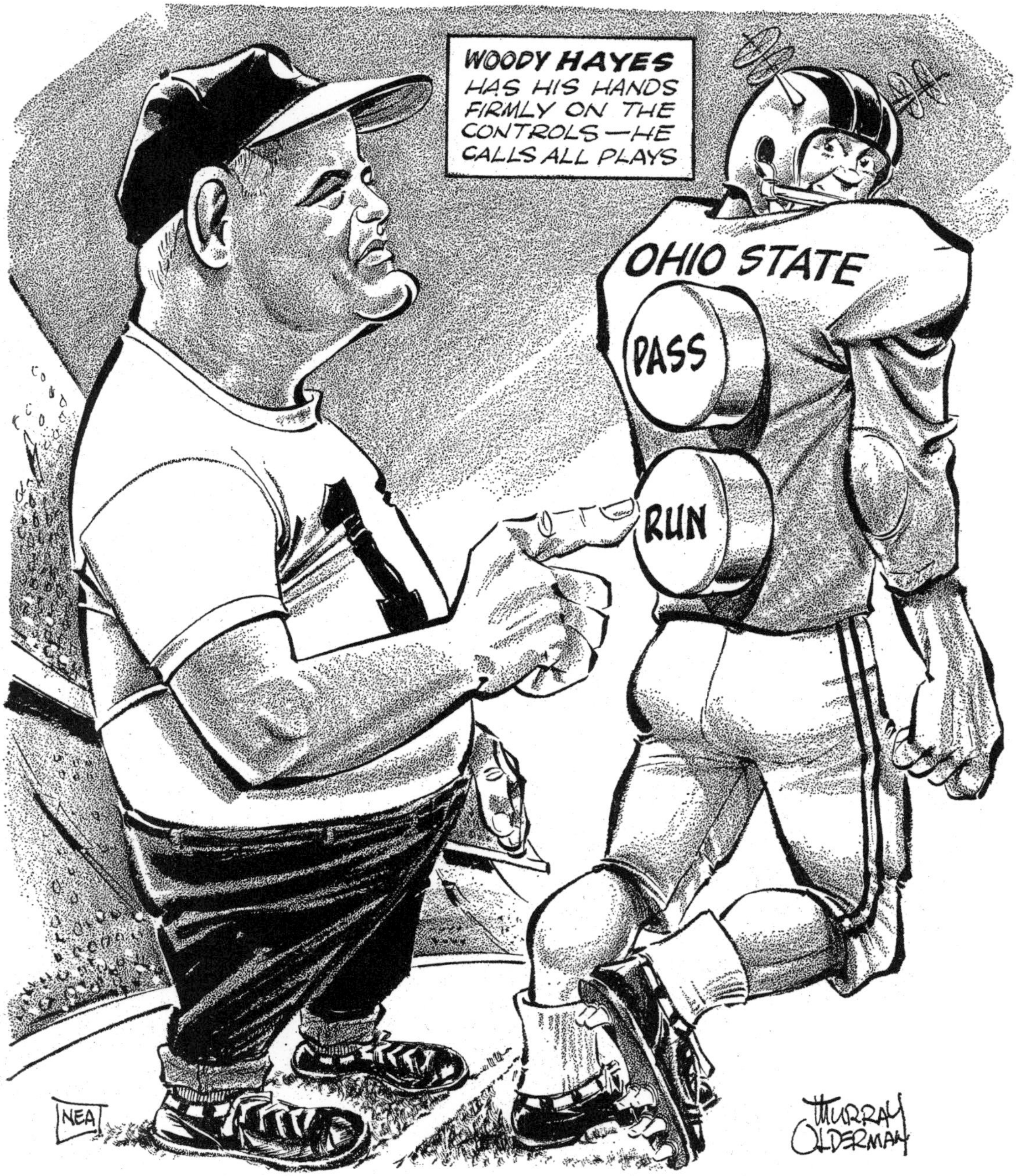
WOODY HAYES
HAS HIS HANDS
FIRMLY ON THE
CONTROLS—HE
CALLS ALL PLAYS
OHIO STATE
PASS
RUN
NEA
MURRAY
OLDERMAN

"Push Button Coach"

Ben Hogan

MY AVENUE TO Ben Hogan was Jimmy Demaret, a legendary golf character. Both were Texans with completely disparate personalities—Hogan was withdrawn, aloof; Demaret was flamboyant, ever-smiling—bound by their passion for the sport and friends for life. Jimmy was good enough to win three Masters titles before World War II. Ben trumped him. He came back from a near fatal auto accident that left him with a limp and became the only golfer in history to win the Masters, the U.S. Open, the British Open in the same calendar year (called the Hogan Slam). Bantam Ben returned from Carnoustie to a New York ticker tape parade. By then Jimmy was a golf pro in the Catskills. Sports editor Harry Grayson contacted Demaret for a story on Hogan. We drove up to Jimmy at the Concord, and the result was a three-part syndicated series, "My Partner, Ben," with Demaret's byline, that I illustrated and helped write. It was expanded into a McGraw-Hill book for which I drew illustrations and wrote some text. (A young Jimmy Breslin, who hung around our office, also worked on it.) Hogan had always been portrayed as stiff-lipped, humorless, and obsessed with his golf swing. "I play golf with friends," he said, "but there are never friendly games." Then I went to a golf clinic put on by the man they also called "The Hawk," at the Englewood, New Jersey Golf Club. He was cordial to the spectators, exhibited sly humor, and was masterful in demonstrating fades and draws as he enthralled them with his shot making. Hogan's quest for perfection in golf led him to return to his native Fort Worth and manufacture a popular brand of clubs that carried his name.

MY PARTNER **BEN**

by *JIMMY DEMARET*

"...the only guy in golf Ben Hogan will listen to."

Jim Lee Howell

THE SUBJECT OF conversation around our dining-room table centered on the kind of snuff their grandmothers dipped down on the farm. That was Jim Lee Howell and my wife Nancy comparing the merits of Red Rooster and Garrett. The Howells lived just up the street from us on the border of Leonia and Englewood, New Jersey, near the George Washington Bridge. Jim Lee was a good ol' boy from Arkansas. Nancy was from rural east Texas. Jim Lee played center on my team in the Leonia recreational basketball league, his 6'5" frame shouldering aside younger players driving to the basket—Jim Lee had been on an Arkansas basketball team that reached the tryout finals for the 1936 Olympic Games. Maybe they were also intimidated by the fact he was head coach of the New York football Giants across the river. He first came to the Giants out of college as a receiver for six seasons, 1937–42, joined the Marines and led a World War II battlefield charge on Okinawa, then played two more seasons. He succeeded Steve Owen as head coach in 1954. Jim Lee had curious standards in assessing talent—he downgraded one young linebacker because "his jaw's too big," and a running

back wouldn't make it because "he's got too much white in his eyes." But Jim Lee had the judgment to hire unknown Vince Lombardi, a contemporary of owner Wellington Mara at Fordham, to run the offense and to make veteran safety Tom Landry his defensive coordinator. He stood impassively on the sidelines with his arms clasped. "When it's fourth and one," he said, "it becomes my decision." The Giants never had a losing record in his head coaching tenure, won three division titles, and captivated New York in 1956 by trouncing the Chicago Bears, 47-7, for the NFL championship. But Jim Lee stepped down abruptly on his own terms after six years, explaining, "I just don't want to make bed check on football players any more." The fuss of dealing with a roster of fifty players burned him out. There was no pretense in Jim Lee, perhaps the most honest man I've met in sports. He always greeted me with a hearty laugh and a direct response to any question. He stayed on as a personnel director and consultant for the Giants, going back to his native Lonoke, Arkansas, between seasons, until he retired there three decades later.

1954
W 7 L 5
1955
W 6 L 5
1956
W 8 L 3
1957
W 7 L 5
1958
W 9 L 3
1959
W 10 L 2
1960
GIANTS
60
FINEST READING SHELF IN THEIR HISTORY IS THE LEGACY LEFT TO THE GIANTS BY VACATING JIM LEE HOWELL
MURRAY OLDERMAN

"Best Years of Their Life"

Lamar Hunt

AFTER TENNIS ON his Dallas estate, Lamar suggested we go out for pizza. There was a popular pizza joint a few blocks away. When we got there, a line had already formed out into the street. Lamar meekly took his place at the end. The multi-millionaire owner of the Kansas City Chiefs, the founder of the American Football League, wouldn't think of pulling rank. That wasn't his way, though he had progressed from the modest tract home when I first met him to the palatial $3.3 million (in 1960's dollars) mansion that he had acquired at half price from industrialist James Ling. And he had forsaken his quirky habit of giving ten-cent tips to Manhattan cabbies. Hank Stram, an assistant coach at Miami University in Coral Gables, told me about this young man watching practice, wearing a tattered coat, wrinkled pants, with holes in his shoes, who shyly introduced himself and asked Hank to coach his new team in the AFL. I took a taxi to see Lamar, then twenty-five years old, in a Dallas suburb, with baby clothes on a line in the backyard. Rosemary, his first wife, made lunch and washed the dishes and sighed, "I sure wish I had a clothes dryer." When it was time to go back to my hotel, Lamar asked me how much the fare would be. Five to ten bucks. "I'll drive you," he said, starting up his five-year-old Olds. The new league was "iffy" and when asked how long Lamar could afford to lose a million a year, H.L. Hunt, his fabled oil billionaire father, responded, "Oh, about 150 years." Though frugal, Lamar didn't skimp in building his franchise, switched it from Dallas to Kansas City, and saw Stram, the unknown he hired, lead the Chiefs to a win in Super Bowl III. Lamar coined the term "Super Bowl" after watching one of his kids bounce a "super ball" over his garage. He also invested heavily in tennis and soccer and ultimately was elected to the Hall of Fame in all three sports. He invited me to dinner one night with his brother Bunker, who tried to corner the world's silver market, explaining with a twinkle in his eyes behind thick lenses, "Bunker thinks he knows everything about football. I need you there when he starts bragging." Bunker was mute for the evening. There was no pretense about Lamar. After his second marriage, his scale of living expanded, but Lamar remained the humble, unassuming man I knew from the start.

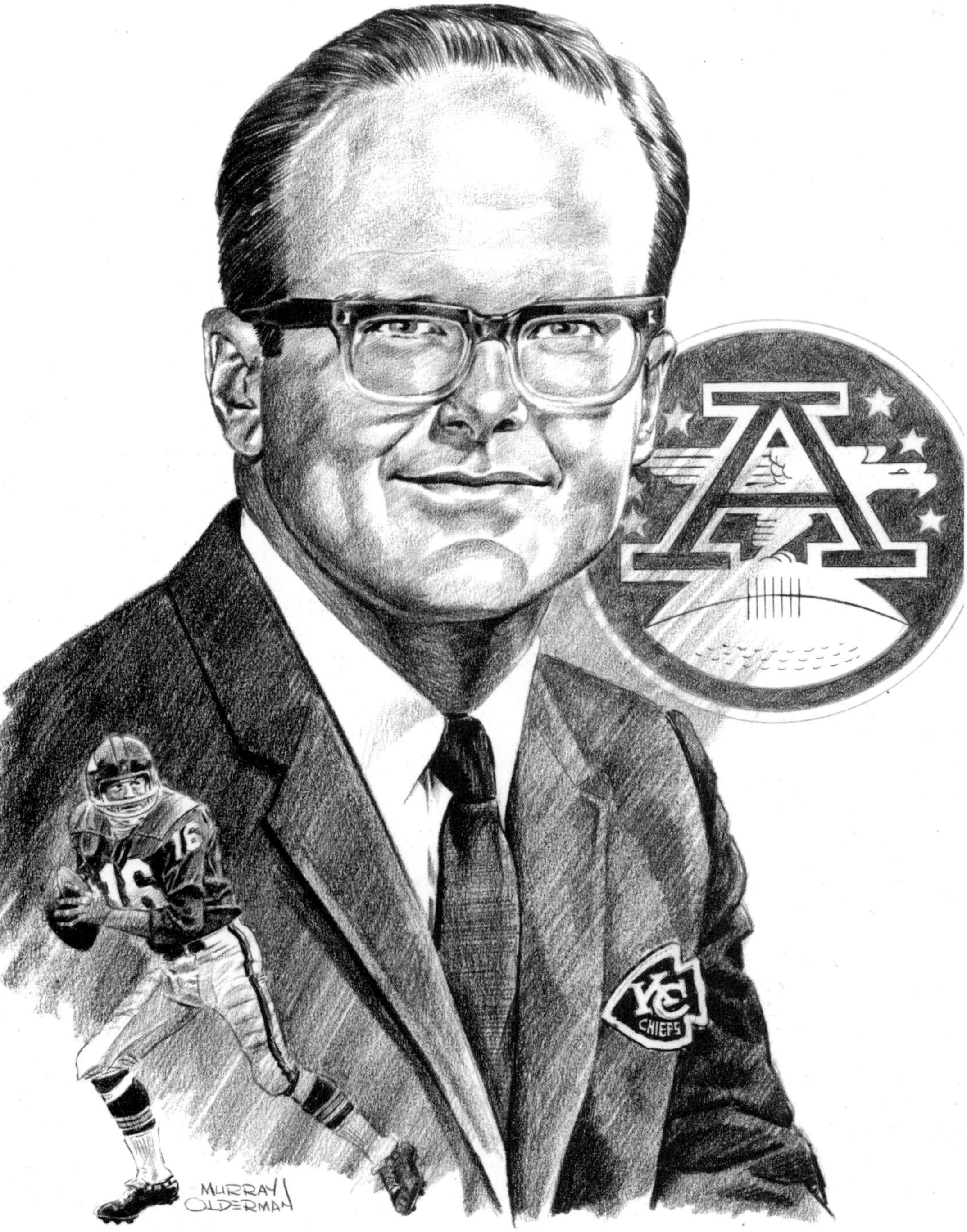
CHIEFS
MURRAY
OLDERMAN

Reggie Jackson

A SMILING VIDA Blue grabbed my hand as I entered the dugout of the Oakland A's and said, "Somebody wants to see you." He pulled me out to the field and up to the batting cage. In it was Reggie Jackson swatting batting practice pitches. "Hey," yelled Vida, the A's star pitcher, with a smirk, "Lookee here." Jackson turned around, saw me, lowered his bat, and let loose a string of four-and-ten-letter words, all directed at me and my heritage. He walked around the cage opening and confronted me, bat still in his hand, and continued his harangue. I was completely startled. I had just returned from a month's trip to Europe and had no idea he was unhappy with me. It turned out that *Sport* magazine had run a cover story on Reggie by me—it was heavily edited by Dick Schaap—during my absence, and Reggie was furious. All around us the nation's top baseball writers and columnists were milling, looking for an off-day story between the second and third games of the 1974 World Series. They had it. Jackson, ingratiating and moody by turn, had given me the run-around when I was researching the story, and I wrote it. While he kept me waiting in his Oakland Hills apartment, I took stock of the contents, including a gun on the TV set. That infuriated him. Months later, we were stuck in an elevator at a Raiders football game in the same stadium. He smiled and stuck out his hand, and whenever I'd see him, like at spring training in Palm Springs, he'd come over and be affable. The slugging outfielder, complex and volatile always, went on to become "Mr. October" with his World Series home-run hitting exploits for the Yankees.

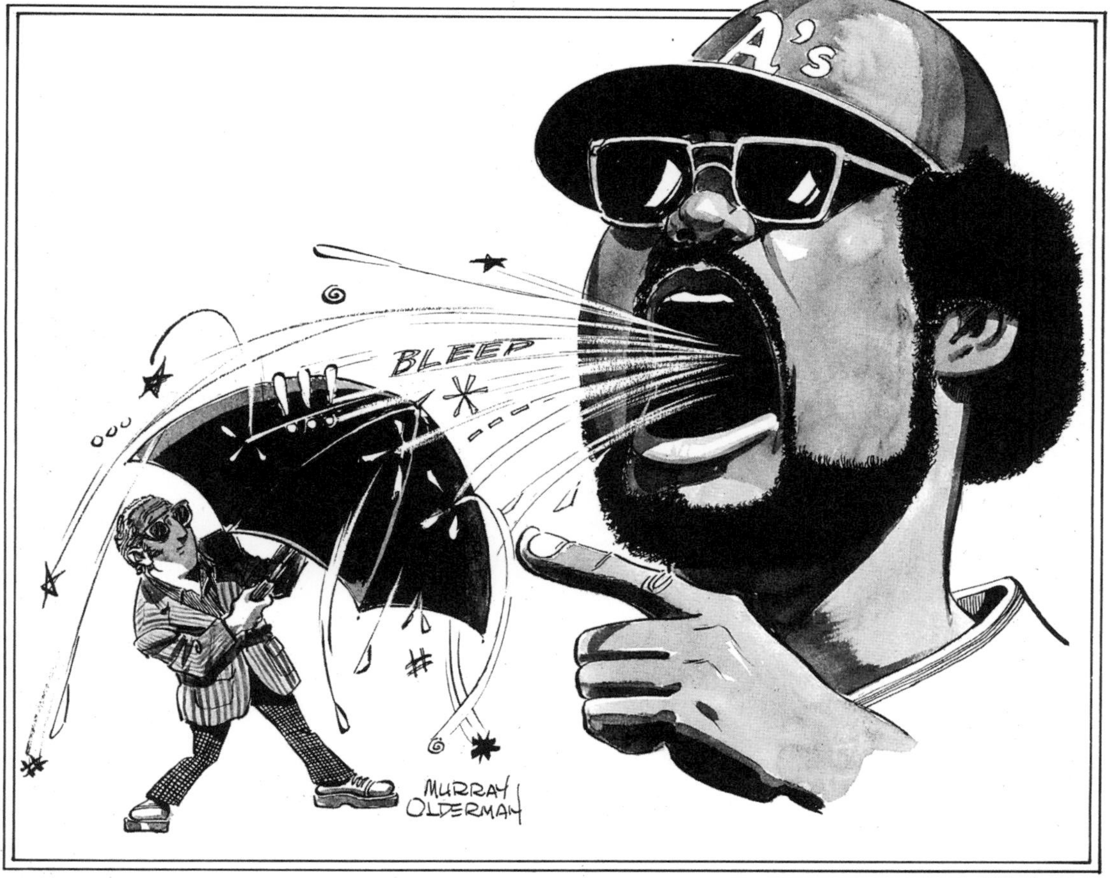
BLEEP
MURRAY OLDERMAN

Don James

THERE WERE PEOPLE you met as a sports journalist with whom you found instant rapport. A little known assistant coach at Florida State had that charisma. I was in Tallahassee on the Seminoles' campus to speak at an annual meeting of Florida sports writers, and as part of the festivities a softball game was arranged. To fill out the lineups, members of the coaching staffs were recruited, and among them, playing in the infield with me, was diminutive Don James. We had a common frame of reference because I knew his older brother Tommy, who played eight seasons in the defensive backfield of the original Cleveland Browns and was the holder for Lou Groza on field goal attempts. The James brothers had both started their football at Massillon High in Ohio, where legendary Paul Brown coached. Don played quarterback at University of Miami in Coral Gables and set five passing records. When I met him, he was in the midst of twelve years as a college assistant, keenly inquisitive, with a good sense of humor. We hooked up again after he got his first head job at Kent State, where the San Francisco 49ers, with whom I was traveling, practiced for a week during a road trip. Don in-

vited me to his home. In his four years there, he tutored Nick Saban of Alabama fame and Gary Pinkel of Missouri. In 1975, he took over the University of Washington program, and in eighteen years he had only one losing record. When an assignment took me to Seattle, Don showed me around the campus, was gracious enough to lose at tennis, and was as cordial as ever. He was also a football innovator, among the first coaches to get wired into the new sideline technology that kept them connected to the field. The Huskies were a perfect 12-0 in 1991 and shared the national title. He spurned big offers to take a pro job. When sanctions were applied to the football program a year later for improper recruiting and booster benefits—Don and his staff weren't implicated—he simply walked away because he felt the school's administration didn't back his regime, and never coached again. His last three teams all went to the Rose Bowl, and he was voted into the College Football Hall of Fame. Our friendly contact continued since Don contentedly spent half the year in a nearby Palm Desert, California, winter residence.

'WE HEAR YOU—LOUD AND CLEAR'

WASHINGTON HUSKIES

COACH DON JAMES

NEA

MURRAY OLDERMAN

WIRED FOR RESULTS

Bobby Jones

GOLF PENETRATED THE national consciousness of sport's Golden Age in the "Roaring Twenties" through the feats of an amateur from Atlanta named Robert Tyre Jones Jr., who competed in tourneys at fourteen, won the U.S. Open at twenty-one, and amassed thirteen major titles. He retired abruptly at twenty-eight to practice law after achieving his Grand Slam version by winning the U.S. Open, British Open, U.S. Amateur, and British Amateur in 1930. But he retained a connection to golf by building Augusta National Golf Course in 1934 to host an invitational tournament that he named The Masters. A crippling, progressive disease of the spinal cord struck him in his mid-30s and incapacitated him until his death in 1971, memorialized in this cartoon. Getting around with great difficulty, using a cane, but alert and communicative, Bobby Jones was the featured guest in the 1950s at a press outing to celebrate the 100th anniversary of the oldest course in the U.S., aptly named St. Andrews, just north of New York. The two of us lounged in the clubhouse while the other writers were out on the course. He puffed on a cigarette in an ornate holder, a Southern in-

carnation of Franklin D. Roosevelt, and in his measured Georgia drawl willingly discussed the big topic of the day, the 1954 Supreme Court decision to integrate education. He was concerned about desegregation of public schools. "I am not in favor of black children attending our grade schools," he said frankly. It was, even for that time, a shocking observation. I didn't pick up on it as a story. Those were more congenial times journalistically, or maybe I was simply naive. At the Masters in 1965, I met Jones again in his home setting, through the auspices of Atlanta columnist Furman Bisher, in his private cottage on the edge of the tenth tee at Augusta National. By this time, he was confined to a wheelchair and cloaked in a green robe. Through the window of his bedroom, he could watch the throngs (as many as 45,000 a day) follow the play. He confined his conversation to golf and the greatness of Jack Nicklaus, who had dethroned Arnold Palmer as number one in the world. "He's always been a sweet, friendly boy," said Jones, "maybe a little shy and overwhelmed by 'Arnie's Army.' Nobody ever combined Jack's power and form." Tiger Woods was not yet born.

..the venerable Bobby Jones no longer can be there, but his spirit remains manifest at Augusta....

"Monument to the Man"

Jack Kemp

I WAS ACCOMPANYING Congressman Kemp when he was in his political mode, on a speaking swing through North Carolina and the Midwest. We weren't strangers. I had listened to Jack years before, just out of Occidental College, lament about his football future at Toots Shor's in New York when he was on the Giants' taxi squad. He turned up as the first quarterback of the Los Angeles Chargers of the new AFL, led them first to a title game and then the AFL crown after they shifted the next year to San Diego. He was peddled to Buffalo on waivers for $100 because of a front office snafu while he was injured. He then lead the Bills to AFL titles in 1964–65. But there was more to Kemp than Xs and Os. I visited his dormitory room in training camp, and next to his playbook were economic treatises on supply-side economics, which he favored, and Keynsian theories, which he opposed. Kemp was a conservative Republican, but very Kennedy-esque in appearance with snub-nosed good looks and a shock of hair over his forehead. As his playing days wound down, politics became his raison d'etre; he was elected to Congress in a blue-collar, heavily Democratic district outside Buffalo—he pointed out that he was a labor leader himself, as the organizing head of the fledgling AFL players union. He was a politician all right. He served eighteen years as a Congressman virtually unopposed, was appointed to the elder George Bush's cabinet, and ran on the Republican ticket as the vice-presidential candidate in 1996. Jack hosted a posh private party at every Super Bowl and always invited me. But I never forgot the original Kemp I knew as a jock because he happened to be a very competent quarterback with a cannonball arm—he could heave it eighty yards downfield—and good mobility.

THE ONLY UNDEFEATED TEAM IN PROFESSIONAL FOOTBALL, SAN DIEGO'S CHARGERS ...
GIVES ME A CHARGE, TOO
... HAS BEEN KEPT THAT WAY ON THE WINGS OF ...
... QUARTERBACK JACK KEMP!
HIS PASSES LEAD ME JUST RIGHT
MURRAY OLDERMAN

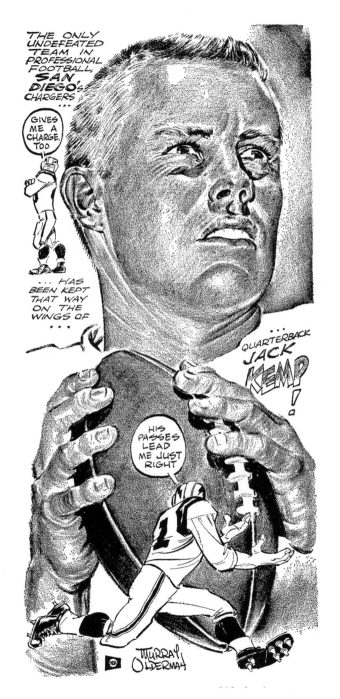

"Lead Charger"

Jean-Claude Killy

LET'S JUST SAY I had an edge on my American colleagues covering the 1968 Winter Olympics at Grenoble, where my focus was on Alpine events and a dashing young Frenchman who was swooping to a covey of gold medals. Jean-Claude Killy's English was nil then. The interviews were conducted only in French at the time. I was fairly fluent and could follow his explanations of navigating through the fog that embraced the slalom and downhill runs at Chamrousse and passed them along to Jim Murray of the *Los Angeles Times*, the only other scribe who bothered to come out to the Olympic site. If Jean-Claude Killy had been American, he would still be lionized as the greatest skier ever—an encomium he rates anywhere there's a snow-covered slope. He grew up in the small French Alpine hamlet of Val d'Isère, where skis are strapped on the feet of children almost as soon as they walk. Killy started winning international events as a teenager and peaked in '68 at age twenty-five. He had already won the World Cup a year earlier. World-class skiers tend to specialize in the variant Alpine races, depending on their techniques and mind-sets. A slalom champ,

expert at carving through gates, rarely excels at the longer downhill. Killy was the world's best at all of them—downhill, giant slalom, slalom. And he accomplished the remarkable feat of winning gold medals in all three disciplines at the Grenoble Games. It made Killy a national hero in France. Of course, he married a movie star, appeared in some films himself, and cashed in on his prominence by lending his name to an American brand of skis. But apparently it didn't suffice to have a chalet in Geneva and swim in neighbor Petula Clark's pool. Four years later—on skis in the interim only ten times for commercials and such—he un-retired to join the U.S. pro circuit. I caught up to him again (or rather, waited at the bottom) at Bear Valley, California, in the High Sierra. He had taken the money lead on the Benson & Hedges Grand Prix tour. "It's fine for me now," he said, in English, "because I'm skiing well. I am before the public now, and it gives me a fantastic life. I have a challenge. Making movies is more work, but more money. I ski because I am a better skier than a movie star."

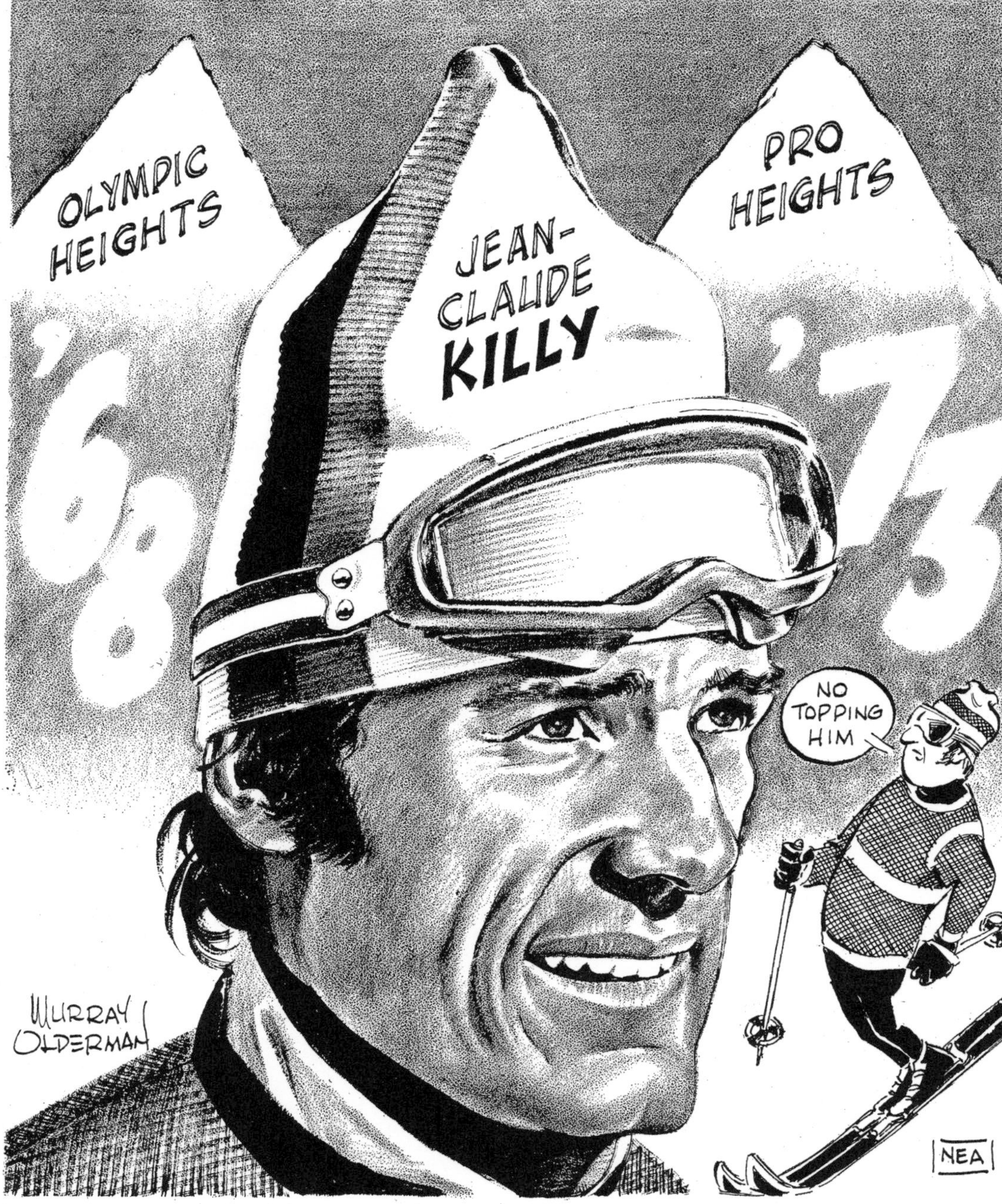
OLYMPIC HEIGHTS
'68
JEAN-CLAUDE KILLY
PRO HEIGHTS
'73
NO TOPPING HIM
MURRAY OLDERMAN
NEA

"Mountain Man"

Billie Jean King

BILLIE JEAN KING was an iconic, revered sports activist who affirmed women's rights and for whom the grounds at the U.S. Open in Flushing Meadows are named. But the Billie Jean King I first knew was a top-rate tennis player with a driving penchant to win and a giggly personality. Athletic genes were in her Moffitt family. Younger brother Randy was a big league relief pitcher of some success. Billie Jean's early mentor was Dennis Vander Meer, a South African pro with whom I wrote a book, *Tennis Clinic*, and together they ran a clinic at Lake Tahoe, where I had a part-time home. Billie Jean's memorable feat, beyond winning six Wimbledon and four U.S. Open singles championships and a total of thirty-nine Grand Slam titles, was a hokey exhibition match in the Houston Astrodome against Bobby Riggs that somehow captivated a nation. Staged with circus hoopla before a crowd of 30,000 and a national TV audience, it was billed as the "Battle of the Sexes," but it really was a twenty-nine-year-old woman who was about to come out of the closet sexually against a chauvinistic 55-year-old has-been who was more noted for his addiction to gambling than the brilliant player he had once been. She was carried into the arena on a lavish Egyptian litter; he arrived in a Chinese rickshaw. Billie Jean won in three straight sets and collected $100,000. It proved nothing tennis-wise, although it gave her image a nice lift. "Before," she said, "people looked at me as a toughie, the villain and the radical. Now they look at me as the heroine." She was probably the most dominant personality in all of women's sports. Her finest achievement beyond her success on the court was her maturation as an admired leader of the feminist crusade that elevated women's tennis to virtual parity with men in prize money at major tournaments.

MURRAY OLDERMAN

MAINLINER MAGAZINE

DECEMBER 1974

131.

Sandy Koufax

FOR HIS LAST six years as an active player, he was the best pitcher in the long history of baseball, bar none. Sanford "Sandy" Koufax absolutely dominated the game from 1961 through 1966, the last half of his twelve-year career with the Brooklyn/Los Angeles Dodgers. Brooklyn-bred Sandy went to Cincinnati on a basketball scholarship, but learned to refine his natural skills as a left-handed flame thrower. His win totals over the final four seasons, when the Dodgers, transplanted to Los Angeles in 1958, won three National League pennants, were twenty-five, nineteen, twenty-six, and twenty-seven. He won four Cy Young Awards and pitched four no-hitters, one of them a perfect game. Every Jewish mother in New York and the Los Angeles basin wanted her daughter to marry Sandy—handsome, personable, well spoken, and, oh, such a pitcher. Before his thirty-first birthday, however, he retired from baseball abruptly because he feared incapacitating, permanent damage from severe arthritis in his left arm. I suspect Tommy John surgery, not yet devised, might have prolonged his career. He shied away from the public the minute he stopped pitching, by choice. Celebrity status left him with a worm's-eye view of America because he never saw much beyond the inside of an elevator. "It's hard to tell Cincinnati from Pittsburgh," he told me. "I know San Francisco because it's so cold, and I know Houston because it's so hot." He measured cities by the quality of their hotels' room service. He hosted an NBC pre-game baseball show in Boston to present an All-Major League team I had assembled, joined by Red Sox outfielder Carl Yastrzemski, and I could see he was neither comfortable nor very good, which surprised me, because as a player he provided thoughtful interviews in a modulated voice that seemed ideal for the airwaves. With the mike in his hand, though, he provided little insight into baseball or its players because he ducked critical comment and protected the jocks. He just dropped out and lived in isolated rural areas such as New Hampshire, emerging from hibernation once a year to advise young pitchers at Dodger training camps. A waste of talent.

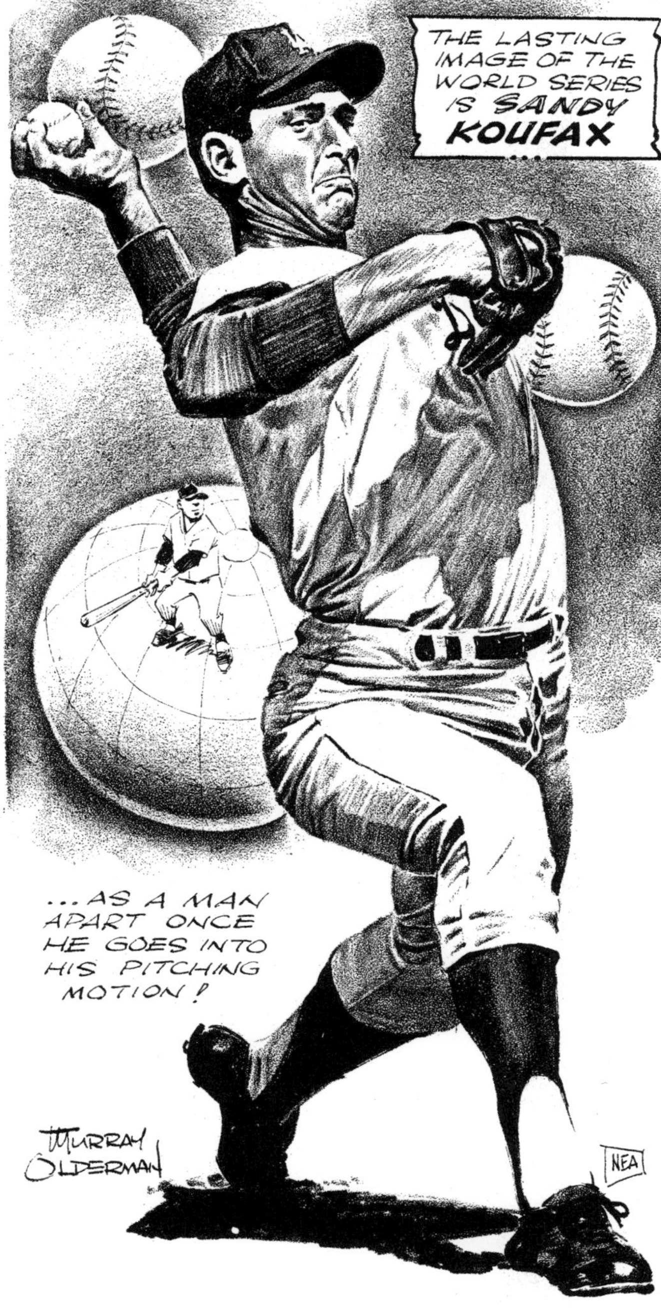
THE LASTING IMAGE OF THE WORLD SERIES IS SANDY KOUFAX
...AS A MAN APART ONCE HE GOES INTO HIS PITCHING MOTION!
MURRAY OLDERMAN
NEA

"In His Own Sphere"

Jack Kramer

MY BIG MOMENT in sports promotion was sharing the title of director of a tennis tournament with the legendary Jack Kramer, the man most responsible for the worldwide growth of pro tennis. The McCulloch Corporation founded Lake Havasu City, California, and enlisted me to organize and direct a pro football players' tournament in the shadow of the original London Bridge (bought and reconstructed stone by stone across the Colorado River). I persuaded some of the greatest NFL stars, from Hall of Famers Franco Harris to Ted Hendricks to Fran Tarkenton, to participate as a lark, just covering their expenses. The second year the event was moved to Apple Valley in the California high desert, where McCulloch had another development, and to add prestige, Kramer was hired to be co-director. It was a blast, and Jack was a great accomplice. I seeded the players and scheduled the matches. Jack smiled and did televised commentary from his vast expertise, having won Wimbledon and a couple of U.S. Opens when amateur tennis ruled. Missing three years during World War II, needing to make a living, he opted to go honest and led pro barnstorming tours, demolishing the likes of Bobby Riggs, Pancho Gonzales, Don Budge, and Frank Sedgman. Tennis served notice it would become the rage the day after Christmas 1947, when a blizzard shut down surface traffic in New York and 15,000 people sloshed through 50 mph winds to fill Madison Square Garden for a Kramer-Riggs showdown. I was flattered that he asked me to do a cartoon of Gonzales for his printed tour program. Jack had the world's best players under contract but, for the good of the game, ceded his tour back to them when the Open era arrived in 1967, turned to broadcasting, and was tops at that.

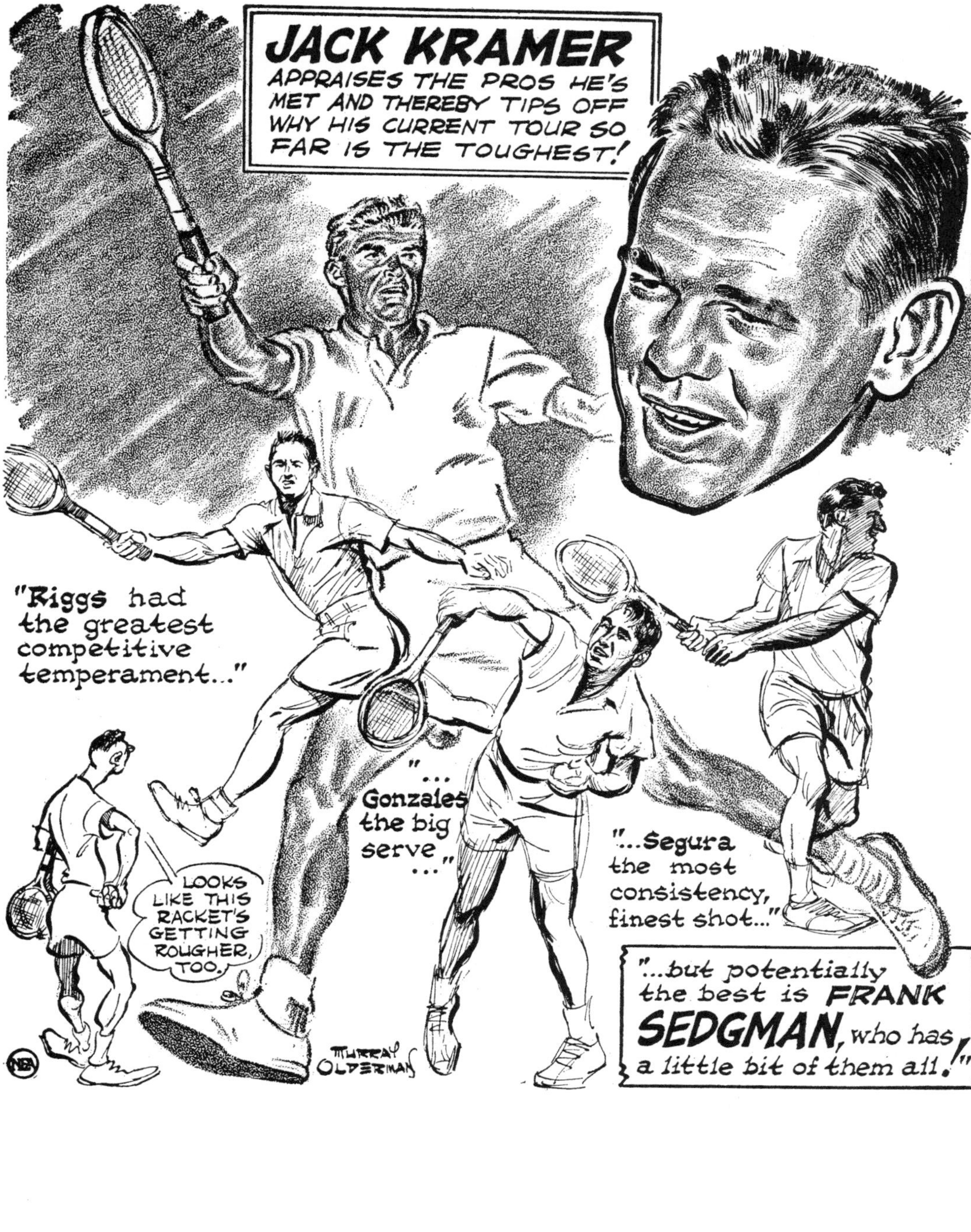
JACK KRAMER
APPRAISES THE PROS HE'S MET AND THEREBY TIPS OFF WHY HIS CURRENT TOUR SO FAR IS THE TOUGHEST!
"Riggs had the greatest competitive temperament..."
"... Gonzales the big serve ..."
"...Segura the most consistency, finest shot..."
"...but potentially the best is FRANK SEDGMAN, who has a little bit of them all!"
LOOKS LIKE THIS RACKET'S GETTING ROUGHER, TOO.
NEA
MURRAY OLDERMAN

"The King Holds Court"

Jack Lambert

SELECTED WRITERS USED to pick the Most Valuable Player in the Super Bowl, with Dick Schaap of *Sport* magazine going around the press box collecting ballots at game's end. Of the eleven votes cast at Super Bowl XIV between the Los Angeles Rams and Pittsburgh Steelers, Terry Bradshaw received six and a Datsun 280ZX for passing the Steelers to a 31-19 triumph. Wide receiver John Stallworth was named on four ballots. I cast the lone dissenting vote—for middle linebacker Jack Lambert of the Steelers. He was the man who stepped in front of a Ram receiver at the Pittsburgh fourteen-yard line to pick off a pass with five minutes to play and the game on the line. It was the Steelers' only interception and the most important play of the game. Lambert was philosophical about being overlooked as MVP. "Leave the cars to Franco Harris (an MVP five years earlier) and Terry Bradshaw," he said philosophically. "They play the glamour positions." I first was aware of Lambert when the San Francisco 49ers, with whom I was traveling, spent a week of practice at Kent State in Ohio between games. The school's sports publicist asked me to do a cartoon of this tall, skinny kid they called "The Stork" for Midwest newspapers. Drafted in the second round, he played eleven full seasons, the ferocious soul of the "Steel Curtain" that took Pittsburgh to four Super Bowl victories. Lambert looked especially fearsome because he played with a gap of four front teeth knocked out from an elbow to the mouth in a high school basketball game. Off the field, bridge in place, he looked like an elongated accountant. In his ninth season, at thirty-one, he won the George Halas Trophy as the NFL's top defender.

I'M ONE SAD SACK

THE VETERAN INSIDE LINEBACKER, IN WINNING HIS FIRST *GEORGE HALAS* TROPHY, HAD HIS BEST SEASON YET AS A PHYSICAL AND EMOTIONAL FORCE!

NEA

MURRAY OLDERMAN

JACK LAMBERT
PITTSBURGH STEELERS

Tom Landry

THE TACITURN TEXAN was the smartest football man I ever knew. He brought to the sport the organized mindset of an industrial engineer and the toughness of a rugged, over-achieving defensive back, both of which he was. The thin-lipped, balding man from the Rio Grande flew a B-17 for the Eighth Air Force over Germany during World War II and then played on Texas teams that went to the Sugar and Orange Bowls. One season with the New York Yankees of the AAC as a 25-year-old rookie defensive back (and fine punter) led to six more seasons with the New York Giants after the 1950 leagues' merger, during which he became a playing coach evolving into a full-time defensive coordinator. He stood on the sidelines against Cleveland and announced before each down what play the Browns' messenger guard was carrying in from the opposite sideline. In a Giant skull session he outlined precisely how the opponent would react to a certain situation, so Giants' owner Wellington Mara wondered what would happen if he was wrong. "There is no way," said Tom, "I can be wrong." Mara concluded, "He was the cockiest quiet man I ever met." Landry was going to quit football to go into executive management when the Dallas Cowboys came into being in 1960 and hired him as their first head coach, a job that lasted twenty-nine years, during which the Cowboys became "America's Team." They had twenty consecutive winning seasons and won two Super Bowls. The iconic coach with the stoic demeanor was derided as "The Great Stone Face," but that wasn't the Tom Landry I knew. As a Giant, he mixed the martinis at Frank Gifford's post-game parties, until he rediscovered religion. He was not an ascetic, however—when the situation called for it, he still had a convivial cocktail. He had a sly grin and a friendly outreach to a young writer. He and his lovely wife Alicia invited me to their home in Dallas. I asked him about coaching "America's Team" in the intense glare of national publicity. "If you're at peace with yourself," he answered, "you handle the pressure. It doesn't bother you that much—I guess because I placed myself in God's hands."

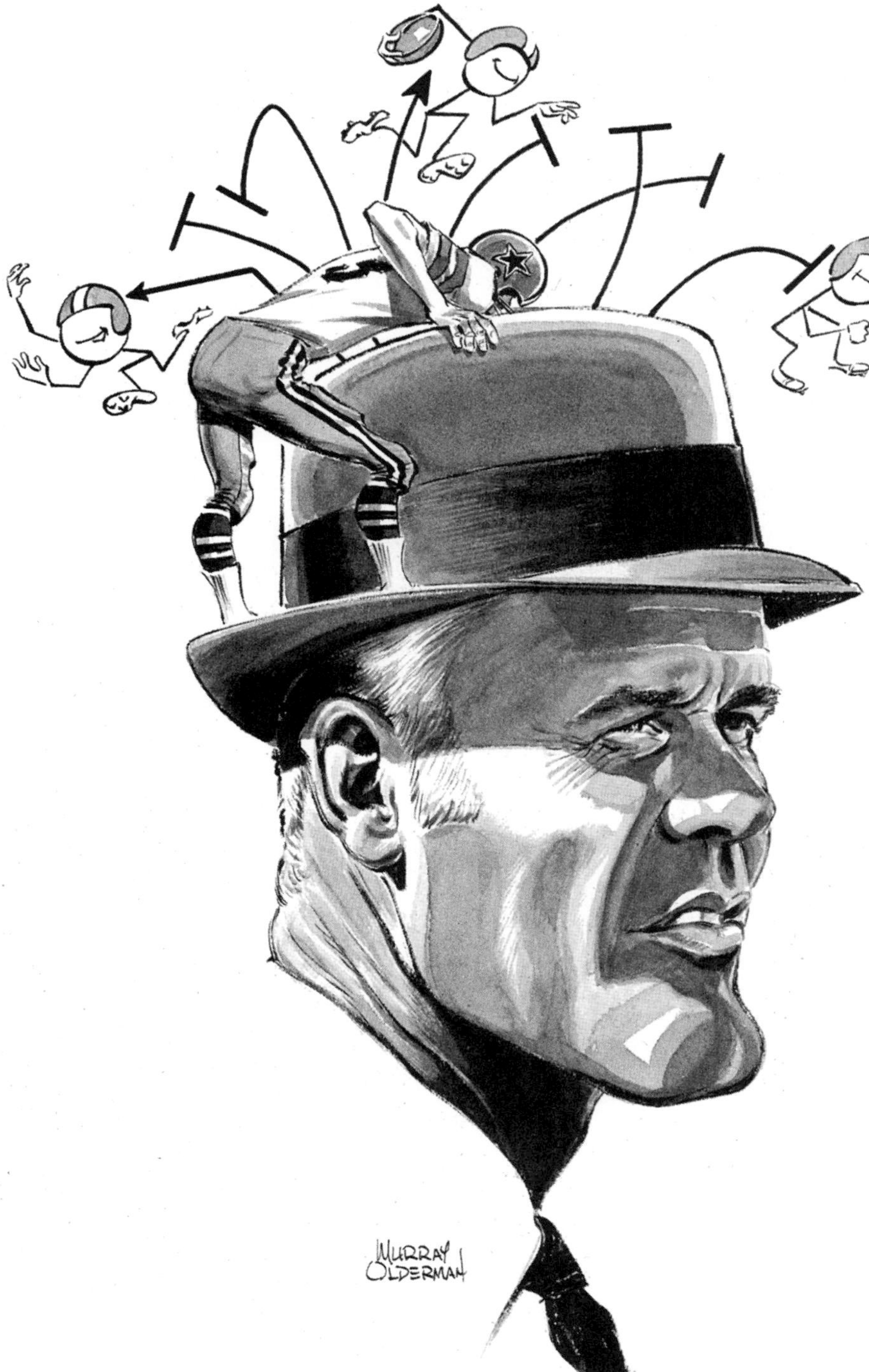
MURRAY OLDERMAN

Rod Laver

IT WAS NOT unusual to see him standing at the end of the checkout line at the Pavilions supermarket when he lived in Rancho Mirage. It's no different in Carlsbad, California, where he moved to a manse overlooking the La Costa resort. Rod Laver was among the most unassuming sports greats. You'd hardly pick him out of a crowd. At 5'8", with a wiry frame, and slightly pigeon-toed, he was among the shorter racket wielders of note in tennis history. Yet the results for this Aussie from Queensland, the son of a cattle man, match those of the best in any generation of the game. You have to put him up there with Bill Tilden, Don Budge, Jack Kramer, Pancho Gonzales, Bjorn Borg, Pete Sampras, Roger Federer, and Rafael Nadal in any discussion of all-time greatness. Laver's career overlapped the transition from amateur to open tennis in the 1960s, and for seven straight years he was the undisputed number one player in the world. No one has come close to his winning all four of the Grand Slam events (Australian Open, French Open, Wimbledon, U.S. Open) in the same year—twice! No one has equaled his feat of winning two hundred singles titles either. The left-handed Laver with the frizzy red-tinged hair and sharp-nosed features was a classic serve-and-volleyer with wristy ground strokes, and a whippet-like backhand. His strength came from his Popeye forearms, and the spring in his legs transformed him to a six-footer on overheads. His slashing style dominated all his contemporaries in head-to-head rivalries, but off the court, he was low-key, reticent. After a serious stroke, the retired and retiring "Rocket," as we called him, recovered ninety-five percent, working assiduously daily with Tommy Tucker, the Mission Hills Tennis Club pro, then would wander over to check out us hackers on the outer courts. He never made a critical comment, but would applaud the rare good shot. Rod Laver was a true tennis gentleman.

JACK
KRAMER

PRO
TOUR

ROD
LAVER

FOREST HILLS

AUGUST 1961

"Audition"

Bobby Layne

WHEN I'M ASKED to name the most memorable athlete I've ever met, my mind automatically goes to Bobby Layne. In 1959, I flew to Lubbock, Texas, to collaborate with the legendary quarterback/playboy on a story for the then prestigious *Saturday Evening Post*. I never even got to my hotel room—but I saw him win $25,000 in a poker game and laugh it off as "Las Vegas money"; turn down a job offer at three times his salary with the Pittsburgh Steelers; drop me off at the airport before going to church for his son's baptism, and say, "I don't know what kind of time you had, but you got to admit it was different." Oh yes, I was also recruited to teach the cha-cha to Lubbock's Junior Leaguers at a party Layne hosted. I was first drawn to Layne when I walked into a Steelers dressing room, and their aging quarterback was fuming over a fourth quarter loss in his first game with them. Layne had led the Detroit Lions to consecutive NFL titles. They were on their way to a third when he fractured a leg and was shunted off to last place Pittsburgh, which had gone eight straight seasons without a winning record. With a potbelly and a scarred shoulder from a horse accident on his Texas farm, the 30-something quarterback was supposed to be playing out the string. The Steelers never lost another game that 1958 season, finishing with six victories and a 7-4-1 record, and I pitched an "as told to" story to the magazine that ran the next year. A writer friend with *Life*, working on a Layne piece, used my name for an intro. He walked into the old quarterback's room in Chicago on a road trip. Layne said, "You know Olderman, huh?" My friend nodded. "He came to Lubbock," smirked Layne, "and for three days I never could get him to sit down and talk football. All he wanted to do was party." Actually, at midnight the last day of my stay at his Lubbock home, Bobby sat down for two hours and cogently offered his football philosophy. The last time I saw him was at Super Bowl XVI at the Pontiac, Michigan, Superdome, where the prodigal Hall of Famer was invited back to conduct the pre-game coin toss. In his mid-50s then, his weathered face showed the effects of hard living, but the crustiness remained. "I want to run out of money and breath at the same time," he philosophized. "When I get up every morning, I say, 'Good morning, God.' I never said, 'Good God, morning.'"

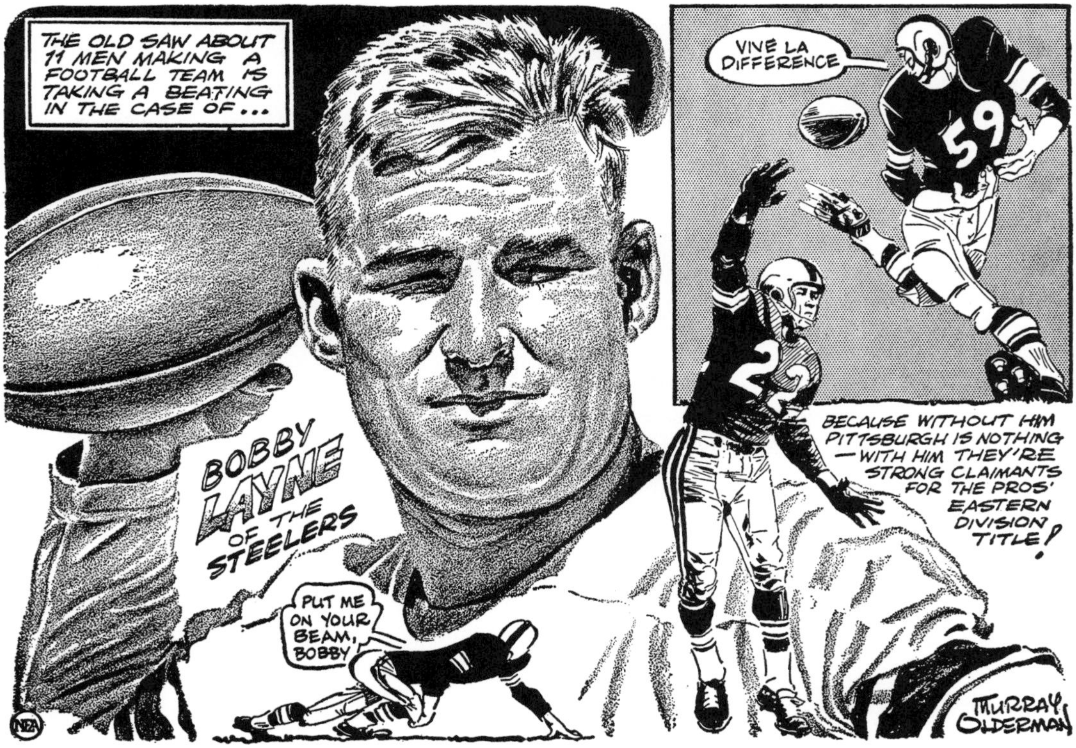
THE OLD SAW ABOUT 11 MEN MAKING A FOOTBALL TEAM IS TAKING A BEATING IN THE CASE OF...
VIVE LA DIFFERENCE
BOBBY LAYNE OF THE STEELERS
BECAUSE WITHOUT HIM PITTSBURGH IS NOTHING —WITH HIM THEY'RE STRONG CLAIMANTS FOR THE PROS' EASTERN DIVISION TITLE!
PUT ME ON YOUR BEAM, BOBBY
MURRAY OLDERMAN

"The Difference"

Eddie LeBaron

AMOS ALONZO STAGG was coaching College of the Pacific at the age of 84 and had a sixteen-year-old playing tailback against Northwestern in a homecoming trip to the area where he practically invented college football at Chicago. I was a graduate student in the stands of Dyche Stadium and saw little Eddie LeBaron, doubling at safety on defense, intercept a pass in the end zone and trigger a 101-yard touchdown play with two laterals. He also threw a scoring pass. The next year, COP converted to the T-formation and made Eddie a quarterback. I happened to get a job in Sacramento fifty miles north and followed him closely as he morphed into a magician ball-handler, and the small Stockton school lost only two games in three years. One of those losses came when a LeBaron touchdown pass was negated because the game officials couldn't follow the ball. "Little Eddie" went into the Marines, led a platoon in battle on Heartbreak Ridge in Korea, and came home with a bronze star and two purple hearts to supplant the great Sammy Baugh as the Washington Redskins quarterback —Eddie introduced me to "Slinging Sammy" in the Skins' locker room at a game in New York.

Eddie played twelve pro years, seven with the Skins, four as the original field general of the start-up Dallas Cowboys, and even worked in a year at Calgary in the Canadian league for his old college coach, Larry Siemering. He also received a law degree in the off-season and played golf with President Dwight Eisenhower. Derogated for his lack of height, LeBaron once led the NFL in passing and was the Redskins' punter in his early years. He was a terrific athlete, compactly built and quick. His biggest handicap was that he never really played on a contending team. In my time with him, he never lost his little-boy look or his impish sense of humor. The Cowboys signed a quarterback, Sonny Gibbs of TCU, who was a foot taller at 6'7". Introduced together at a Dallas luncheon, Eddie asked the rookie, "What do you think, Sonny—would you be a better quarterback if you were six inches shorter?" Gibbs never played a down. After his active football career, astute Eddie practiced law and became the general manager and executive vice-president of the Atlanta Falcons for a decade, then reverted to the practice of law in Nevada and California.

OF THE AWARDS PASSED OUT THIS BANQUET SEASON WE CAN THINK OF NONE MORE FITTING THAN THE TRIBUTE OF "MOST COURAGEOUS" TO KOREAN PURPLE HEART HERO, WASHINGTON REDSKIN QUARTERBACK **EDDIE LE BARON!**

MURRAY OLDERMAN

Vince Lombardi

WE WERE SITTING around the "Five O'clock Club," cocktail hour at an annual NFL meeting in Philadelphia, when an assistant coach of the New York Giants turned to me and said, "I'm taking an early train home to New Jersey. Why don't you come along?" I said, "Naw." And missed the biggest scoop of my life. The next day, Vincent Thomas Lombardi was appointed head coach and general manager of the Green Bay Packers. It was clear he had wanted to talk about this career change. I was never a confidant of Lombardi, but knew him as an intelligent, driven, moody man who had transformed the Giants' offense to championship caliber (they won the NFL title in 1956 and played in the famous "sudden death" game against Baltimore in '58). You could be bantering with him one minute. Five minutes later he'd walk by, absorbed in thought, and act like he never saw you. I preferred to keep my distance. But there was no mistaking his genius for leadership once he took control of the Packers. They finished 7-5 his first year as he settled on Bart Starr, a seventeenth round draft choice, at quarterback. They reached the NFL title game his second year, losing in the last minute to Philadelphia. That was the last post-season defeat ever for the Packers under Lombardi. They won five NFL crowns in seven years, including Super Bowls I and II. The Super Bowl trophy is in his name. Overlooked is the brevity of his career. He was an altar boy from Brooklyn (his father was a butcher) with plans for the priesthood who became an under-sized guard on Fordham University's famed "Seven Blocks of Granite" in the 1930s. He didn't get a head coaching job until he was forty-six years old. He died at the age of fifty-seven. Lombardi was consistent in his pursuit of excellence. "He treats us all alike," said defensive tackle Henry Jordan, "—like dogs." But there was a gentler, shy side to the private Lombardi. Raised near Belmont Park, he loved the ponies. He was like a little kid when I introduced him once at Toots Shor's to jockey Eddie Arcaro, one of his heroes.

OLDERMAN

NEA

Joe Louis

THE TESTIMONIAL DINNER was for the man in the wheelchair spending his last days greeting customers at Caesar's Palace in Las Vegas. My portrait of him was in the printed program of the celebrity gathering that ranged from actor Cary Grant to former heavyweight king Max Schmeling from Hamburg, Germany. Joe Louis Barrow (he dropped "Barrow" when he launched his ring career) was one of America's first black national sports heroes. Before him, Jack Johnson in the ring and football's Paul Robeson exemplified athletic greatness, but were controversial because of their social stances and not accepted by the general population at the time. Louis literally embodied the rags-to-riches dream (though the riches sifted through his fists to the greedy managers and promoters who infested boxing). He rose from a rural Alabama shanty—his grandparents were slaves—to the boxing rings of Detroit that nurtured his fighting ability. By 1935, at age twenty-one, he was the vaunted "Brown Bomber" for his fistic prowess, but was temporarily derailed by Schmeling, who discerned that Louis dropped his left hand after jabs and nailed him with overhand rights in a 12-round knockout, the first of only three losses in his career. In 1937, he won the heavyweight title by knocking out Jim Braddock, and a year later got his revenge by stopping Schmeling with a ferocious barrage two minutes and four seconds into the first round. Joe was a man of few words, but pithy. "He can run," said Louis of upcoming speedy opponent Billy Conn, "but he can't hide." He reigned through World War II, retired, and lost a comeback decision to Ezzard Charles for the vacated title, and in his final bout, his skills eroded by age, was knocked out by Rocky Marciano, who apologized to him. His post-ring years were marked by money and other problems—I deplored his brief venture into phony wrestling to make a buck, portrayed here—but he retained his dignity to the end.

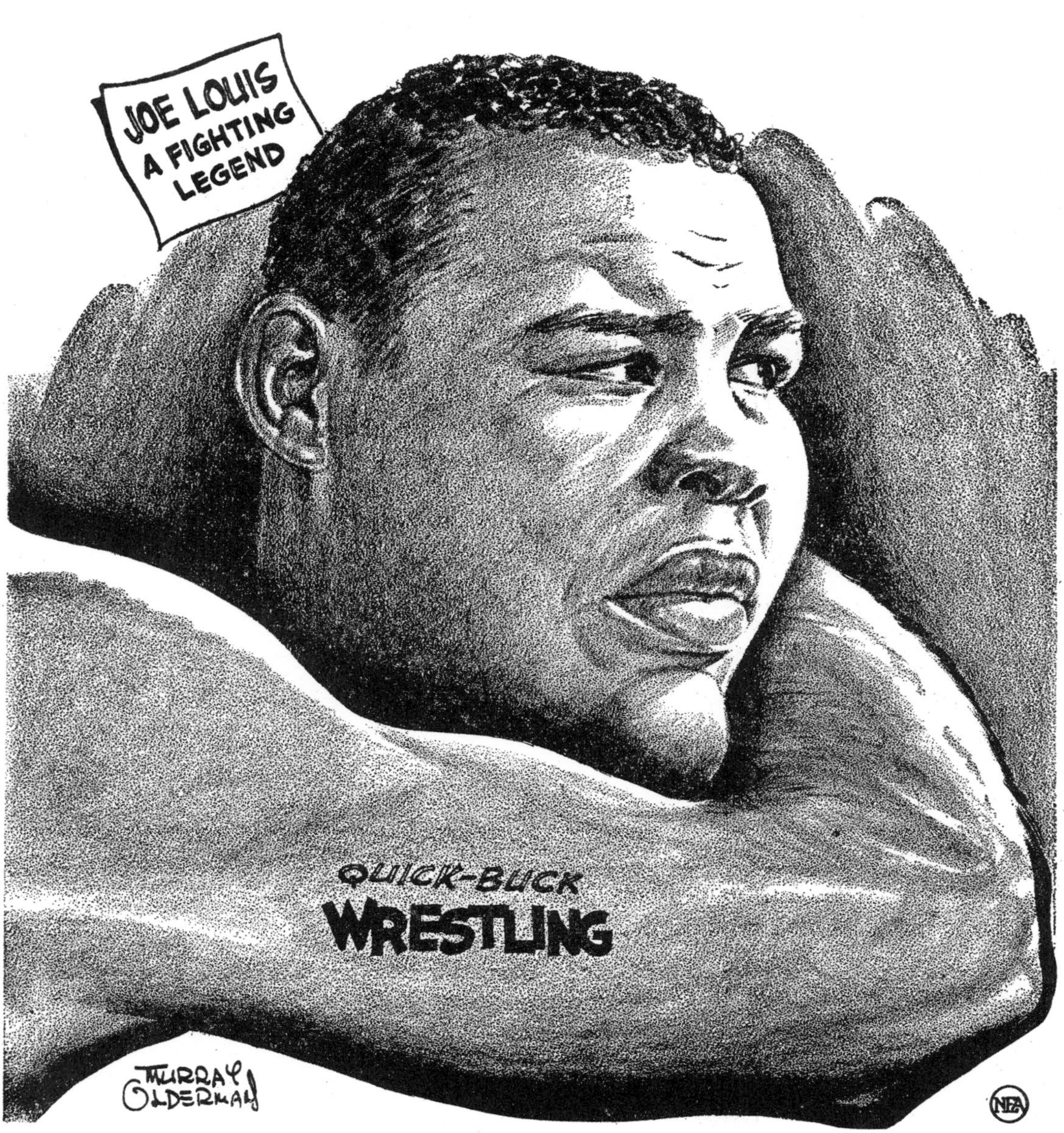
JOE LOUIS
A FIGHTING
LEGEND
QUICK-BUCK
WRESTLING
MURRAY
OLDERMAN
NEA

"Stranglehold"

Sid Luckman

A BIG BLACK limousine awaited us as we descended from his office high in the concrete maze of Chicago's Loop, and the chauffeur steered us to a round dinner table at the fashionable Drake, where we were joined by the CEO of a national vending company, the founder and president of a national bakery chain, and a multi-millionaire oil magnate. That was my introduction to Sid Luckman, one of my boyhood idols. Sid was the vice-president of a packaging corporation and doubled as coach-advisor to "Papa Bear" George Halas, founder and owner of the fabled Chicago football franchise. Sid was a Brooklyn boy, a high school star who once drew 30,000 spectators to a game. He took the subway to Morningside Heights in Manhattan to enroll at Columbia University and emerged as an All-American triple-threat tailback in the single wing. Halas envisioned him as quarterback for his newly devised T-formation, and Sid in his first year at the helm led the fabled 73-0 rout of the Washington Redskins in the 1940 NFL championship game. The Bears won three titles in his first four seasons. On "Luckman Day" in New York in 1943, Sid was the first to throw seven touchdown passes in an NFL game, a feat duplicated sev-

eral times, most recently by Peyton Manning in 2013, but never exceeded. I managed to get to Brooklyn for a Bears' pre-season game against the old football Dodgers in Ebbets Field and saw Luckman rip off a forty-four-yard run. My next Luckman sighting was in Chicago, described above, to research my first big book, *The Pro Quarterback*—the pencil crayon rendition, opposite, was the heading for the chapter on the legendary quarterback. Another time, I ran into him unexpectedly at a fabulous country restaurant near Versailles, outside Paris; he was accompanied by Irv (Kup) Kupcinet, the esteemed Chicago columnist and TV personality. Post-football, he became a bon vivant, and I would bump into him in the aisles ringside at heavyweight championship fights in Las Vegas. He was always immaculately dressed in a tailored black suit, white shirt and silk tie, hair still black—I'm not sure it was natural—unfailingly gracious and friendly, enjoying the good life. Listed at 6'0" and 195 pounds in his playing days, he then looked slight by comparison. "All those hits over the years compressed my spine," Sid explained, "so now I'm two inches shorter."

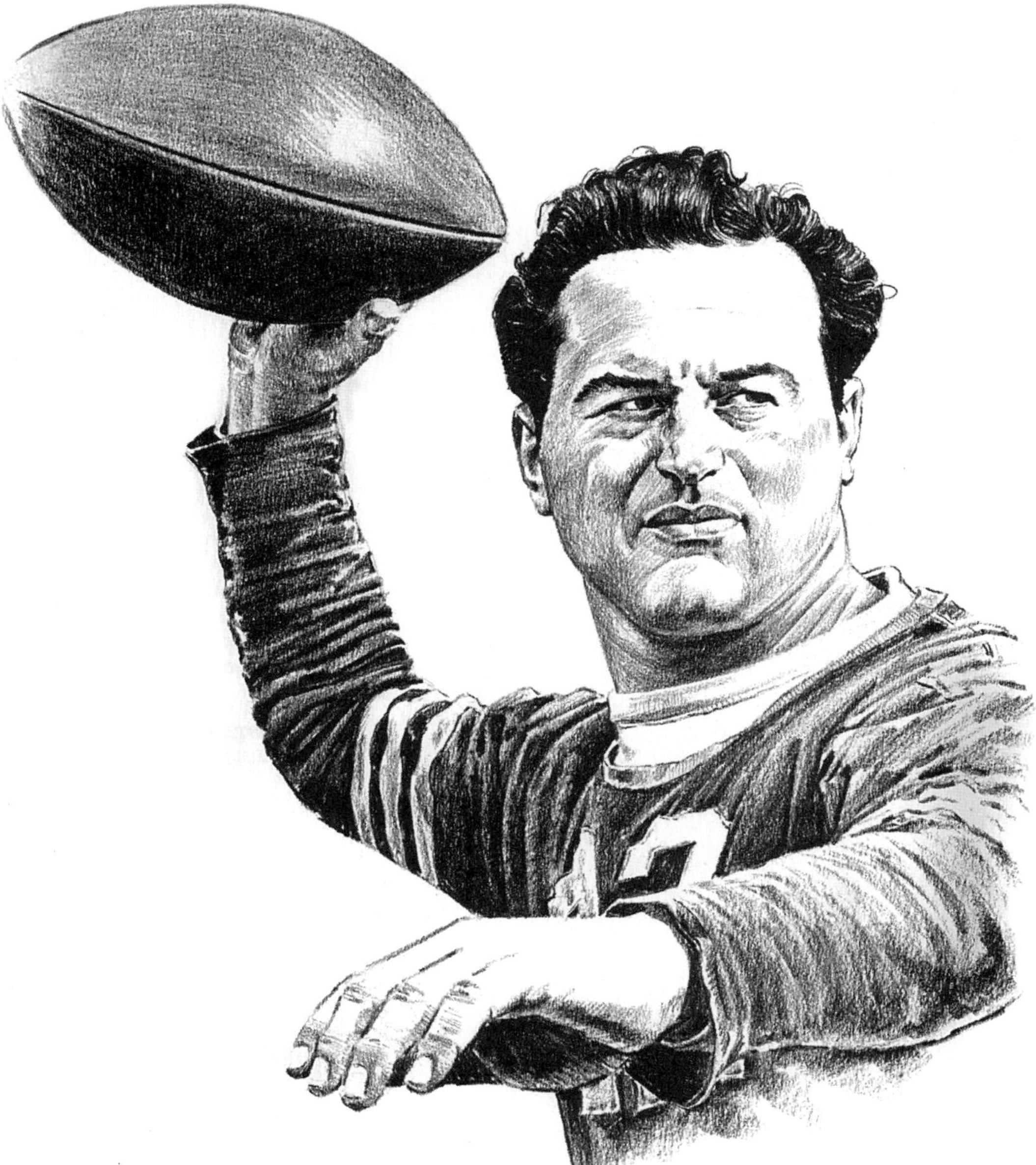

John Madden

AL DAVIS FIRST became aware of the beefy, bombastic coach when, taking over the Oakland Raiders in 1963, he received a call from Madden offering Hancock Junior College as their training site. He declined, but was intrigued by the young coach's verbal football knowledge. On a recruiting trip to San Diego State, Davis bumped into Madden—he had moved on—and hired him for the Raiders. When head coach John Rauch shuffled off to Buffalo, the Oakland Raiders' managing general partner bypassed three assistants with vast experience and chose obscure John Madden, on the Raider staff just two years, to be the new field boss. Why? Davis was impressed with the flair of Madden's chalkboard talks to Raider linebackers. This gift of gab, and an enthusiasm for the game, abetted by leadership skills, kept Madden at the helm of the Raiders for the next decade and brought him election into the Pro Football Hall of Fame, plus even greater renown as a national telecast analyst. It also got him an apartment at the Dakotas off Central Park West in New York, an ocean-side getaway in Carmel, California, a sprawling ranch home in the east Bay of Northern California, plus a customized bus

to ferry him around the country. Madden had developed a fear of flying, a major factor in his retirement from coaching. He never had a losing season with the Raiders, secured their first Super Bowl triumph, and was the youngest coach ever to attain one hundred NFL victories. Sometimes derided as a puppet coach because of Davis's presence, he ran the show on the sidelines—with his florid complexion, rumpled clothes, and wild gestures, he was almost a cartoon character—and rationalized his boss's input: "I got an owner who's the smartest football man in the league. I'd be stupid if I didn't take advantage of it." He was no beacon of enlightenment, at least at first. When women were entering sports journalism, I heard him declare, "They got no place around football. They got no business going in the players' dressing rooms. I won't allow it as long as I'm coaching." Of course, he never followed through on that. He was only forty-two years old when he quit the Raiders and, with his boom-boom style of football commentary, gained national popularity and ancillary business success from the broadcast booth.

THE COACH

THE PLAYER

NFL FUTURE

JOHN MADDEN

MURRAY OLDERMAN

HE'S GOT THE KID'S WHOLE WORLD IN HIS HANDS

Mickey Mantle

BENEATH HIS OKIE "aw, shucks" demeanor, genuine enough, Mickey Charles Mantle was a sentimentalist. That's how I got to him early on. In this cartoon, I included his father, Mutt Mantle. Before Mutt died at 40 from Hodgkin's disease after years in the lead and zinc mines of eastern Oklahoma, he taught little Mickey—so named because Mutt greatly admired Hall of Fame catcher Mickey Cochrane—baseball fundamentals. Mickey idolized his father. Mutt made him a switch-hitter, regarded as the greatest in the history of baseball. In the footsteps of legendary Yankees Babe Ruth and Joe DiMaggio, Mantle was an immediate New York sensation, but the country boy from Commerce, Oklahoma, was dismayed by the clamor of the press. He later confessed to me, "I was scared to death of the writers. Now I don't give a shit. I say what I want." He didn't regard me as one of them: "You're the guy who did the drawing of my Paw." In the spring of 1956, I drew a cartoon of Mantle projecting

him as the batting triple-crown winner. That fall, after the results were in, he inscribed on the original drawing, which hung in his Oklahoma home: "BA—.353; HR—52; RBI—130." There never was a player who better combined massive power and amazing speed. Mantle also had a droll side. He might give writer-intruders a baleful stare or even rudely walk away, but within the Yankee family he was warm and without pretension, the butt of a lot of joshing. They called him "Elmer" because of his Okie twang. One of the provocateurs was infielder Phil Linz, part owner of a Manhattan boîte. Mantle asked me to do a drawing of Linz pulling Joe Pepitone around the city. Mickey and Joe displayed the art at the ballpark. Despite debilitating injuries and a reckless lifestyle, Mantle played eighteen years in a Yankee uniform. And when I last encountered him, as a cable TV analyst for their games, he invited me to lunch with him in the Yankee press room and remained mellow and self-deprecating.

Behind the budding greatness that is MICKEY **MANTLE** hovers the image of his late father, "Mutt"— a father who selflessly devoted his life to his son's future.

MURRAY OLDERMAN

Gino Marchetti

MY MEMORY OF him is not of the fearsome defensive end who flattened quarterbacks with such ferocity that I still think of Gino Marchetti as the best pass rusher who ever lived, among greats that have ranged from Deacon Jones to the present-day J.J. Watts. No, I remember Gino sitting on a plane going from Baltimore to San Francisco for the Colts' season-ending trip to the West Coast. Beneficent owner Carroll Rosenbloom let Gino take his family on the flight because their off-season home was in the Bay area. Cradled in Gino's arms, head draped over one shoulder was his sizeable toddler son, and the stoic father never moved once from his seat the entire non-stop, cross-country passage so that the kid wouldn't wake. I first drew a cartoon of Marchetti in the *Modesto Bee* when he was a junior college tackle. He had been an eighteen-year-old infantryman in the WWII Battle of the Bulge, and he was recruited by the University of San Francisco—arriving on a motorcycle and studded leather jacket with fifteen zippers—joining a team that produced eleven future NFL players. He was primarily a nondescript offensive tackle for disbanded New York and Dallas franchises that became the Baltimore Colts, where Weeb Ewbank converted him to defensive end. At weigh-ins, lanky 6'4" Gino, at 225 pounds, put lead weights in his jock strap to meet Weeb's minimum 240 for defensive linemen. He filled out in his prime; fast, quick, strong, he became the prototypal pass rusher. In the famous 1958 overtime game with the New York Giants, he fractured his tibia and fibula with seconds remaining, but on that play stopped Frank Gifford inches short of a first down that would have clinched a Giant victory in regulation. Wheeled off the field, he insisted on stopping at one end zone to watch the Colts tie the game (and subsequently win). On a late-season visit by Gino to hometown Antioch, California, brother Itzy noticed Gino's leg twitching and asked, "How come you're so nervous?" Anxiously ruffling his black hair, Gino muttered, "It's the day before a game." Gino was thirty-five and had been all-pro nine straight years. At forty-two, two years after he officially retired, Don Shula persuaded him to return for a few games to bolster the Colts' front four. In the meantime, Gino teamed with fullback Alan Ameche to open a chain called "Gino's Hamburgers" that was eventually in 313 East Coast locations.

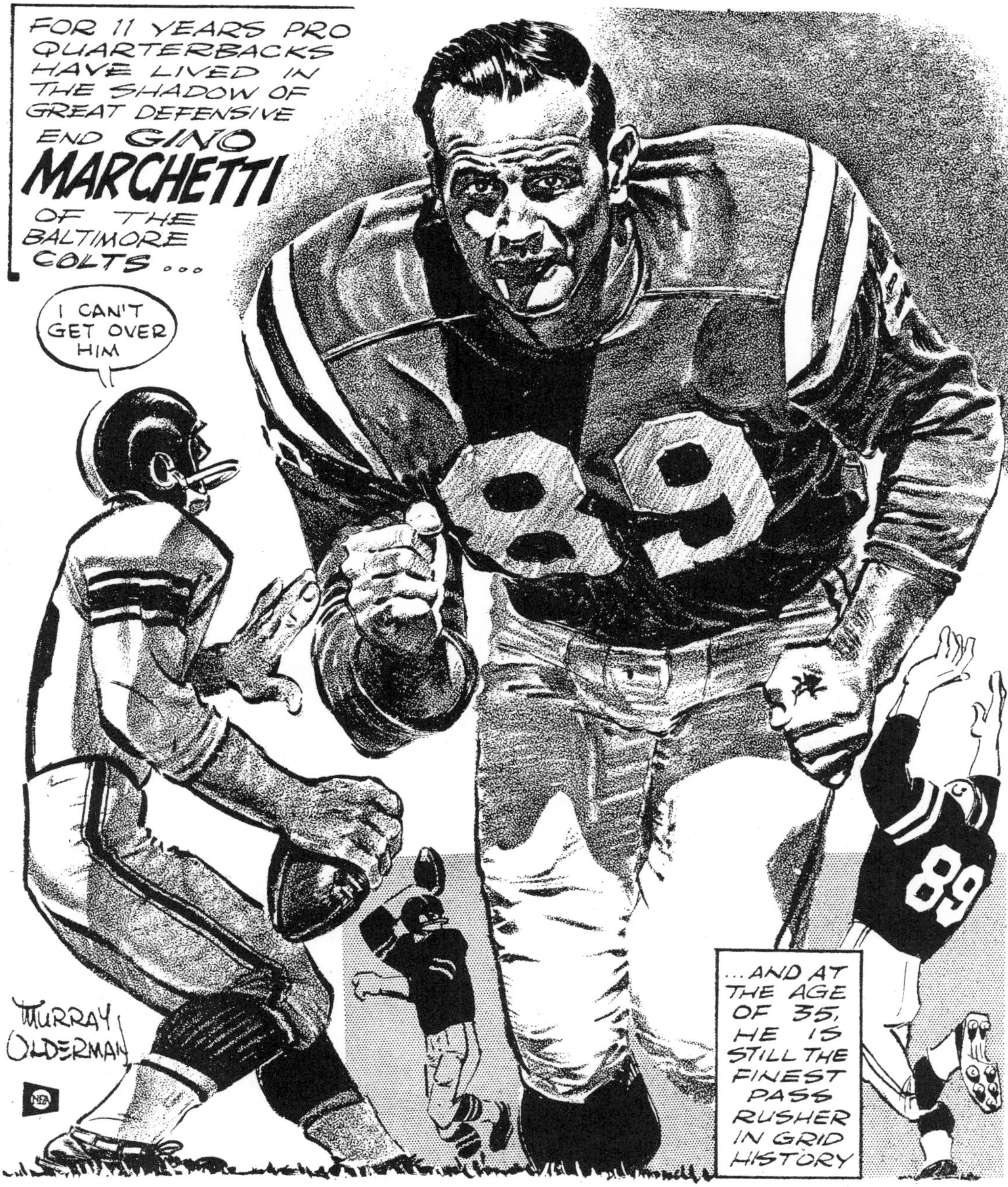
FOR 11 YEARS PRO QUARTERBACKS HAVE LIVED IN THE SHADOW OF GREAT DEFENSIVE END GINO MARCHETTI OF THE BALTIMORE COLTS...
I CAN'T GET OVER HIM
...AND AT THE AGE OF 35, HE IS STILL THE FINEST PASS RUSHER IN GRID HISTORY
89
89
MURRAY OLDERMAN
NEA

"They Shall Not Pass"

Rocky Marciano

WE WERE JOGGING near his Grossingers training camp—I was the only writer his age—when Rocky Marciano paused and asked, "Tell me, Murray . . . am I a good boxer?" He was training to fight Archie Moore in his forty-ninth, and last, pro bout. "Well," I artfully dodged the question, "you've never lost a fight." Rocky pondered and concluded, "I guess I am a lousy boxer." He remains the only heavyweight champion in history never to lose a fight. The one press question he hated while preparing for a fight was, "How do you feel, Rocky?" He grimaced. "How do they expect me to feel?" Rocky took me to a prison where he was surrounded by the thousand inmates at Napanoch in the Catskills. With stubble on his face, he looked like one of them. "I had trouble getting started, too, fellas," he said. "I'm from Brockton, Massachusetts. All they got there is a shoe shop, and I didn't want to work in a shoe shop. I tried twenty different jobs and decided to become a fighter. They told me physical condition is ninety percent of the battle. I can have the best corner men in the world, but once I climb through the ropes there's no one to help. It's either me or him." He fought with desperate, violent aggression. He simply at-tacked with sledgehammer fists until he penetrated the other guy's armor. In his second title defense, he hit NYU-educated Roland LaStarza's forearms with such force that La Starza could no longer raise them to ward off punches. Rocky took me in a limo to a swank New York nightclub for the post-fight party and chortled, "I 'learned' the sonuvabitch a few things he didn't get in college." It was the closest he ever came to boasting. Playing ping-pong with him, I cut my head retrieving the little ball from under the staircase in a farmhouse at Grossingers and required a couple of stitches. This was just before the Ezzard Charles fight that was almost stopped in the seventh round because Rocky's nostril was completely slit. He KO'd Charles the next round. After the fight, his head swathed in bandages, completely red from oozing blood, surrounded by writers, he looked up at me and in his high-pitched voice asked, "How's your cut, Murray?" Always frugal, he mooched a private plane ride to a personal appearance, pocketing the expense money. The small plane crashed in a storm over Iowa, ending Rocky's life a day before his forty-sixth birthday.

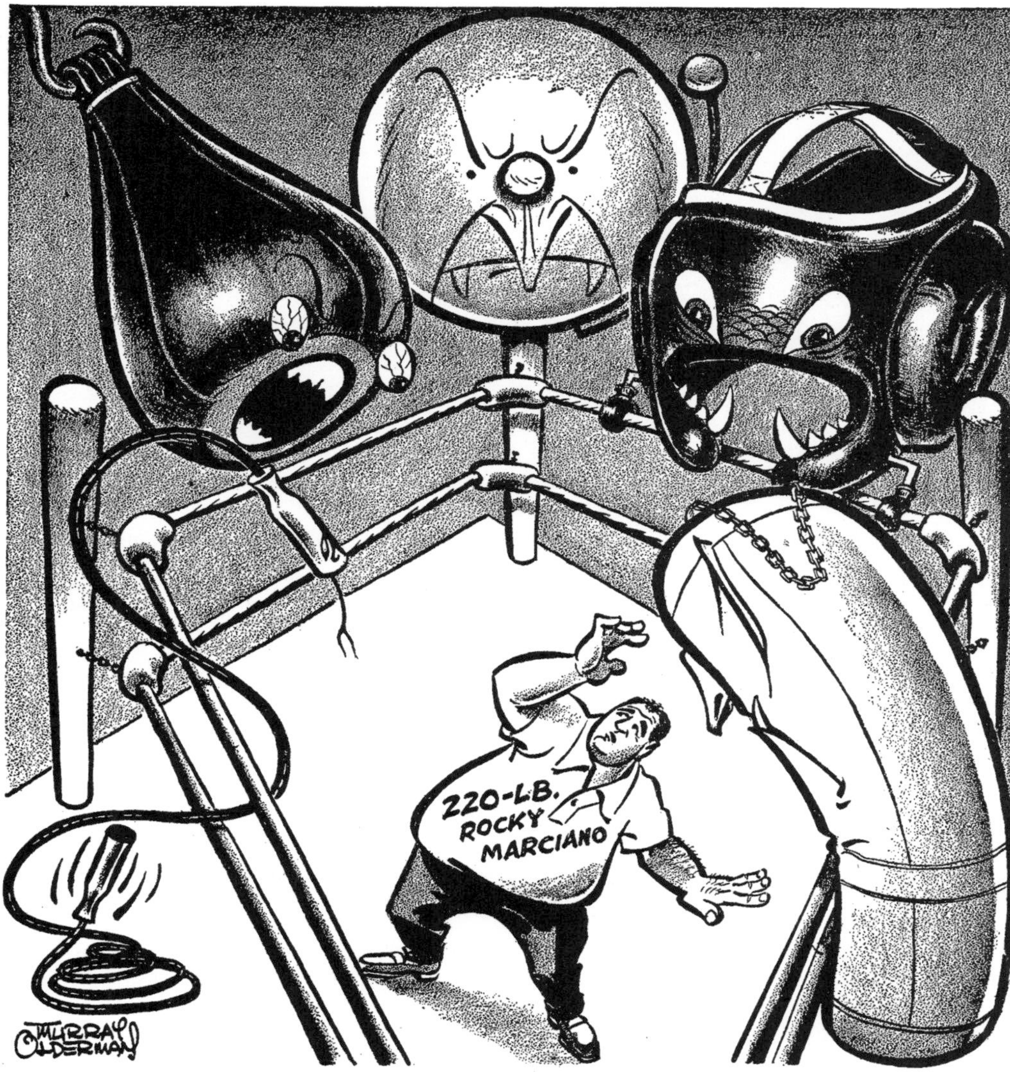
220-LB. ROCKY MARCIANO
MURRAY OLDERMAN

"Chamber of Horrors"

Roger Maris

THE FOLLOWING TABLEAU about Roger Maris is lifted from Gay Talese's highly acclaimed and anthologized story on Joe DiMaggio in the July 1966 issue of *Esquire* magazine:

> *"Hey, Rog," yelled a man with a tape recorder, Murray Olderman, "I want to do a thirty-second tape with you."*
>
> *Maris swore angrily, shook his head.*
>
> *"It'll only take a second," Olderman said.*
>
> *"Why don't you ask Richardson? He's a better talker than me."*
>
> *"Yes, but the fact that it comes from you . . ."*
>
> *Maris swore again. But finally he went over and said in an interview that [Mickey] Mantle was the finest player of his era, a great competitor, a great hitter.*

I was writing Chris Schenkel's ABC radio show then and doing spot interviews for it. Roger Maris, a blue-collar home run hitter, just wanted to go to work with his lunch pail, finish his shift, get paid, and go home without any fuss over him. When he broke out with his remarkable 1961 season, walloping sixty-one home runs, and became a national sensation, he didn't know how to handle it. Roger was a decent guy, a good family man, plainspoken, not unfriendly. He was a bit of a square with a crew cut hairdo. There was no animosity between him and Mantle. Like Mantle, he considered me primarily as a cartoonist who wouldn't zing him. When they didn't want to bring their families into the cauldron of New York publicity, they shared a Queens apartment with outfielder Bob Cerv. Notwithstanding his fame for breaking Babe Ruth's home run record, he was an underappreciated talent. As a high school back in North Dakota, he was offered and turned down a scholarship to ranking gridiron power Oklahoma. He took a small baseball bonus from Cleveland, was traded to Kansas City, and then New York. His first Yankee year, 1960, he led the American League in RBIs and was its MVP. He was also bull-headed. If he didn't want to be bothered, he couldn't be bothered. He ducked an interview with a United Press columnist and was skewered nationally. He wasn't gracious as demands increased during his pursuit of Ruth's record. His hair fell out in clumps under the tension. And then Commissioner Ford Frick ordained that his new record would carry an asterisk because it wasn't accomplished, like Ruth's, within a 154-game season.

"Now There is an Asterisk"

Willie Mays

IN THE SPRING of 1951, a nineteen-year-old outfielder was promoted from Class B Trenton in the New York Giants farm system to the Triple-A Minneapolis Millers, just after I went to work for the *Minneapolis Star*. I saw Willie Mays run up a wooden fence at old Niccolet Field to make the most brilliant catch I ever witnessed. My cartoon appeared in *The Sporting News*, the national baseball publication which took credit for getting Willie, batting .477, called up to the Giants a few days later to patrol center field in the Polo Grounds. Owner Horace Stoneham took out ads in both the morning and afternoon Minneapolis papers, apologizing to the fans for taking away their phenom. I followed him to New York and saw him make the fantastic catch of Vic Wertz's drive to deep center against Cleveland in the 1954 World Series, running with his back to home plate 460 feet away, pulling in the ball over his left shoulder. The Willie of that period was refreshing and engaging; he played stickball with kids on the streets of Harlem. In the Giants' dressing room, pitcher Sal Maglie would snap a towel at a squealing Willie as he went by to shower. Willie was the life of a continual party. He couldn't remember names so he addressed all, "Say, hey!" and became the "Say Hey Kid." Although I was around for his entire career—twenty-two seasons, 660 home runs, 338 stolen bases, lifetime .302 batting average—I don't think Willie ever really placed me. He certainly didn't call me by name. There was a transition in his temperament, especially after the Giants moved in 1958 to San Francisco, home turf of the great DiMaggio. Willie didn't feel accepted; he withdrew. He didn't ingratiate himself to locals. I went to a Giants' training camp in Arizona and found him a reluctant, suspicious interview. The once bubbly, eager-to-please Willie even got into a fight on the field that so shocked us in New York I drew a cartoon the next time the Giants came to town to play the Mets. He also reflected social change. Manager Alvin Dark appointed him team captain at thirty-three, piously proclaiming, "Baseball is ready." As if the man who led them to four World Series needed validation. The next spring, I was standing with Willie around a batting cage as he exclaimed petulantly, "Why everybody ask me about my age? Bet you don't talk to [Mickey] Mantle that way."

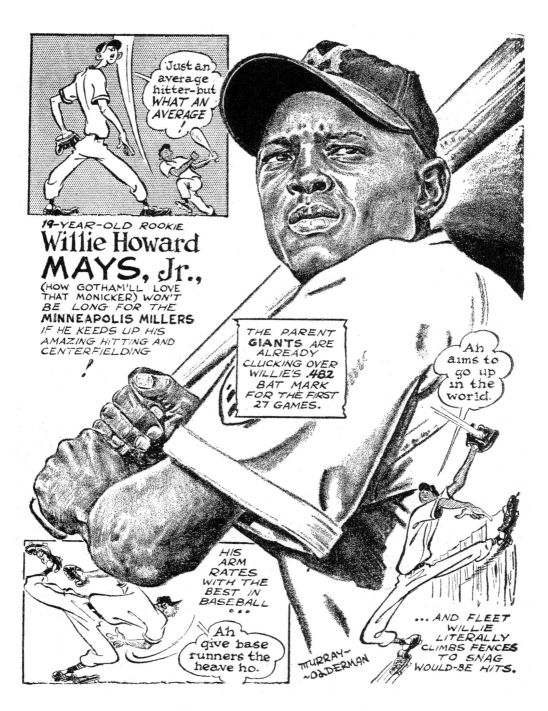

"Pounding Path to Polo Grounds"

Gil McDougald

EVERY CHRISTMAS, AFTER transplanting from northern New Jersey to northern California, we would get a card from the McDougalds with a longhand message to tell us what Gil and Lucille and their brood of children were doing. They lived in Tenafly, where many of the Yankee players rooted during baseball season because it was near the George Washington Bridge and a quick hop to Yankee Stadium—and New Jersey had no state income tax. We didn't really socialize, but occasionally Gil and Lucille had come by with their kids, who'd play with ours. Gil was a versatile infielder in the Casey Stengel era. In his decade of play the Yankees were in eight World Series, and Gil started at second base, third, shortstop, wherever needed, twice batting over .300. Incongruously, he is remembered for hitting a line drive in 1957 that caught pitcher Herb Score in the left eye and effectively ended the Cleveland lefthander's career. "If Herb loses his eye, I'm quitting baseball," said Gil, a religious and compassionate man. Score recovered to pitch briefly again and became a sportscaster. Ironically, two years earlier, Gil himself was hit in the head by a line drive during batting practice. The blow broke a hearing tube, but didn't affect his playing career. He retired at thirty-two because, he said, he was tired of traveling and groveling before the owners. He operated a successful office cleaning business and coached baseball at Fordham. But progressively, since the batting practice accident, he lost his hearing and stopped coaching because he couldn't hear the thwack of a ball coming off a bat, then gave up his business because he couldn't use a telephone. For twenty-five years he was virtually stone deaf and became a recluse, moving to the Jersey shore, shunning old-timers' games and player reunions. A poignant *New York Times* story by Ira Berkow in 1994 about Gil's world of silence caught the attention of a Baltimore ear surgeon, who contacted the McDougalds and apprised them of a relatively new procedure called a cochlear implant that might restore his hearing. Gil had the operation, and when the healed implant was activated a couple of months later, Gil miraculously could decipher sound. He was interviewed on the *Today* show and made appearances. From afar, we reveled in the McDougalds' good fortune and were happy continuing to get that Christmas card reminder of old times.

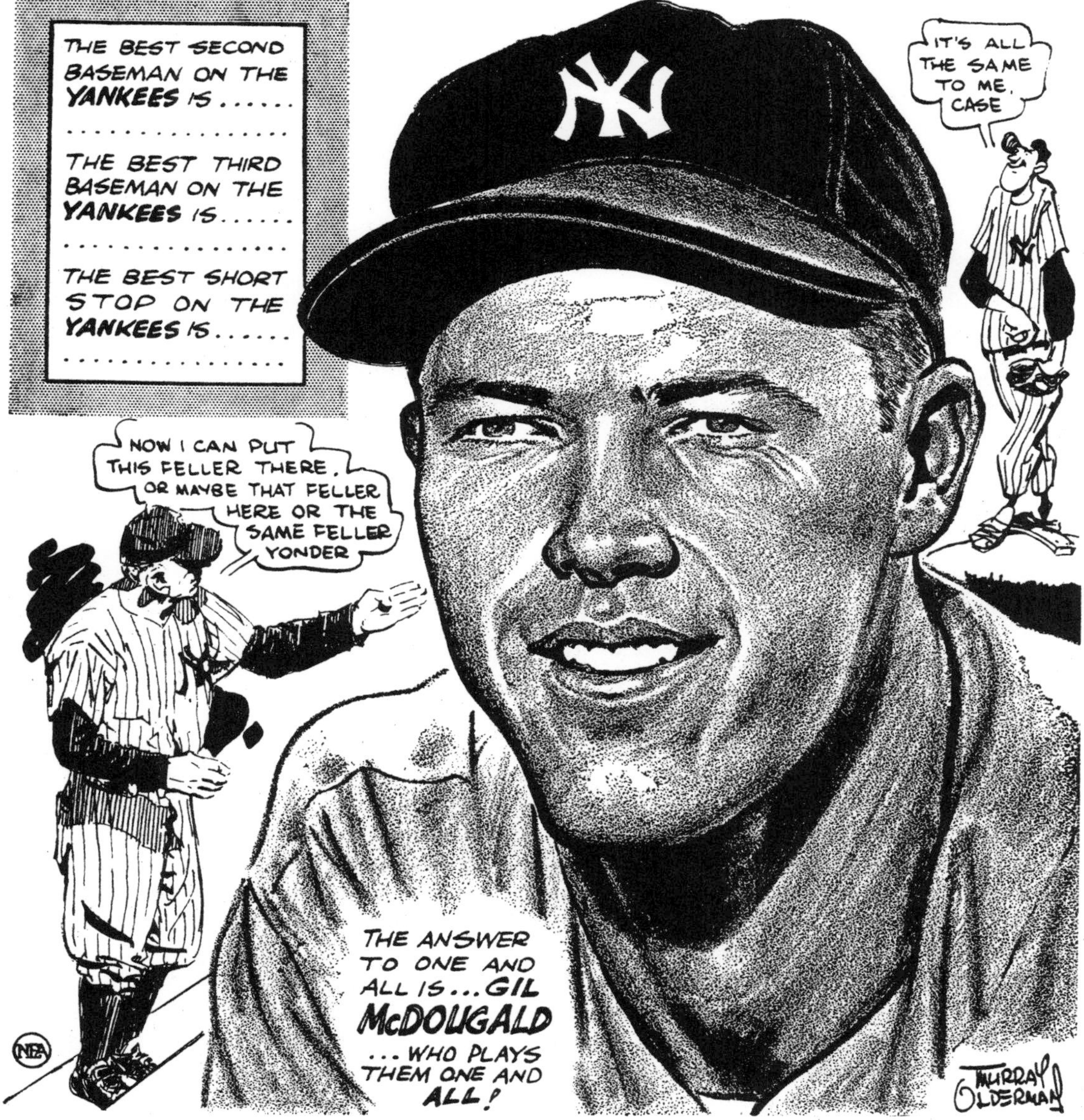
THE BEST SECOND BASEMAN ON THE YANKEES IS ......
THE BEST THIRD BASEMAN ON THE YANKEES IS ......
THE BEST SHORT STOP ON THE YANKEES IS ......
IT'S ALL THE SAME TO ME, CASE
NOW I CAN PUT THIS FELLER THERE, OR MAYBE THAT FELLER HERE OR THE SAME FELLER YONDER
THE ANSWER TO ONE AND ALL IS... GIL McDOUGALD ... WHO PLAYS THEM ONE AND ALL!
NEA
MURRAY OLDERMAN

"Filling in the Spaces"

John McEnroe

HE WOULD BE the first to tell you he was churlish, boorish, and disruptive on a tennis court. "You cannot be serious" became his mantra in harangues directed at courtside officials. But the outbursts don't diminish the fact he was among the finest players to wield a racket, in any era. Once in London, Gene Mako, a doubles partner of Don Budge, shared a cab to Wimbledon with me and alerted me to McEnroe's wonderful talent. "The kid is the only one out there who hits the ball on the rise," Mako said. "He's got the hands and reflexes to dominate this game." And McEnroe did in the 1980s, taking it over from Sweden's Björn Borg, a gentler soul who retired abruptly at age twenty-five. McEnroe shouted at umpires and lines people and stormed around the court, but never directed his ire at the guy on the other side of the net. He was often contrite and embarrassed by his behavior. Late in his career, he amused me at a press conference with a rambling, stream-of-consciousness dialogue: "It amazes me that no one ever listens to me about tennis, the one thing I definitely know about . . . If I miss a tennis ball, it's not going to change society. Take firemen, policemen, pilots, bus drivers—where lives are on the line. Give those people more money and come down in sports. Because we get this incredible amount of money, people think it's OK to do anything. I'd rather have less money and some sanity to the whole thing . . . In a certain sense, I'm overpaid. What can I do? I'll make the best of the situation. I'm a tennis player."

The lithe left-hander from Queens, also a fine soccer player in his youth, used a vast array of spinning shots and superb volleying to make his millions while winning seventy-seven tournaments, fourth highest in the Open era, stretched over thirteen years. Those are significant achievements in a period when the competition, besides Borg, consisted of such tennis greats as Jimmy Connors, Ivan Lendl, and Vitas Gerulaitis. He was one of the few who didn't shun doubles play, winning nine Grand Slam doubles titles. He also married a movie star, Tatum O'Neal, and a rock star, Patty Smyth, and dabbled in music. The self-deprecating, but always candid television commentator who emerged after he retired from the tennis tour—and in my view the best tennis analyst in the business—was a likeable John McEnroe.

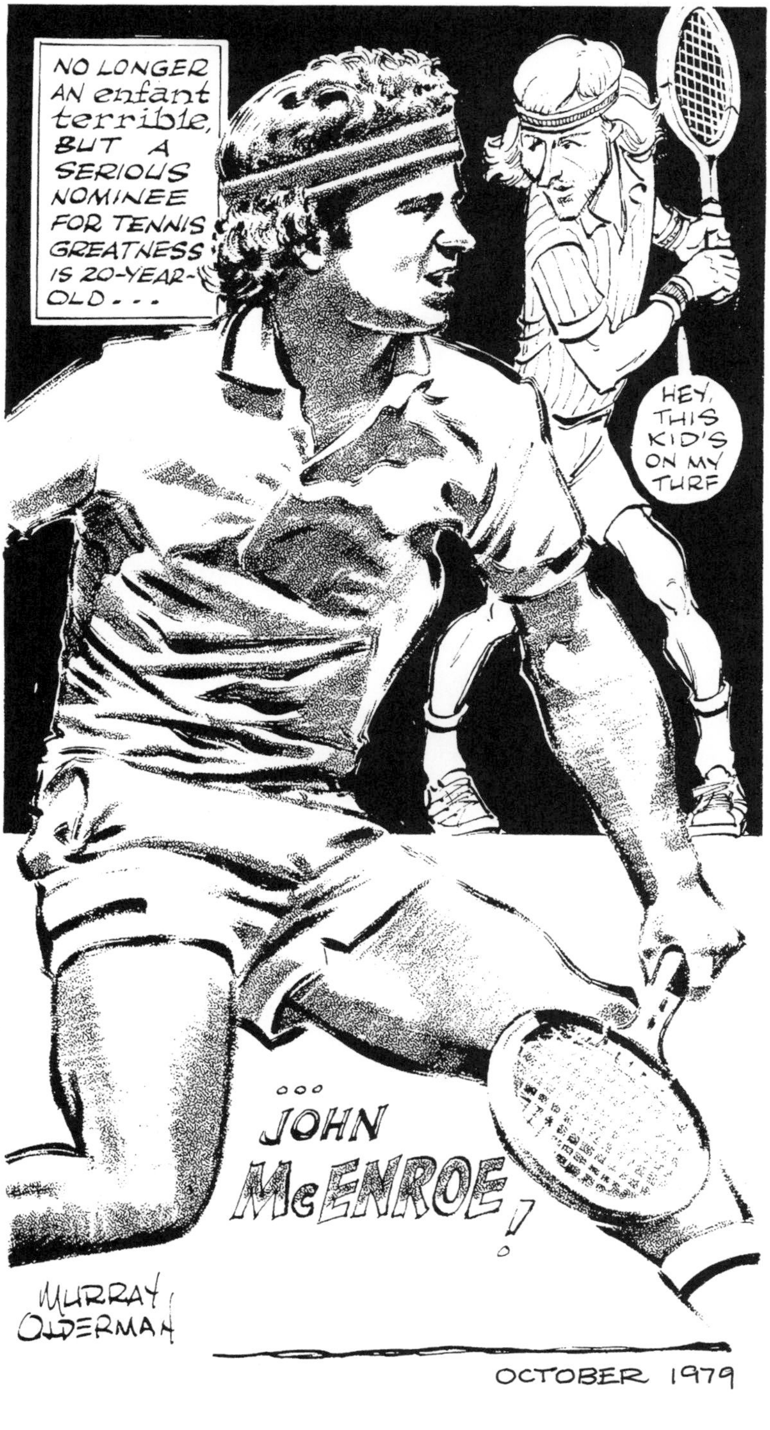
NO LONGER AN enfant terrible, BUT A SERIOUS NOMINEE FOR TENNIS GREATNESS IS 20-YEAR-OLD . . .
HEY, THIS KID'S ON MY TURF
. . . JOHN McENROE!
MURRAY OLDERMAN
OCTOBER 1979

George Mikan

THE MAN FROM Peoria, Illinois, was my introduction to big-time sports. The editor of the *Minneapolis Star* who hired me in early 1952 said I could move from sleepy (at that time) Sacramento to the Twin Cities at my leisure. I figured I'd report March 1st after the worst part of the winter was over. It snowed thirty inches in March, but I slogged through icy streets and shifting snow drifts to a drafty downtown arena to watch the Minneapolis Lakers, the best team in pro basketball. It was a strange operation, run by a restaurateur/fight manager, Max Winter, who later was a founding partner of the Minnesota Vikings. But the man who hustled and signed players was a sports writer, Sid Hartman, once banished from the press section for baiting referees. George Mikan, an awkward giant whose broad shoulders seemed to protrude from his neck at a ninety-degree angle, was the dominant figure in pro basketball, then just starting to catch on. He wore glasses with coke-bottle-thick lenses, braces on his knees, and lurched down the court. He was considered monstrous in size at 6'10" and no one could cope with Mikan's physicality and sharp elbows. There was no twenty-four-second clock to step up the pace, no three-second rule, and the foul line was narrower. By camping under the basket, shooting short hooks and layups, Mikan averaged more than twenty-eight points a game to lead the NBA in scoring. He was abetted by good guys like versatile Jim Pollard, rebounding power forward Vern Mikkelsen, point guard Slater Martin—all friendly to a young journalist. I moved to New York the next year but retained emotional ties to the Lakers. When they beat the New York Knicks in Madison Square Garden for the league title—the Lakers won four in the first five years of the NBA—they invited me to the post-game celebration at the Copacabana Club. Mikan retired after the 1954 season at the age of thirty, coached briefly, but was fired. The big guy really wanted to be a lawyer and pursued it as doggedly as he had overcome his awkwardness in basketball. It took him a few tests to pass the bar, and the newly formed American Basketball Association made him its first commissioner.

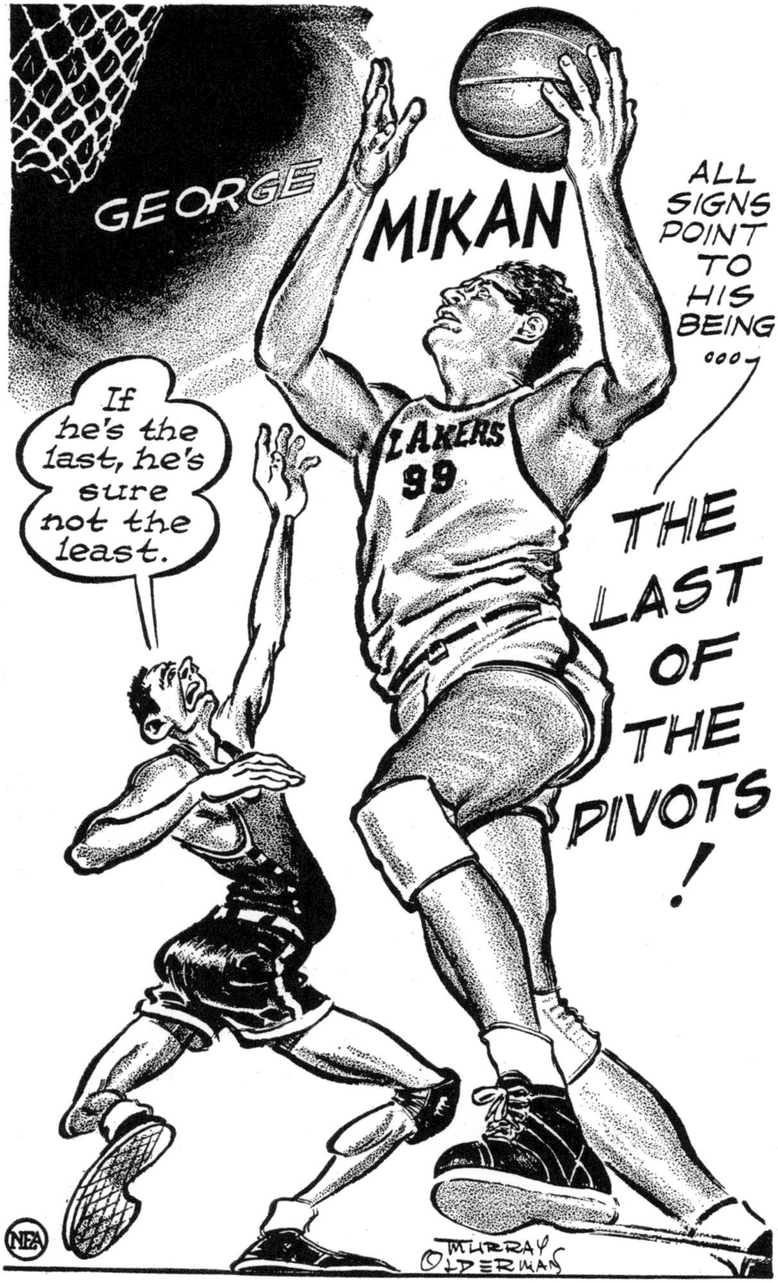
GEORGE
MIKAN
ALL SIGNS POINT TO HIS BEING ...
If he's the last, he's sure not the least.
LAKERS
99
THE LAST OF THE PIVOTS!
NEA
MURRAY OLDERMAN

"All With Mighty Mikan"

Ron Mix

ON AN EASTERN trip to play the Buffalo Bills, the San Diego Chargers stayed at a hotel in Niagara Falls, but practiced on a high school field on the Canadian side. Separate buses took the players and coaches to the training site. One day the coaches' bus was held up at the border, leaving the players stranded on the practice field. "It was a typical winter day," offensive tackle Ron Mix recalled for me, "about fifteen degrees, wind blowing." The players stood around, shivering, until quarterback John Hadl suggested, "Let's play some touch football." Running back Paul Lowe chimed in, "Yeah, offense against defense." "Nah," said gigantic defensive tackle Ernie Ladd. "Let's play Blacks against Whites." The players started laughing and yelling exuberantly. Blacks ran to one side, Whites to the other. "They wouldn't let me play," said Ron Mix, "because I'm Jewish. I was the referee." He put the story in a serious context by adding,

"This diverse group of players had become so comfortable with each other, we could joke about it. I'm convinced sports has done more to advance racial and religious relations than any singular movement." Ron was an atypical football player—he was myopic and at USC had to switch from tight end to tackle because he couldn't see the ball. He was scholarly in demeanor; through dedicated study of offensive line technique he became a devastating blocker, perhaps the fastest ever off the snap of the ball. He gave the fledgling AFL immediate cachet by signing with San Diego instead of the NFL defending champion Baltimore Colts, who made him their number one draft choice. He wrote a story, "Why I chose the AFL," for a football annual I edited. He studied law while playing, passed the bar, and has been a successful attorney, specializing in workmen's compensation.

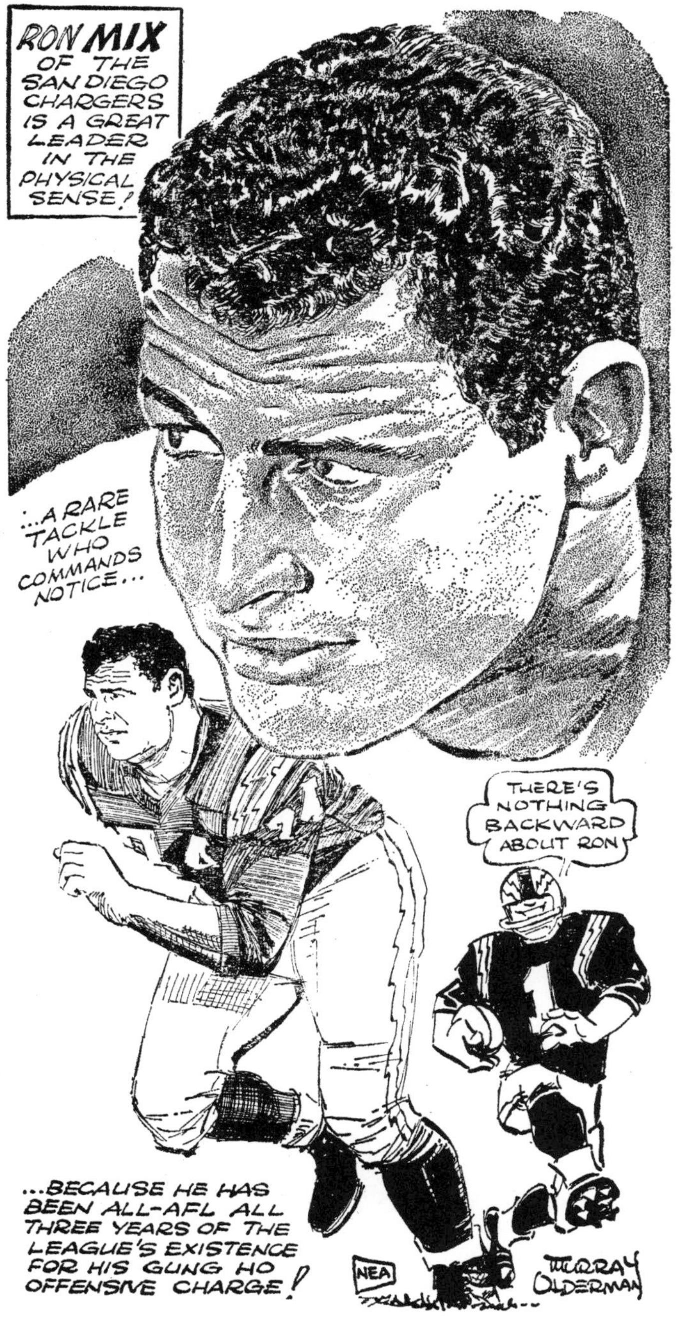

RON MIX OF THE SAN DIEGO CHARGERS IS A GREAT LEADER IN THE PHYSICAL SENSE!
...A RARE TACKLE WHO COMMANDS NOTICE...
THERE'S NOTHING BACKWARD ABOUT RON
...BECAUSE HE HAS BEEN ALL-AFL ALL THREE YEARS OF THE LEAGUE'S EXISTENCE FOR HIS GUNG HO OFFENSIVE CHARGE!
NEA
MURRAY OLDERMAN

"Strong Mix"

Joe Montana

HIS FIRST TWO years with the San Francisco 49ers, he was backup to someone named Steve DeBerg. Not even Bill Walsh, who drafted Joe Montana number three in his debut as 49ers coach, envisioned what he had. Montana appeared slight, a vague Barry Manilow look-alike, and at Notre Dame, coach Dan Devine frequently benched him, although he warded off hypothermia to produce a dramatic victory in the Cotton Bowl. He threw a football well, but without the zoom of a Joe Namath, who came from the same western Pennsylvania coal district. He was quick, but no speed burner. He was so colorless as a personality that he was married three times without a whiff of scandal. Yet the combo of Walsh and Montana invented and perfected the West Coast offense that has pervaded football since the 1980s with short, controlled passes interspersed with quick-opening running plays. In Montana's first year as a starter, he drove the 49ers eighty-nine yards against Dallas in the final two minutes, capped with the celebrated "Miracle Catch" by Dwight Clark that upset the Cowboys and put them in Super Bowl XVI, where he led the 49ers over Cincinnati, again in the last two minutes. Seven years later, in Super Bowl XXIII, with under four minutes to play and the 49ers backed up to their eight-yard line, trailing the Bengals by three points, he took them all the way on eleven plays. Mr. Excitement, right? Hardly. After games, he was polite, but bland. I can't recall a memorable quote Montana ever uttered, even one-on-one. The most I ever elicited from him about his role was this: "I'm not a fiery guy, but on the field I have to know exactly what has to be done and how to get everybody to do it. I guess it has become second nature to me because I have been doing it since high school. You have to know you are right, and if you are wrong, you have to act like you're right, at least until the coach yells at you." There had to be a lot of "right" for Montana to collect four Super Bowl rings in his fourteen seasons with San Francisco and be named the MVP in three of them. He closed out his career with two years in Kansas City.

It's in his hand(s) by MURRAY OLDERMAN

IN THE WINNING SCHEME OF THE SAN FRANCISCO 49ERS, THE KEY IS TO LET JOE MONTANA SPRINT INTO ACTION.....

49ers offense

I REALLY WOULDN'T CARE TO WALTZ

...AND THEN RELY ON THE QB'S UNCANNY INSTINCT, MOBILITY AND SHARP PASSING TO DO THE REST

NEA

173.

Stan Musial

HE DIDN'T NEED a degree in political science to master the art of diplomatic denial and become baseball's most beloved personality. Stan Musial spent twenty-two years with the St. Louis Cardinals with never a speck of controversy—he was never even thrown out of a game for arguing with an umpire. Faced with a thorny question, he'd give you that warm smile and politely decline to answer, or skip around it. No one ever took offense. He was, after all, Stan the Man, a revered icon in St. Louis. Late in his career, almost every at-bat produced a new baseball record. Not bad for a kid from Donora, Pennsylvania, whose first three years in organized baseball were spent as a left-handed minor league pitcher in the Cardinal farm system. Because he wasn't an automatic out like most pitchers—he hit .311 over those years—managers also played him in the outfield, but a fall chasing a fly ball injured his shoulder. He converted full time in 1941 to the outfield at Springfield and Rochester and hit over .400 when the Cardinals called him up briefly in September. The following spring he was starting in left for the parent club, which won the World Series against the Yankees, and he batted .315. That started a string of sixteen straight .300-plus seasons—he missed 1945 for a stint in the Navy. "He could have hit .300 with a fountain pen," said Joe Garagiola. His lifetime average was .331. He led the National League in hitting seven times and played in twenty-four All-Star games. Musial amassed 3,630 hits, fourth all-time, among them 475 home runs. The power of this slim slugger derived from a unique stance that resembled a coiled spring, described by old-time pitcher Ted Lyons as a "kid peeking around the corner to see if the cops were coming." He also was named the National League MVP three times. Whenever I saw "Stash"—the Polish derivative of his given name, Stanislaw—away from the ballpark, he invariably showed up with his buddy, second baseman Red Schoendienst (whose own career span was nineteen seasons), two guys who always looked like they were having a blast. Musial was also an accomplished harmonica player. After retirement, he had a brief run as the Cardinals' general manager, taking them to a World Series title, but quit because he didn't want to be tied down to a desk. He also had numerous business interests, among them a landmark St. Louis restaurant.

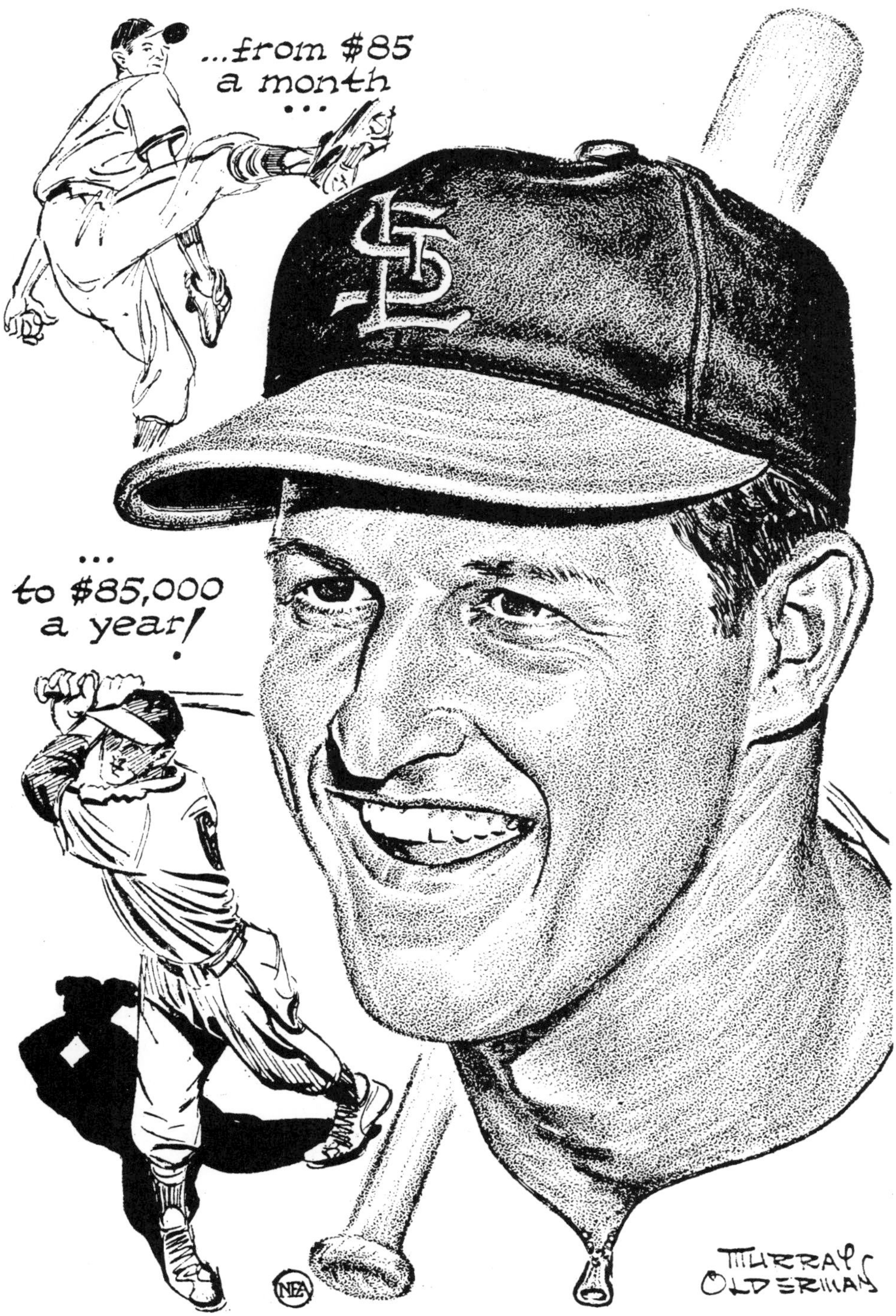
...from $85
a month
...
...
to $85,000
a year!
NEA
MURRAY OLDERMAN

Joe Namath

IN THE ALABAMA locker room after a victory over Georgia Tech in Atlanta, the quarterback of the Crimson Tide sat on a bench, smoking a cigar in celebration—a startling ritual for a college kid. "Look over here," he said to backup Steve Sloan, pointing to my trousers. "No cuffs. That's New York." Cuffless pants were a sartorial fad at the time. It was my first sighting of Joe Willie Namath of Beaver Falls, Pennsylvania. The next summer, he was in the training camp of the New York Jets at Peekskill, New York, swimming in the pool with my son Mark during a practice break. Johnny Carson had just visited the Jets' camp and tossed a few footballs with the rookie quarterback. I asked Namath for his impression. "Oh, you mean the little old gray-haired guy?" Namath shrugged. Carson was 40 years old. I was on the *Tonight Show* that fall to plug a book, *The Pro Quarterback*, and told Carson about Joe's reaction to him. He wasn't amused. Sonny Werblin, the Jets' managing owner, had been set to sign record-breaking college passer Jerry Rhome of Tulsa and flew him to New York for an interview. After taciturn "Yups" and "Nopes," show-biz savvy Sonny told Coach Weeb Ewbank,

"Get me the kid from Alabama," traded for the rights to Namath, and signed him to a stupendous (for the time) $400,000 contract. Joe Willie was a smash hit from the start, despite a damaged knee from college—brilliant passer, super-quick release, natural field general—and immediately transformed to "Broadway Joe," with a bachelor lifestyle to match. I visited his hospital room after knee surgery, along with a continuing parade of lovelies; Joe sipped champagne and ordered Scotch. He also took the Jets to an astounding 16-7 upset of the Baltimore Colts in Super Bowl III that legitimized the AFL brand of football; he received greater fame with his pre-game victory "guarantee." There was always a twinkle in his green Hungarian eyes, as if Joe knew it was a put-on, and it was a kick bantering with him. On the side, he dabbled in television and movies, and once starred opposite Ann-Margret. He managed to survive thirteen battle-scarred seasons on his bad legs, the last with the Los Angeles Rams. That led me to re-dub him "Hollywood Joe." He hardly played for the Rams, but his career was good enough to make the Pro Football Hall of Fame.

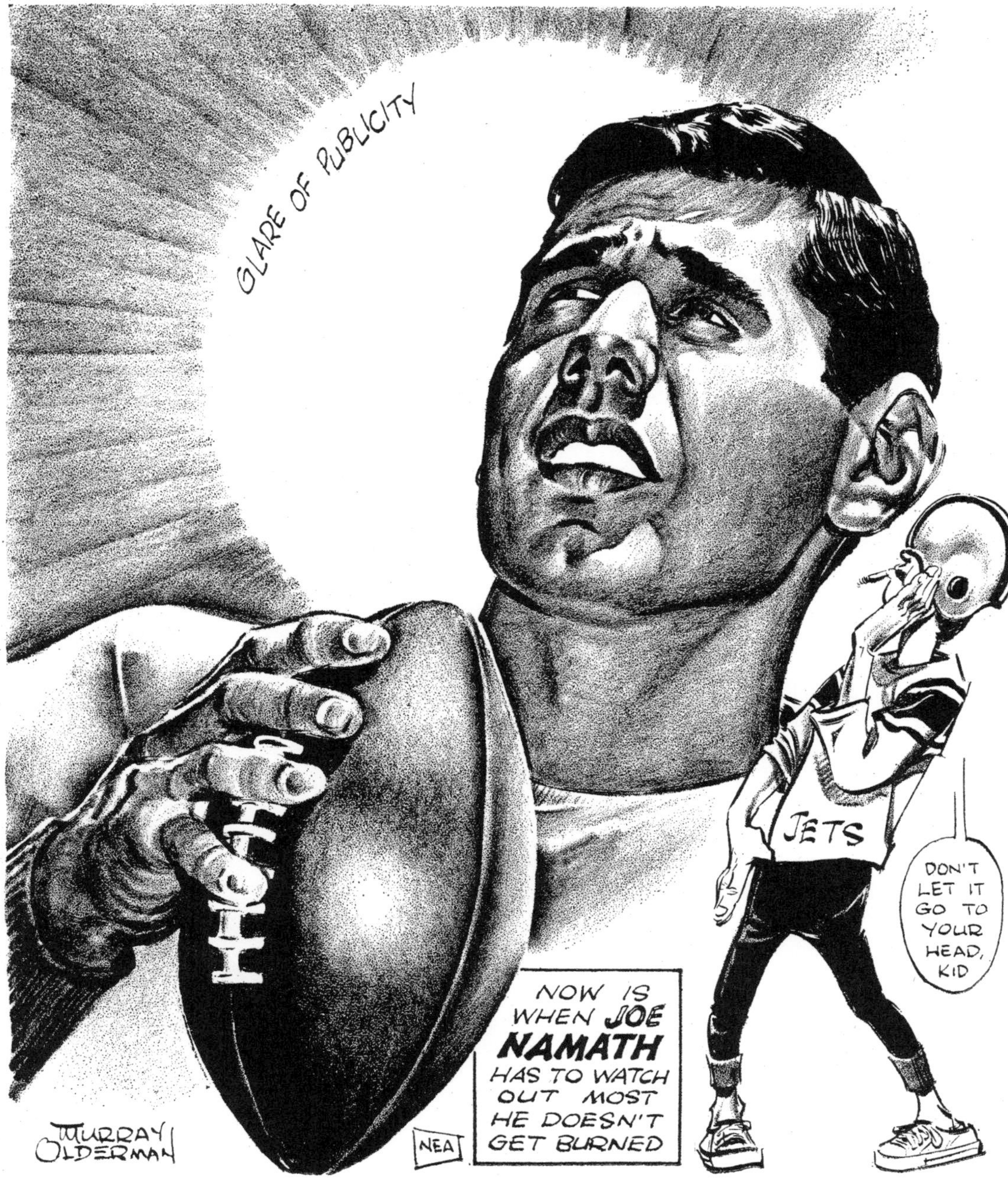
GLARE OF PUBLICITY
JETS
DON'T LET IT GO TO YOUR HEAD, KID
NOW IS WHEN JOE NAMATH HAS TO WATCH OUT MOST HE DOESN'T GET BURNED
MURRAY OLDERMAN
NEA

"His Day in the Sun"

Jack Nicklaus

I FOLLOWED JACK Nicklaus for the seventy-two holes of the first professional golf tournament he played, the Los Angeles Open at El Rancho, and saw him mis-club, spray shots, butcher chips, and misread putts. With Nicklaus hacked out of contention, playing partner Art Wall noticed me still slogging along on the fourth day and said, "You must be doing something on him." I was. I had a magazine assignment for *Sport* magazine. He finished tied dead last with two other golfers and shared last place money of one hundred dollars. His total purse was just over thirty-three dollars. That ultimately accrued to five million dollars in career prize money and a recent net worth of some $300 million. I'll write it right now—Jack Nicklaus is the greatest golfer ever. The immortal Bobby Jones, also called the greatest, said, "He plays a game of golf that I don't recognize." Nicklaus won a record eighteen major Grand Slam titles, including the Masters at age forty-six. As a twenty-year-old amateur, playing with Ben Hogan, he finished second in a U.S. Open to Arnold Palmer. After his stumbling pro start, he soon supplanted charismatic Palmer as the top golfer in the world—not the most popular. His rivalry with Arnold Palmer was real, but never acrimonious. Nicklaus was wide-bodied, squat, rumpled. In college, they called him "Ohio Fats." I did a color cover for an annual issue of *Golf Digest* and was complimented for my acuity in showing a rotund Nicklaus with his right elbow flying, an unorthodox aspect of his swing. I had no idea how Nicklaus swung a club, but I winged it cartoon style. His wife Barbara was more impressed that I captured his girth—she called him "Fat Boy." Flying back from a British Open triumph, he turned to her and said, "That's it. I can go home and gain twenty pounds in three weeks. Why not go home and lose twenty?" On a self-imposed diet, he went in three weeks from 210 to 185 pounds, dressed more modishly, let his blond hair grow out, and with the new gestalt became the "Golden Bear," with greater appreciation for his golf prowess. Jack was one of the rare athletes who wasn't self-absorbed. He always bothered to ask me how I was doing. After a round at a U.S. Open at Baltusrol, he beckoned to me and confided, "I had to deny the quotes I gave you because I'd get in trouble with one of my sponsors." I don't even remember the subject matter of that long-ago column, but he had the decency to let me know that I had gotten it right.

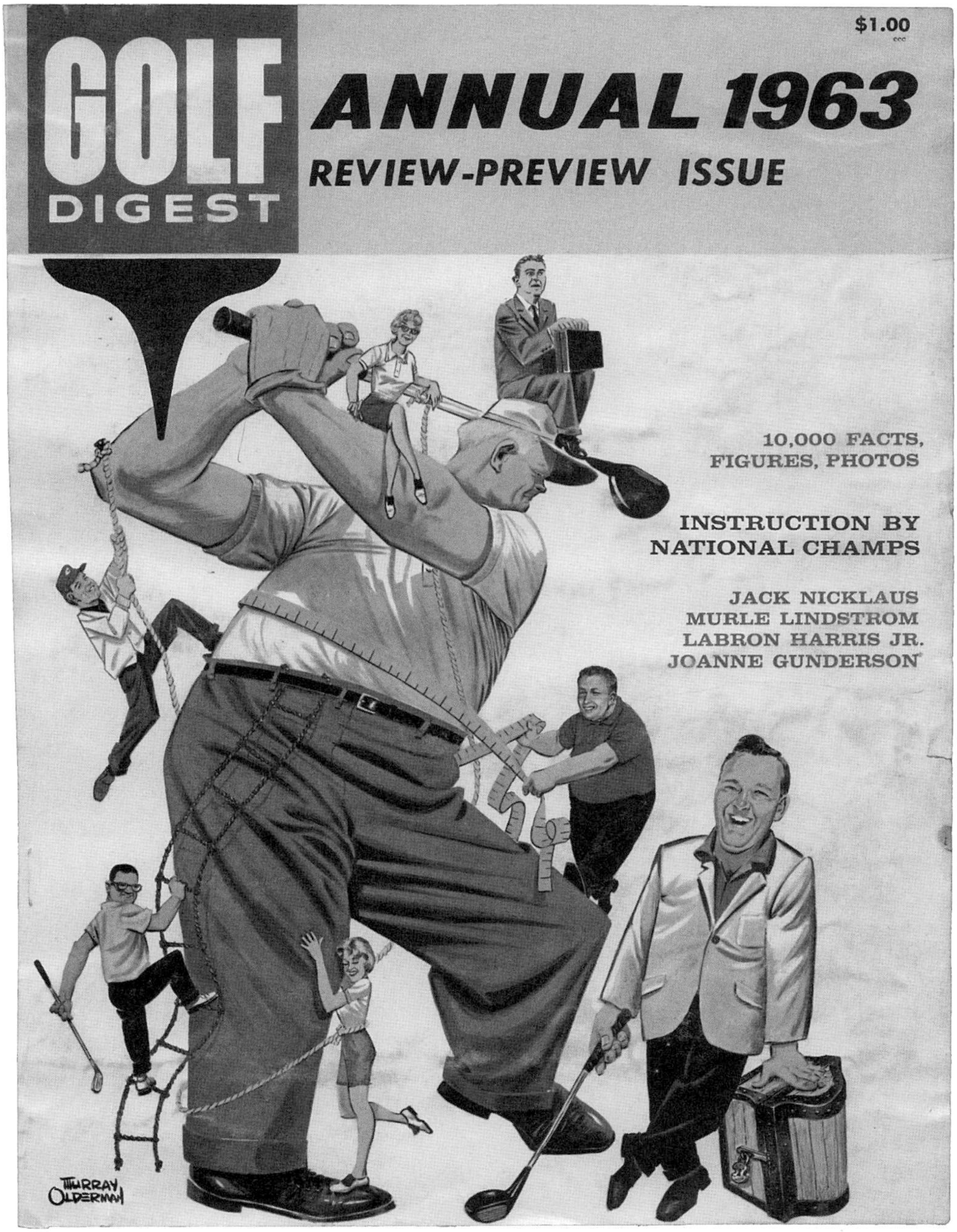
$1.00
GOLF DIGEST
ANNUAL 1963
REVIEW-PREVIEW ISSUE
10,000 FACTS, FIGURES, PHOTOS
INSTRUCTION BY NATIONAL CHAMPS
JACK NICKLAUS
MURLE LINDSTROM
LABRON HARRIS JR.
JOANNE GUNDERSON
MURRAY OLDERMAN

Merlin Olsen

THE LONG FORGOTTEN Gotham Bowl in the Big Apple signaled Merlin Olsen's debut as a compelling sports personality. The All-American lineman, 285 pounds of muscular force and speed (he was a high school hurdler and sprinter), led bucolic Utah State into New York and began talking, with wit and intelligence, the moment he arrived. The physical and the verbal facets sustained him through a long career. The Los Angeles Rams drafted him number one and put him at defensive tackle alongside end Deacon Jones for the most formidable combo ever seen in the NFL. Olsen was selected for fourteen straight Pro Bowls and, predictably, the Hall of Fame. The ability to verbalize got him guest shots on TV. "I understand you're one of the most articulate men in all of sports," said a talk show host. "Okay, articulate!" Merlin looked at him blankly a few seconds, smiled broadly, and started talking. He never really stopped. While I was writing the book *The Defenders*,

the Rams, on a road trip, were lodged in a New Jersey hotel a few miles from my home. Merlin came over the afternoon before the game and gave me a four-hour dissertation on the specifics of playing defensive tackle. Harland Svare, a Rams coach, criticized him: "You think too much." Merlin admitted, "It was probably legitimate. You've got to establish the physical factor. I want the guard opposite me to know that if I want to run over him, I can." But he added, "The old image of the stupid defensive lineman is dead. A stupid man cannot play our sophisticated game successfully." While playing pro ball, Merlin obtained a master's degree with a thesis on the world sugar crisis. He went from the NFL to esteemed network football analyst, veered into a popular TV series star, and finally abandoned Hollywood to return to his Rocky Mountain roots and become a persuasive bank spokesman. Never at a loss for words.

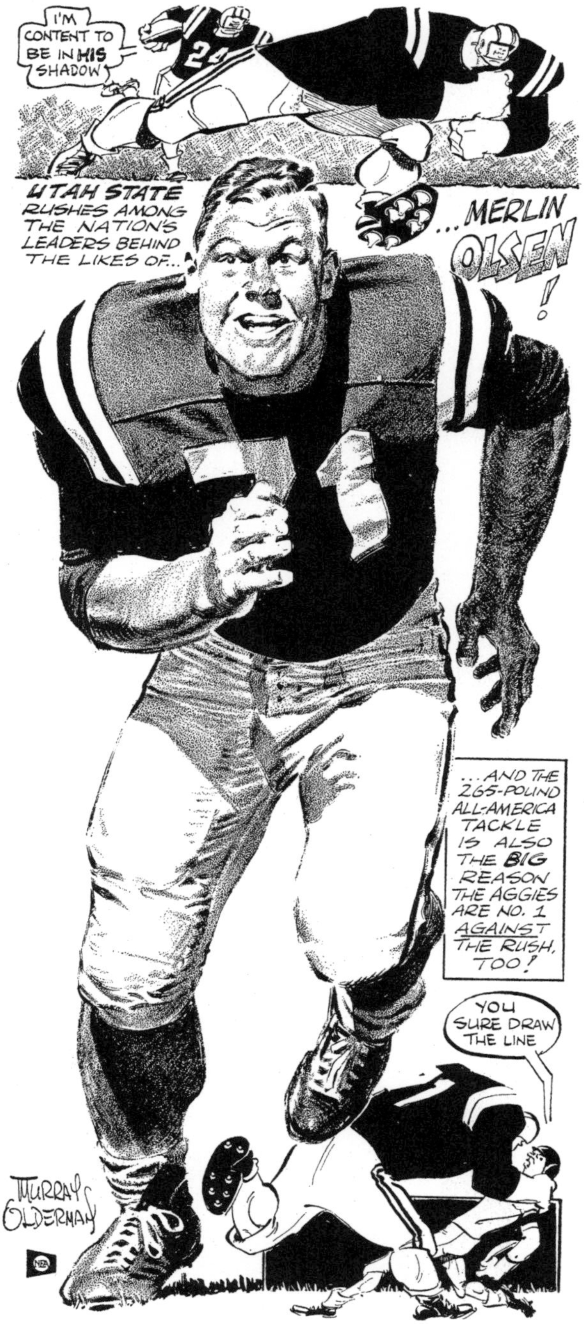
I'M CONTENT TO BE IN HIS SHADOW
UTAH STATE RUSHES AMONG THE NATION'S LEADERS BEHIND THE LIKES OF...
...MERLIN OLSEN!
...AND THE 265-POUND ALL-AMERICA TACKLE IS ALSO THE BIG REASON THE AGGIES ARE NO. 1 AGAINST THE RUSH, TOO!
YOU SURE DRAW THE LINE
MURRAY OLDERMAN

"Big Both Ways"

Walter O'Malley

HE TRANSFORMED BASEBALL nationally by moving the Brooklyn Dodgers to Los Angeles in 1958, the first major league penetration west of Kansas City. But Walter O'Malley really wasn't a visionary, but just a lawyer looking for the best deal he could get. O'Malley was a Bronx-bred, Fordham law grad, and a New York Giants fan who became the Dodgers' general counsel and by 1950 bought out the minority Brooklyn owners and took over the club. He wanted a new stadium to replace antiquated Ebbets Field, but couldn't get the local Brooklyn politicians to cooperate. He was wooed instead to a ravine near downtown L.A. O'Malley wore double-breasted suits and smoked cigars and typified a new breed of owner. Until then, baseball and football clubs were run by men raised in the sports or super-rich magnates on an ego trip. O'Malley was florid, genial and accessible. I visited him in his office overlooking home plate after the Dodgers blew the '62 pennant in the ninth inning of the final playoff game against the Giants. "We didn't do so badly," he said. "More than four million fans paid to come into this stadium last year. I don't take the criticism [of how we played] serious." He took a phone call and assured the caller that "I took care of Jack Benny's seat locations." The Dodgers later won the 1965 World Series, and I wrote a three-part syndicated series the next spring, focusing on O'Malley's hands-on leadership and his attained recognition as the most influential and successful owner in baseball.

"The whole 1962 season was so dramatic...I don't take the criticism serious...we didn't do so badly...."

— Walter O'Malley CHAVEZ RAVINE

"Reflections of Buddha"

Jesse Owens

THIS SKETCH OF the famed sprinter, who won four gold medals at the 1936 Olympic Games in Berlin, was part of a double truck (two facing pages) layout I did for *True* magazine on "Olympic Highlights." It featured great champions in the history of the Games—decathlete Jim Thorpe, distance legend Paavo Nurmi, sprinter Charley Paddock, 17-year-old decathlete Bob Mathias, hurdler Harrison Dillard—and appeared in the August 1952 issue. It was the first art I ever did for a national magazine, a breakthrough for a young cartoonist, and its publication coincided with my move from the *Minneapolis Star-Tribune* to NEA (Newspaper Enterprise Association), the Scripps-Howard national syndicate, in New York. A couple of years later, I actually met Jesse Owens at a luncheon at Toots Shor's on 52nd Street in Manhattan, the favorite sports hangout in the city. Owens was doing motivational speaking by then after varied ways trying to capitalize on his Olympic glory. I don't remember what company he was plugging, but do recall the staccato cadence of his spiel. He talked almost as fast as he ran, with a rehearsed patter. Later he slowed down in a congenial private conversation to tell me how he had been influenced by Paddock's success and how he in turn had first encouraged Dillard, meeting the youngster at a parade in his native Cleveland, Ohio.

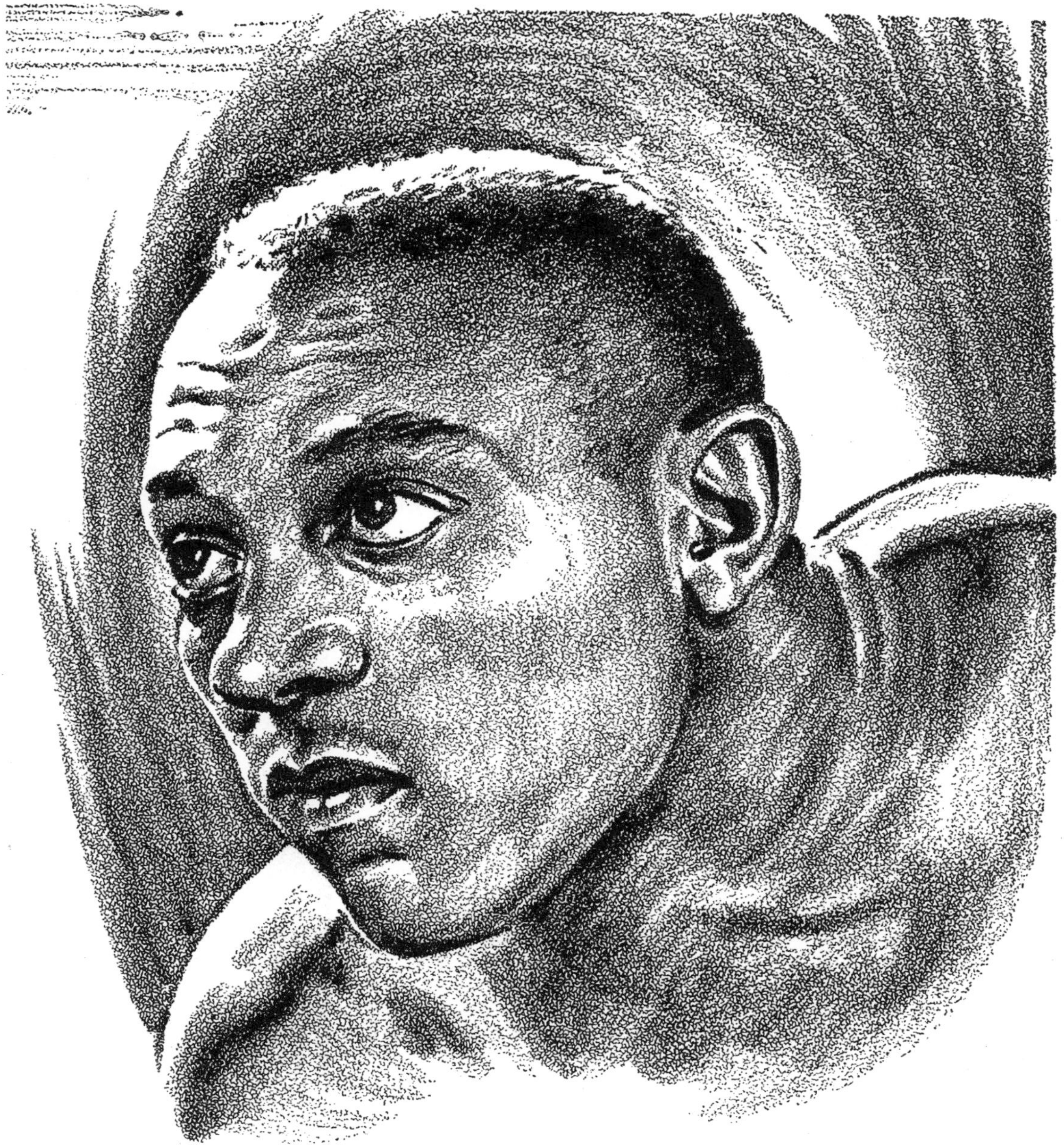

Arnie Palmer

IN HIS LONG reign over golf, starting with famous charges to win both the Masters and the U.S. Open in 1960, his popularity never diminished, no matter the result. The man last won a regular tour event in 1973, and yet more than a quarter of a century later, he was still commanding thirteen million dollars a year in endorsement income. Palmer had a flair, a knack for the dramatic, for saying the right thing. In Florida for baseball spring training, I detoured to a St. Petersburg Open at DeSoto Lakes and caught up to him on the sixteenth hole. He hooked his drive into under-growth behind a clump of moss-covered palmetto. The flagstick, dogleg left, was almost hidden from sight. A frown on his snub-nosed face, he strode out to the fairway to check the angle. Back into the rough, he grabbed a seven-iron, took a sharp swing, and the ball screamed through a birdcage opening in the hanging moss, curled onto the green and stopped five feet from the cup—the greatest golf shot I've seen in person. A few years later, at a Puerto Rican resort, I watched him film a segment of *Shell's Wonderful World of Golf*. His private jet was down the road in San Juan. He was the first pro golfer to earn more than one million dollars in prize money. A relaxed Palmer shot a magnificent sixty-five as "Arnie's Army" followed him the entire round, among them a little, gray-haired lady. She walked up to him and grimaced, "You're the only man I'd walk eighteen holes for." Palmer beamed and said, "Let's go have a beer." She melted. The years dwindled down, and I trudged down a fairway after Palmer at a Diners Club match in La Quinta, California, my energy flagging, my head drooping. "Arnie," now sixty-six and white-haired, strode over and chided me, "You're looking down at the grass." Pause. Sardonic grin. Then he added, "But it's better than looking up at the roots." That was a line I hadn't heard before.

"The General Plots His Campaigns"

Floyd Patterson

ONE OF ELEVEN children brought up in the dangerous Bedford-Stuyvesant area of Brooklyn, Floyd Patterson had a troubled childhood—habitual truant, total loner, so emotionally disturbed his mother sent him to a corrective school in upstate New York. At fourteen, he was hanging around Cus D'Amato's Gramercy Gym in lower Manhattan because his brother Billy boxed there. "Never opened his mouth," said Cus. "Just hung his head and grunted when you asked him something. But I noticed his determination when he got in the ring. He'd get hit on the chin, blink, shake his head, move right in again." Cus taught him the peek-a-boo style of boxing, gloves alongside his head. By seventeen, he won a gold medal as a middleweight in the 1952 Olympics. As a pro, Patterson grew into a heavyweight, and, after Rocky Marciano retired, beat old Archie Moore to become the youngest champ ever—another D'Amato disciple, Mike Tyson, later won that honor at age twenty. Patterson fought three memorable bouts with Ingemar Johansson, losing the title to the Swede's "Toonder and Lightning" barrage of rights, regaining the crown, surviving a knockdown to win the third, depicted here—I drew it on deadline, distributed on the United Press wire from Miami Beach that night. As he matured, Floyd became more communicative, with a bemused, pleasant demeanor. Although quick, with fast hands, Patterson was exposed as an under-sized 185-pound heavyweight when he came up against brutish Sonny Liston and was KO'd in the first round. Mortified, he slunk away in shame, disguised with a fake beard. In a rematch, Liston decked him again in the first round. After he retired, Patterson served as head of the New York state boxing commission.

"After 'Toonder and Lightning,' RAIN!"

Bob Pettit

AS THE NATIONAL Basketball Association was spreading its wings in the 1950s, to honor a new breed of star in the wake of the Lakers' George Mikan—hot-shot scorers like Paul Arizin of the Philadelphia Warriors—I called Haskell Cohen, the NBA publicity chief, to institute a Most Valuable Player Award, under the auspices of my feature syndicate. I sent ballots to every NBA player, stipulating one could not vote for a teammate. The first winner in 1956 of the President's Cup, as I called it then, was Bob Pettit of the St. Louis Hawks, a second-year forward who was cut from his Baton Rouge, Louisiana, high school team as a sophomore and learned to play in a church league. He received thirty-three votes; Arizin had twenty-one; Bob Cousy eleven. He received the trophy from Commissioner Maurice Podoloff in a halftime presentation at the NBA All-Star game. A few years later, I changed the name to the Podoloff Cup, now the official NBA tribute to its MVP, but the league ultimately took over the voting process and gave it to its writers. "Pettit right now," said Joe Lapchick, an original Celtic who coached the New York Knicks, "is a better player than Mikan at his best. He's more of a basketball player." An All-American at hometown LSU, he had to be convinced to try pro ball by his cousin Frank Brian, a star with the Fort Wayne Pistons. Pettit was a graceful scorer and led the NBA with twenty-five points per game and stayed at a twenty-plus pace through his eleven-year career. He was handsome and articulate and a jitterbug of some note back in Baton Rouge. His only reaction to getting that MVP trophy: "Gosh."

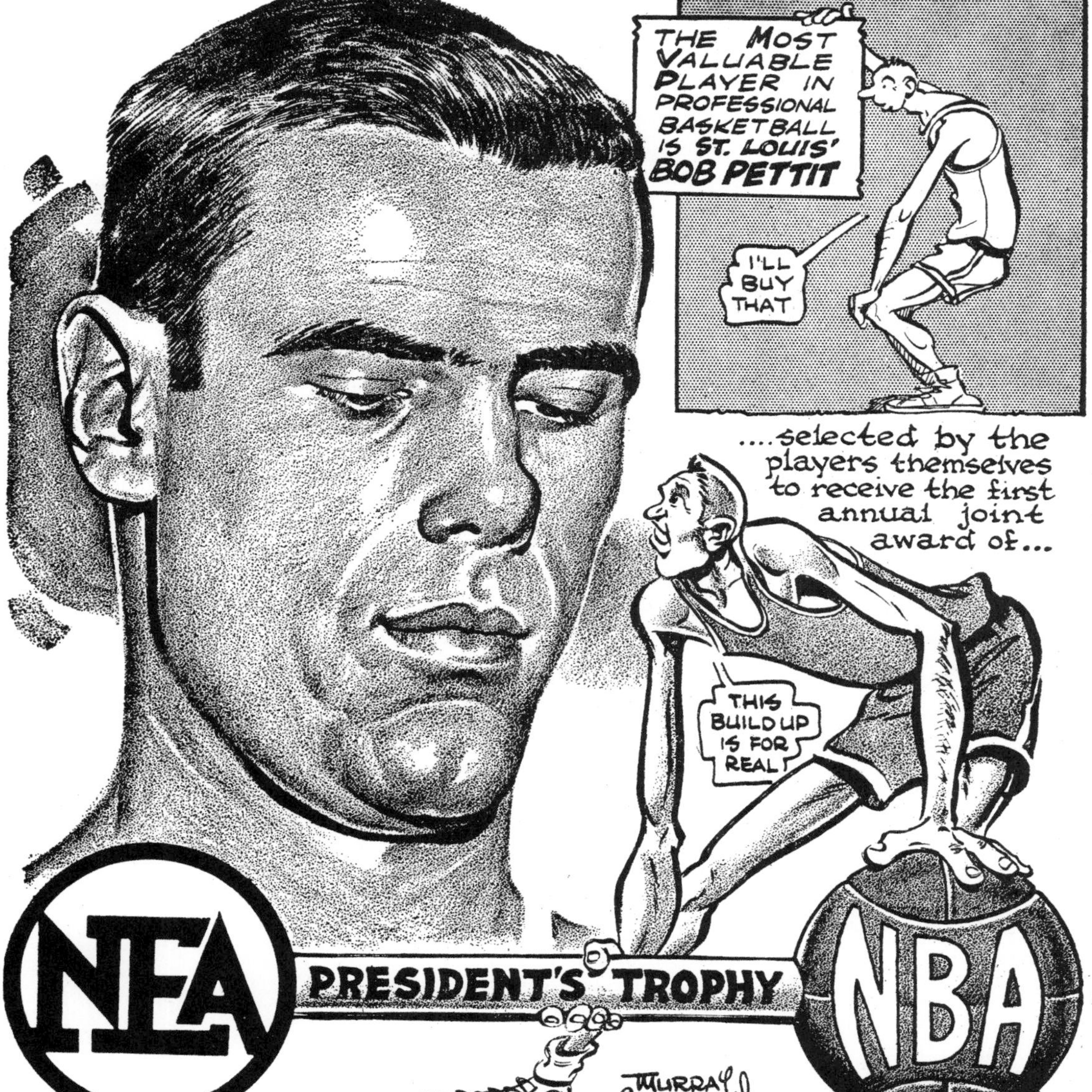
THE MOST VALUABLE PLAYER IN PROFESSIONAL BASKETBALL IS ST. LOUIS' BOB PETTIT
I'LL BUY THAT
....selected by the players themselves to receive the first annual joint award of...
THIS BUILD UP IS FOR REAL
NEA
PRESIDENT'S TROPHY
NBA
MURRAY OLDERMAN

"Exerting a Strong Pull"

Jim Plunkett

IN THE SUMMER of 1978, Jim Plunkett could have been claimed by any one of twenty-seven NFL teams for the waiver price of one hundred dollars. All passed on the battle-scarred seven-year veteran, and the San Francisco 49ers released him. Mind you, this was a Heisman Trophy winner for Stanford and the first player picked in the 1971 draft. I saw his first pro game in which the rookie quarterback led the Patriots to an upset over the tough Oakland Raiders. But he never played on a winning team in five years with New England, was traded to the 49ers, lasted two seasons, and was let go as damaged goods, after three knee operations and a bruised psyche from weak protection. The Raiders' Al Davis reached across the Bay and brought Plunkett in for a tryout, signing him as a backup. He sat around for two more years, barely playing, but in the fifth game of the 1980 season, starter Dan Pastorini suffered a leg fracture, was replaced by Plunkett, and the faltering Raiders rallied to reach and win the Super Bowl— he was the first Latino quarterback to achieve that feat. Adversity was in his DNA. Both of

his parents, of Mexican descent, were legally blind and on welfare. As a kid in San Jose, he had to scramble to make a buck. When he started to make big money as a pro, the first thing he did, as a bachelor then, was buy a home in posh Atherton on the Peninsula. "We always had to move when the rent went up," he explained. "I wanted my own place." Jim was also crafty. I invited him to play in an off-season pro football players doubles tennis tournament. He cajoled me into letting him team with his old Stanford and Patriot teammate, Randy Vataha. I didn't realize Vataha was by far the best tennis player among the jocks; they won the event. As a field general, Plunkett had a big arm and stood strong in the pocket. And he got better as he got older. In 1983, supplanted by young Marc Wilson, he took over again when Wilson fractured a shoulder and led the Raiders to a second Super Bowl triumph. Plunkett managed to last sixteen pro seasons and has remained with the Raiders ever since, on their broadcast team, and delving into successful businesses.

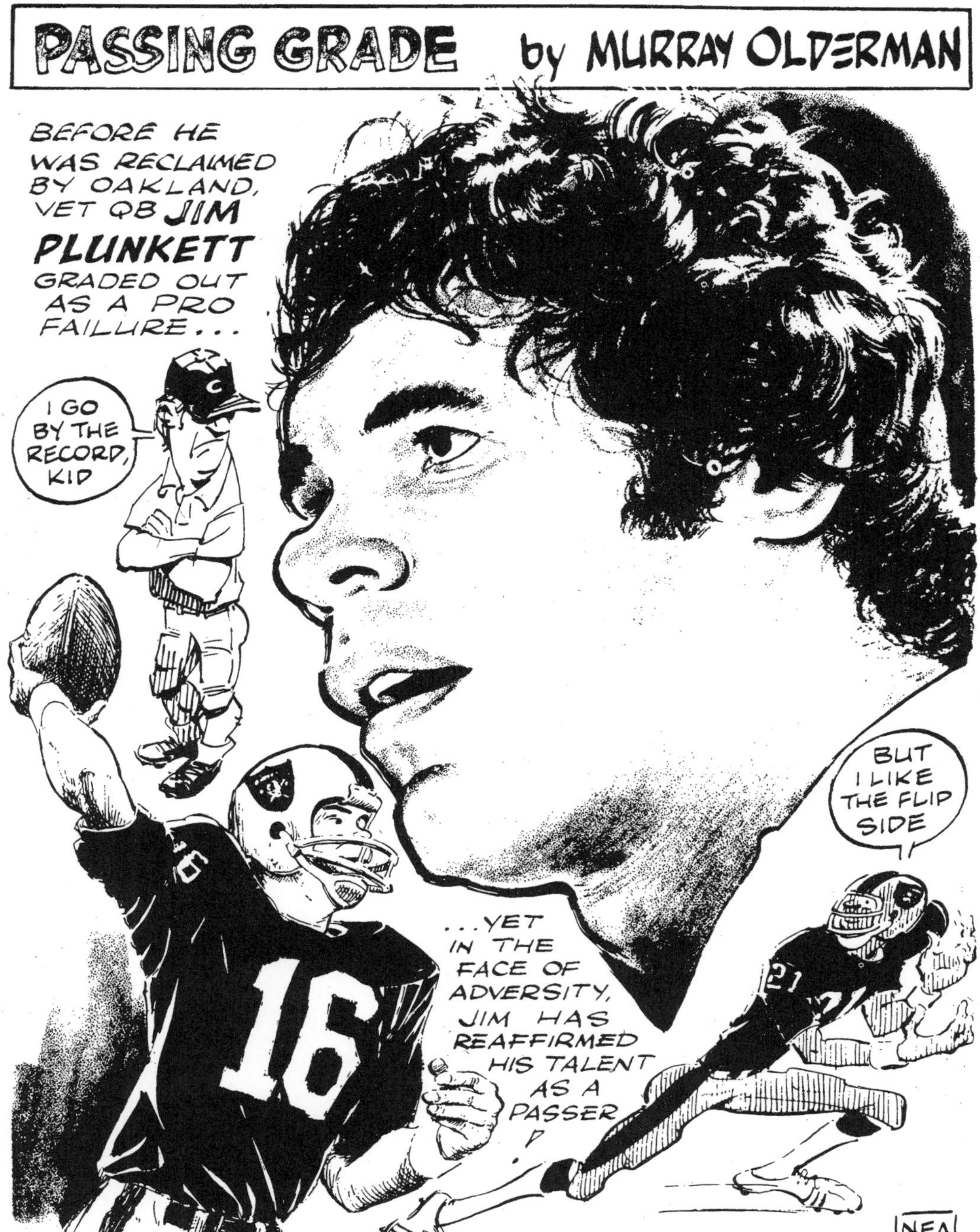
PASSING GRADE by MURRAY OLDERMAN
BEFORE HE WAS RECLAIMED BY OAKLAND, VET QB JIM PLUNKETT GRADED OUT AS A PRO FAILURE...
I GO BY THE RECORD, KID
BUT I LIKE THE FLIP SIDE
...YET IN THE FACE OF ADVERSITY, JIM HAS REAFFIRMED HIS TALENT AS A PASSER
16
21
NEA

Jackie Robinson

NEW TO THE New York sports scene in the early 1950s, I was a little in awe of Jack Roosevelt Robinson. He was at the peak of his playing career as a second baseman and iconic leader of the legendary Brooklyn Dodgers, the man who broke the racial barrier in organized professional sports. Baseball probably wasn't his best sport. He had been an All-American back in football and high scoring guard in basketball—both at UCLA—as well as a world-class long jumper in track. Some, such as sports-writing savant Ira Berkow of the *New York Times*, claim he was the greatest athlete ever. As a condition of signing him as the first black player in organized baseball, Branch Rickey, the Mahatma of the Dodgers, had instructed him not to fight back at the abuse he would face. And at first he held his tongue. But Jackie was no longer a "turn-the-other-cheek" guy when I first encountered him five years later in the Dodgers' dressing room at Ebbets Field after a World Series game. Jackie was completely assertive, the combative soul of a championship team. What really astounded me, though, was his language. Jackie Robinson was the most profane man I ever heard in the privacy of a locker room, dishing out obscenity-laced hyperbole with high-pitched stridency. Most amazing to me, however, was that he never slipped up in public. Robinson morphed into a corporate executive and social activist before his death in 1972 at fifty-three from diabetes complications—though his aggressiveness enveloped him in disputes and controversy even as he slid into retirement from baseball after an historical decade with the Dodgers.

Labels in image: CONTROVERSY, POP-OFFS, RHUBARBS, FEUDS, DISPUTES, RETIREMENT

"To the End, a Cloud of Dust"

Sugar Ray Robinson

ONE OF MY most unusual encounters in sports was taking Darrell Royal to Harlem to meet with Sugar Ray Robinson at his restaurant on 125th Street. Darrell was a football coach at the University of Texas, a national champion during his tenure. Sugar Ray was considered pound-for-pound the greatest fighter in the history of boxing. They couldn't have been more disparate, but it was fascinating to hear them compare notes on the discipline and dedication it takes to be a winner. Sugar Ray was a professional fighter for an amazing twenty-five years and in his first decade lost only one of 131 fights, to Jake LaMotta. He was the welterweight champion of the world for five years and then graduated to the middleweight class, winning the title at thirty by stopping LaMotta. (They had six memorable bouts, with Sugar Ray winning the last five, causing Jake to lament, "I fought Sugar Ray so many times I almost got diabetes.") I was at ringside when Sugar Ray challenged Joey Maxim for the light heavyweight crown a year later in Yankee Stadium on a hot June night with the temperature at 103 degrees. Referee Ruby Goldstein had to quit

from heat exhaustion in the middle rounds. Sugar Ray was leading on the cards of all three judges when, dehydrated, he wobbled crazily and collapsed after the thirteenth round, unable to come out from his corner for the fourteenth—the only KO in his long career. He grew up Walker Smith Jr., in Detroit on the same street as Joe Louis, but moved to New York in his teens. Too young to get a boxing license, he borrowed the birth certificate of his friend, Ray Robinson, and that became his name. As much as Floyd Mayweather epitomizes ring greatness for modern boxing fans, Sugar Ray, with his speed and instincts and punching power, embodied the ideal for all generations. Neither one was really likeable—there was an arrogance in their personas. Sugar Ray was flashy and flamboyant. He lived his life conspicuously and was accompanied on world travels by an entourage. He tried acting and becoming a song-and-dance man but flopped. At thirty-seven, he regained his middleweight crown from Carmen Basilio, another serial adversary. But fighting into his forties took its toll and left him with late-life dementia.

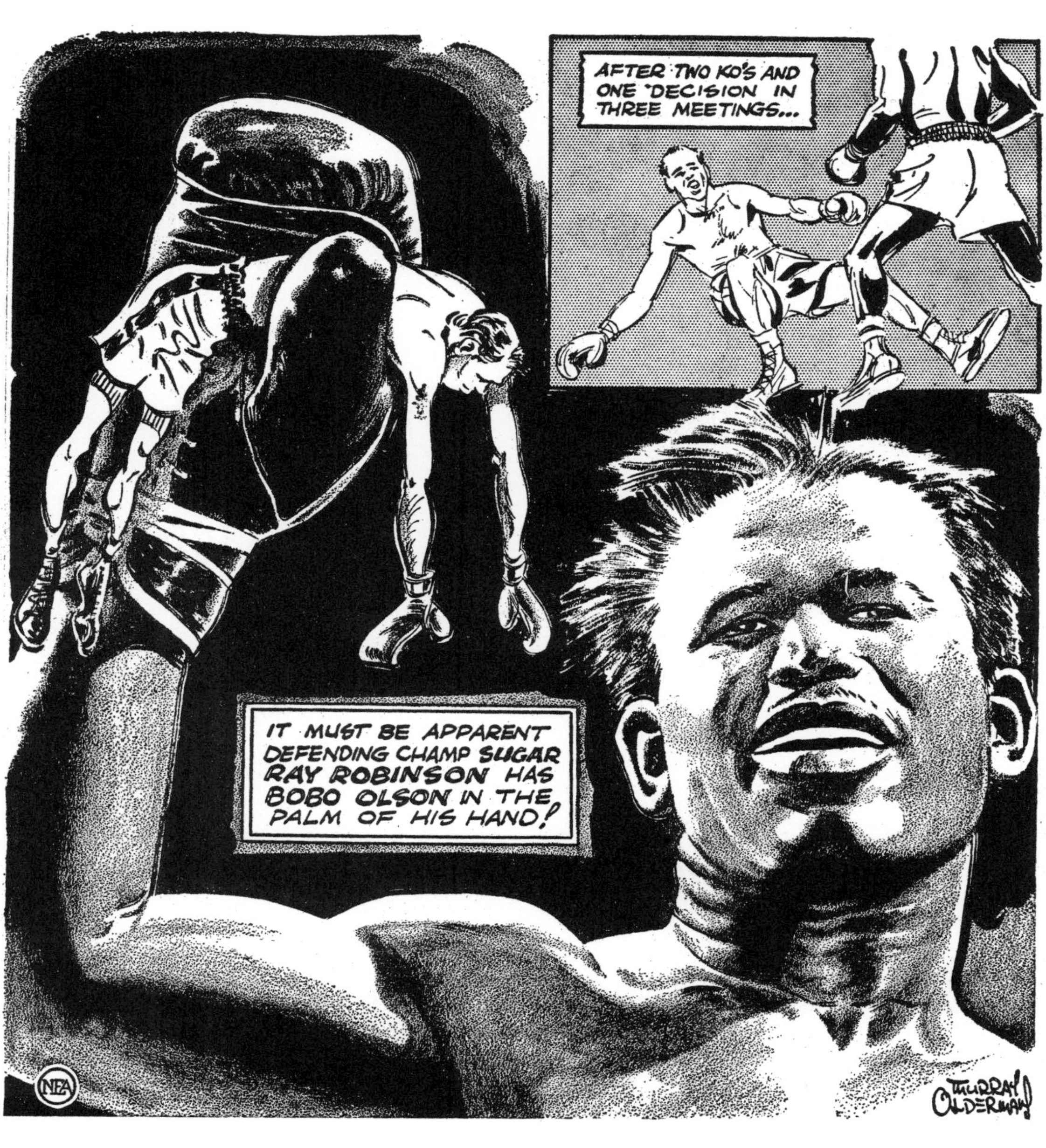
AFTER TWO KO'S AND ONE DECISION IN THREE MEETINGS...
IT MUST BE APPARENT DEFENDING CHAMP SUGAR RAY ROBINSON HAS BOBO OLSON IN THE PALM OF HIS HAND!
NEA
MURRAY OLDERMAN

"Hold Him Lightly"

Pete Rose

A GROUP AT the Cincinnati training camp was driving from dinner one night on the long causeway across Old Tampa Bay and glimpsed a young guy trudging towards the city. We couldn't make out his face in the darkness. "That looks like our rookie second baseman," said Earl Lawson of the *Cincinnati Post*. "Naw, can't be," said Coach Dick Sisler, driving the car. Fifteen minutes later, Sisler, in the hotel lobby, saw young Pete Rose walk through the swinging door. "Was that by any chance you out there on the causeway?" he asked the rookie. "Sure was," said Pete. And he explained, "I was at this restaurant on the other side of the Bay and thought I'd get a cab back. But when the dinner bill came I didn't have any money left. My pop told me before I came here that major leaguers don't hitch a ride." He simply walked the six miles. Later that season, after flying out to Willie Mays, on the changeover the brash rookie said to Willie, "You better play me deeper." Scoffed Willie, "Man, you can't hit the ball over my head." Next time up, Pete lashed a double to deep center over Willie's head. Pete Rose simply willed his way to greatness and collected more hits than any batter in the history of the game. He had an encyclopedic memory and could recall each of them, like the triple off pitcher Bob Friend in his second game, his first big league hit after going 0-for-3 in the opener. At forty, he related that anecdote in a dugout pre-game chat and regaled me for an hour with statistical records, both significant and arcane. He even noted he had the highest fielding average ever for an outfielder with more than a thousand games. When I interjected that this obsession with personal records might be construed as selfish, he shrugged, "Most people don't talk about records because they don't get the chance to accumulate them." Every conversation I had with Pete, as player or manager, devolved down to stats, but the anomaly of Rose was his classic team traditionalism. He was nicknamed "Charlie Hustle" for running out every play. An All-Star at second base, he suggested the shift to the outfield for the good of the club, then moved without complaint to third base and then first base. As a citizen, he wasn't a model. His carousing and gambling have been well documented, and betting on baseball got him banned for life and kept him from the Baseball Hall of Fame.

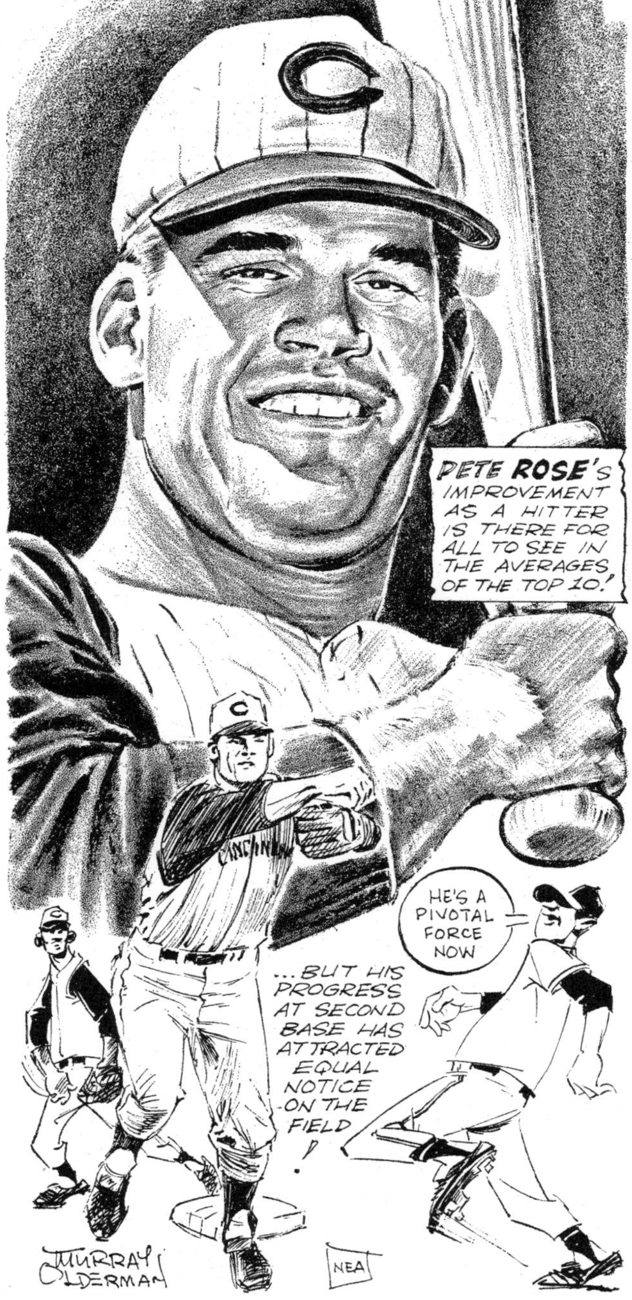
PETE ROSE's IMPROVEMENT AS A HITTER IS THERE FOR ALL TO SEE IN THE AVERAGES OF THE TOP 10!
...BUT HIS PROGRESS AT SECOND BASE HAS ATTRACTED EQUAL NOTICE ON THE FIELD!
HE'S A PIVOTAL FORCE NOW
MURRAY OLDERMAN
NEA

"Second to None"

Carroll Rosenbloom

IT PUZZLES ME that Carroll Rosenbloom is not in the Pro Football Hall of Fame. From the time Commissioner Bert Bell, his old coach at Penn, convinced him to buy the Baltimore Colts in 1953 for $25,000, he was the most powerful owner in the NFL. His Colts spurred the national popularity of the sport when they won the famous sudden-death overtime against the Giants in 1958; he engineered the election of Pete Rozelle as commissioner; he pulled off the amazing trade of the Baltimore and Los Angeles franchises and raised the Rams to Super Bowl level before his death by drowning off his beach home in Florida. My profession gave me the chance to meet and know and study actual millionaires, a breed that controlled sports as they became big business the last half of the twentieth century. Rosenbloom was an authentic high roller as a gambler and in the financial world. He made his first millions by buying a denim factory at the outbreak of World War II, converting it to manufacture GI uniforms. Although Baltimore was home, he kept an apartment on Central Park South in Manhattan, where I'd hear him arranging parties with Ambassador Joe Kennedy (father of President JFK), and his girlfriend Georgia down the street. I traveled with the Colts and became friendly enough with Rosenbloom to be the "beard" for Georgia at home games—although separated from his first wife, Rosenbloom still had to keep up appearances—until he finally married her. In 1972, fed up with media criticism in Baltimore, he arranged to swap the Colts for the Rams and moved to Los Angeles, where he was a big Hollywood investor, and emerged as the squire of Bel Air with a yellow-gray hairpiece, designer jeans, and Guccis without socks. I played tennis on his court with the likes of trumpeter Ray Anthony and guested at his home on trips to L.A. We vacationed once with the Rosenblooms in Hawaii. The pro football team was his big passion, but he clashed with Rozelle on league issues and became disenchanted with the archaic Coliseum as home field, so in 1978 worked a deal to move the Rams to Anaheim. He never saw them play there because on April 2, 1979, at seventy-two, he waded alone into the surf at Golden Beach, Florida, and got swept up in an undertow. There were rumors of foul play, never authenticated. To avoid estate taxes, he left seventy percent of the team to his widow and the rest to his five children. A wake at Bel Air, with comedian Jonathan Winters as M.C., was held up an hour for Georgia's arrival.

IT'S NO COINCIDENCE THAT THE RISE OF THE **COLTS** TO CHAMPIONSHIP STATUS STARTED WITH THE ACTIVE INTEREST OF PRES. CARROLL **ROSENBLOOM** ...

BECAUSE HE USED TO GET THE JOB DONE ON THE FIELD AS A **PENN** HALFBACK ...

HOW'S THE WIFE 'N' KIDS, JOHN?...AN' YOU HAVING MUCH LUCK ON YOUR Z-OUT PATTERNS?

SOME GUYS GET A RISE OUT OF THE BOSS — WE GET A RAISE

MURRAY OLDERMAN

...AND HE'S EXERTED THE SAME DYNAMIC FORCE AS A FRONT OFFICE EXECUTIVE, WITH KEEN PARTICIPATION IN ALL COLT ACTIVITIES !

Kyle Rote

AS A SOPHOMORE playing his first season at Southern Methodist—freshmen weren't yet eligible—he became a national hero in one game, the finale of the 1949 season against mighty Notre Dame, when colleges mattered more than the pros. He replaced injured All-American Doak Walker at tailback, passed for three touchdowns, and had a last-minute throw knocked down on the goal line that would have spoiled Notre Dame's perfect season. This put Kyle Rote on the cover of prestigious *Life* magazine, a big deal in that era. His rookie year with the Giants, he stepped into a gopher hole before an exhibition game in Arkansas and tore up his left knee. That ended his running back days. Switching to wide receiver, he played gimpy for all eleven of his pro seasons, with no speed but great moves and improvisational skills that produced 300 receptions and forty-eight touchdowns, a leader on a New York team that won the NFL crown in 1956 and was in two other title games. He was so popular on the Giants that teammates all named their new babies "Kyle." He was just as talented out of uniform, composing songs and writing poems. He was a fine raconteur with an impish sense of humor; it was inevitable he'd get into broadcasting. He became a New York personality, doing network pro football broadcasts for several years. But Kyle had two drawbacks—his voice retained the flat nasal drawl of his native San Antonio and a drinking problem caused his professional and personal lives to deteriorate. I had lost touch with him for more than three decades when I spotted a white-haired man sitting in the VIP Pavilion of the Bob Hope golf tourney at Bermuda Dunes, California. The face was lined, the physique shrunken, but the twinkle in his eyes familiar. It was Kyle Rote. He was visiting from his residence on Maryland's eastern shore because of a favor he had done for a little kid who once sent a fan letter, asking if Kyle could get him on the Giants' sideline. Kyle sent back a note to write Wellington Mara, the team president, saying he was covering for his high school paper. On the sideline on a cold November Sunday, Kyle felt a tug on his poncho. The kid introduced himself. He invited Kyle to his high school graduation, later his wedding, then rose to CEO of a national steakhouse chain. Wherever one opened, Kyle was invited and could get a small piece of the action. Rote was at this golf tournament because his friend's company catered the golf event.

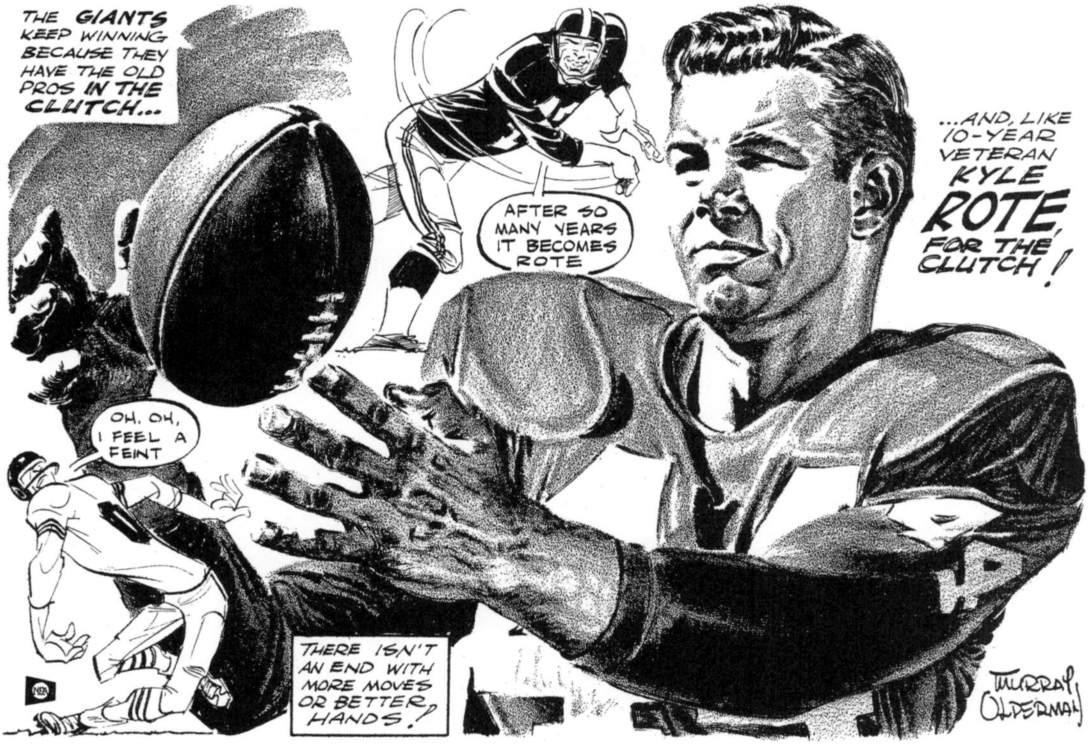
THE GIANTS KEEP WINNING BECAUSE THEY HAVE THE OLD PROS IN THE CLUTCH...
AFTER SO MANY YEARS IT BECOMES ROTE
...AND, LIKE 10-YEAR VETERAN KYLE ROTE, FOR THE CLUTCH!
OH, OH, I FEEL A FEINT
THERE ISN'T AN END WITH MORE MOVES OR BETTER HANDS!
MURRAY OLDERMAN

"Receiving Benefits"

Darrell Royal

COUNTRY MUSIC WAS Darrell Royal's passion, so if you were his house guest in Austin, where he served as coach of the University of Texas football team, a visit to the Soap Creek Saloon was on the agenda to hear the likes of Willie Nelson and Charlie Pride and Jerry Jeff Walker. Once when I bumped into him in Las Vegas we wound up in the dressing room of country singer Roy Clark after a casino performance. I first met Darrell when I commiserated with him at a Mexican restaurant in Dallas after a Cotton Bowl loss to Syracuse. Darrell was what I call a professional country boy from Hollis, Oklahoma, who didn't mind courting writers such as Furman Bisher of Atlanta and Blackie Sherrod of Dallas—former Football Writers Association of America presidents. Darrell was also a shrewd football coach. Coming out of the service in World War II, he had been an undersized run-option quarterback for Bud Wilkinson at Oklahoma, then coached at diverse outposts Edmonton in the Canadian League, Mississippi State, and Washington. At Texas, he produced two national champions and was twice national Coach of the Year, introducing the Wishbone T as a way to grind out victories on the ground. A Texas professor said to him accusingly, "You want more power (on campus) than I've got." Responded Royal, "There's no other faculty member checking to see his boys are in bed so they can get enough rest to function well in class. There's no one else conducting exams before 65,000 people." Royal was a realist. Even after two decades without a losing season and consecutive perfect records in 1969–70, he felt football success was cyclical, and he wasn't going to get caught in a downswing. So, at fifty-four, fed up by the hypocrisy of recruiting and cheating in the college game, he quit, served the university as an advisor to the president, had the Texas stadium named for him, and enjoyed retirement for the next thirty-five years with Edith, his childhood sweetheart. He also played golf out my way in the Coachella Valley every winter, mostly with former archrival Frank Broyles of Arkansas. They got into a cart at dawn and raced around the courses at PGA West at a breakneck pace, and by nightfall they had finished 90 holes of golf, five full Odyssean rounds. It got his mind off football.

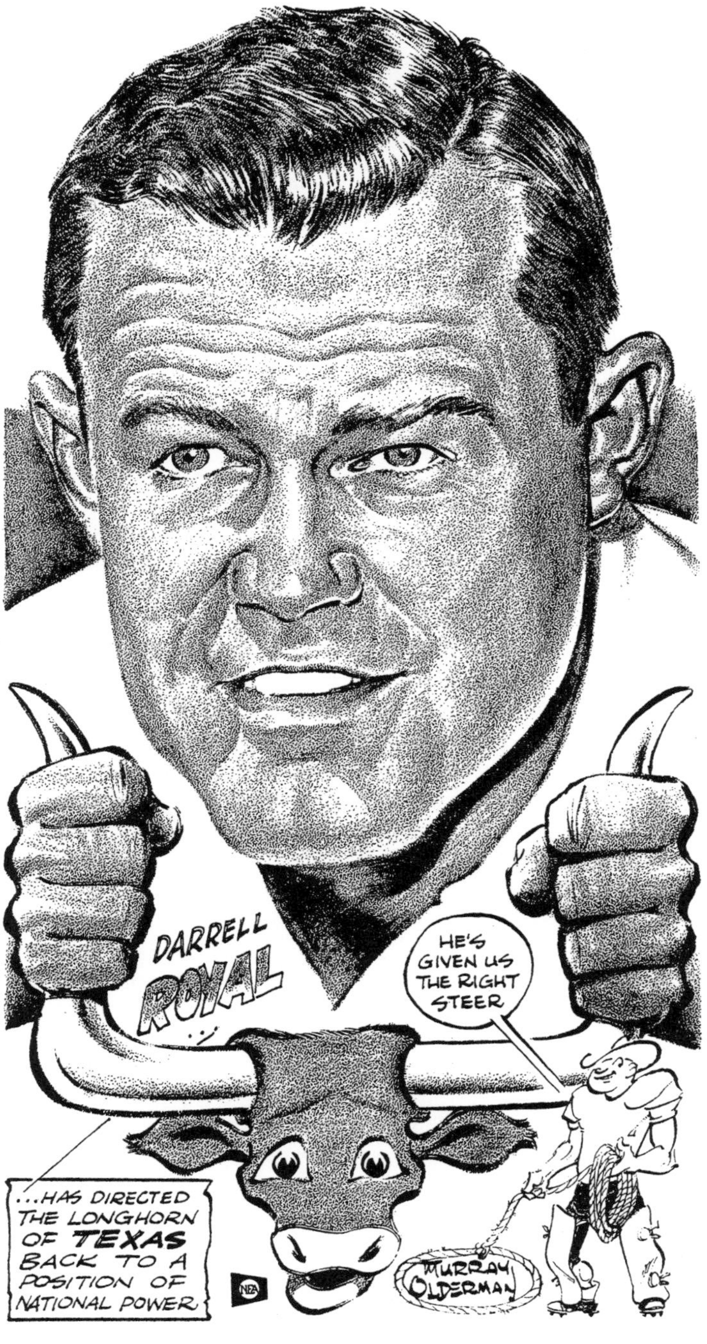
DARRELL ROYAL
HE'S GIVEN US THE RIGHT STEER
...HAS DIRECTED THE LONGHORN OF TEXAS BACK TO A POSITION OF NATIONAL POWER
NEA
MURRAY OLDERMAN

"By the Horns"

Pete Rozelle

I KNEW PETE Rozelle had it made when he arrived for a dinner party at my house in Leonia, New Jersey, across the George Washington Bridge, with his first wife, Jane, in a chauffeured black limousine. When the party broke up a few hours later, the chauffeur was still there outside waiting to take them back to Sutton Place in Manhattan, neighbors of such as Irving Berlin. Rozelle was a lower-middle-class kid from Compton, California, who was christened Alvin; an uncle mercifully decreed he was to be called Pete. He set the standard for modern commissioners who, until his ascendancy to the NFL top post, were politicians like Happy Chandler or judges like Kenesaw Mountain Landis or society scions like De Benneville "Bert" Bell, his predecessor. He was the first to tap the real possibilities of TV revenue and transform pro football into big business and a cultural icon. My first dealings with him were on the press row of University of San Francisco basketball games where Pete, who started as a student public relations man, doled out pencils and score sheets. He matured as the sports information director of the Los Angeles Rams and then their general manager until he was chosen in 1960 to lead the NFL because first choice Marshall Leahy, the 49ers lawyer, wouldn't move the league office to New York. The "boy commissioner"—age thirty-three when he took over—was smooth, (nattily dressed, with a cigarette holder) but firm and directed as he lorded over the colossus of pro football for the next thirty years. But he didn't forget old friends. He invited me along on his private jet back to New York from a Hall of Fame game in Canton. He'd relax with his drink of choice—a "Rusty Nail" (scotch and Drambuie)—in the privacy of his Park Avenue office and share confidences and show his puckish sense of humor. The increasing legal hassles that went with the job wore him down. I last had breakfast with Pete in posh Rancho Santa Fe, where he retired and was battling cancer that claimed his life at seventy. I still feel his role in sports was under-appreciated.

Hornung

Karras

"Indefinite Suspension"

Bill Russell

IN KEZAR PAVILION, a little bandbox where the University of San Francisco Dons played their home games, the featured attraction was a sinewy 6'10" center on an illusory pogo stick. I went there after LaSalle's Tom Gola, hitherto the top collegian, told me, "Every time I put up a shot, there was this big snake of an arm to block it. The guy's all-world." Bill Russell led the Dons to fifty-five straight victories and two NCAA titles. He brought a new dimension to defense in basketball. No big man before him had the agility and quickness and anticipation to block shots and dominate around the basket, hoard rebounds, and run the court with anyone. In 1956, coach Red Auerbach of the Boston Celtics traded bona-fide stars "Easy" Ed Macauley and Cliff Hagan to St. Louis for the rights to draft Russell, although he wouldn't report until mid-season because he helped the U.S. team to an Olympic Gold Medal in Melbourne. When he showed up in December, the Celtic spurted to an NBA championship, the first of eleven titles during Russell's thirteen-year Celtics tenure. The last three he was a player-coach. Growing up in the hardscrabble projects of Oakland, California, where the family moved after a racially charged childhood in Louisiana, Russell was sensitive to slights. Abe Saperstein wanted him for the Harlem Globetrotters but, sidestepping Russell, dickered with the USF coach. Russell lividly ignored his offer. He was intense and aloof, tough to approach. His personal foible was never to sign an autograph. I felt he tolerated me because year after year I kept presenting him with official NBA MVP trophies, five in all. It was amazing to me how he consistently bested Wilt Chamberlain in their head-to-head duels although Russell gave up height and weight and strength to his perennial rival (of course, Russell also had a better supporting cast with the likes of Hall of Famers Bob Cousy, Tommy Heinsohn, and John Havlicek). The key to Russell's success was fierce pride, inherent will, shrewd positioning, and instinctive timing. Not much of an offensive threat early in his career, Russell improved his shooting skills and raised his career average to over fifteen points per game. Only after he retired did we engage in any bantering, though he could be giggly and jocular if you caught him in the right mood. In 2011, he received the Presidential Medal of Freedom.

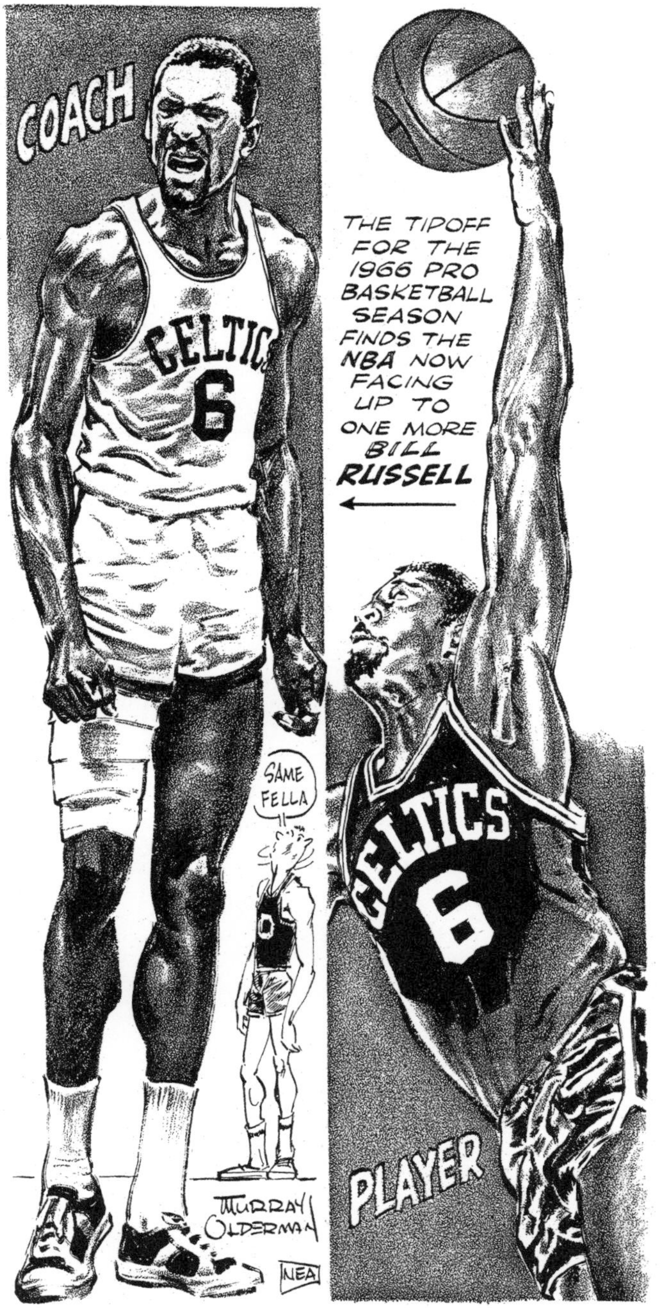

COACH
THE TIPOFF FOR THE 1966 PRO BASKETBALL SEASON FINDS THE NBA NOW FACING UP TO ONE MORE BILL RUSSELL
CELTICS 6
SAME FELLA
CELTICS 6
PLAYER
MURRAY OLDERMAN
NEA

"Split Personality"

Babe Ruth

I REMEMBER COMING through the grand-stand turnstile and gawking at the emerald carpet of a baseball field, greener than anything this twelve-year-old country bumpkin had ever seen. Yankee Stadium in the Bronx; my first major league game. But the real attraction was the blimpy figure playing his last season with the New York Yankees in 1934. George Herman Ruth Jr.—also known as "Babe," "the Bambino," "Sultan of Swat," "Jidge," "The Big Fellow"—was and remains the most recognizable figure in sports history. Sy Weintraub, a Missouri classmate and television-movies mogul, asked me to design the brochure cover of a TV series he was producing, a quarter of a century after Babe played his last game. I used the same image, juxtaposed with Roger Maris, who broke Ruth's season home run record, for the jacket of the first book I wrote in 1963, *The 20th Century Encyclopedia of Baseball*. In it, there was a chapter heading of Ruth as the savior of baseball after the scandal of the 1919 fixed World Series, but the Babe was no angel. My NEA colleague Harry Grayson was an occasional running mate and regaled me with tales of their nocturnal forays. No one matched Babe's feats by day (before night baseball). As a young Boston Red Sox pitcher, he won twenty-three and twenty-four games in 1916 and '17 and hurled over twenty-nine scoreless innings in a World Series. Traded to the Yankees in 1919 because Red Sox owner Harry Frazee needed money to finance the Broadway show *No, No, Nannette*, and placed fulltime in the outfield, the Bambino set a home run record of twenty-nine during the dead ball era, raised to fifty-nine in 1921 and sixty in '27. When told his then astronomical salary of $80,000 topped that of Depression-beleaguered President Herbert Hoover, Babe shrugged and said, "Well, I had a better year than he did."

BABE RUTH

BLACK SOX SCANDAL

Nolan Ryan

ALTHOUGH HE THREW a baseball with velocity reminiscent of the great Bob Feller, his
career was jeopardized right at the start by a
proneness to develop blisters on the fingers
of his pitching hand. The New York Mets
didn't know if their husky young rookie from
Refugio, Texas, a twelfth round draft choice,
would be able to grip the seams for those one
hundred mph fastballs. Sidelined for stretches
by the blisters, he searched for a remedy and
started soaking his right hand in pickle brine.
The skin hardened enough to sustain him for
twenty-seven seasons in the majors, a modern
record. The Mets, not sure of his durability,
used him primarily as a spot starter and re-
liever, and he had his moments, pitching over
two scoreless innings against the Baltimore
Orioles in Game 3 of the 1969 World Series,
which the Mets took in five games. It was the
only World Series he ever played in. The next
year, he struck out fifteen batters in a game,
with a fastball that topped out at a record
100.9 miles mph, and yet amazingly in December 1971, the Mets traded him and three
other players to the California Angels for
shortstop Jim Fregosi (who would later manage Ryan in Anaheim). Taking his pickle brine
with him, Ryan won nineteen games in '72,
twenty-one in '73, and twenty-two in '74 for
Angel teams with losing records. That's when
he became established as baseball's premier
fastball pitcher, a man who could be mentioned in the same breath as Feller or Walter Johnson or Sandy Koufax. And he started
his string of seven no-hitters—his last when
he was forty-four years old—not to mention
eleven one-hitters. In 1980, he declared free
agency and signed with the Houston Astros
in the National League. Eight years later he
became a free agent again and shifted back
to the American League with the Texas Rangers, where he finished out his career in 1993,
tearing a ligament in his pitching arm two
starts before he was going to announce his retirement. By then he had 5,714 strikeouts, a
record that might last as long as DiMaggio's
fifty-six-game hitting streak. On the side,
Ryan was a rancher with a profitable beef
business. In 2008 he became president of the
Rangers, and soon part owner of the team,
but stepped down in 2013 and then became
a special assistant to the Houston Astros. He
also lectured on using pickle brine to combat
blisters.

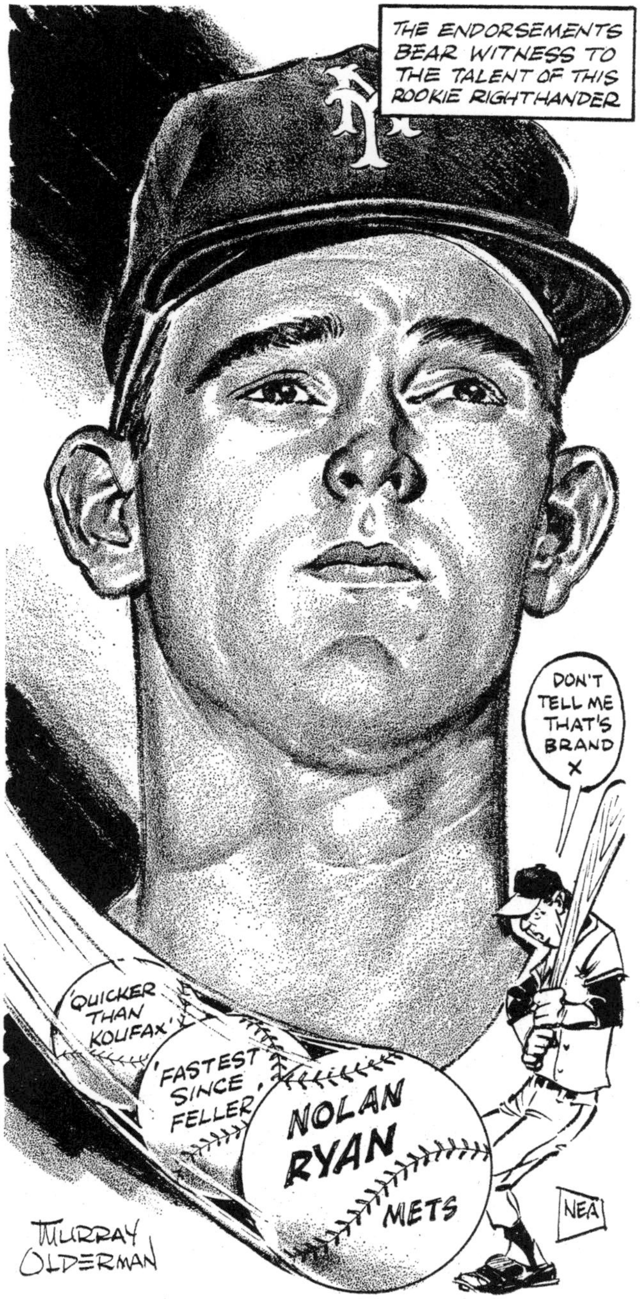
THE ENDORSEMENTS BEAR WITNESS TO THE TALENT OF THIS ROOKIE RIGHTHANDER
DON'T TELL ME THAT'S BRAND X
'QUICKER THAN KOUFAX'
'FASTEST SINCE FELLER'
NOLAN RYAN
METS
MURRAY OLDERMAN
NEA

"High Velocity Pitch"

Gale Sayers

IN COLUMBIA, MISSOURI, to speak at the journalism school and take in a University of Missouri football game, I ambled out to the practice field on a Friday afternoon to watch a freshman game between Mizzou and archrival Kansas—first-year students weren't eligible to play on the varsity. Missouri was touting new halfback Johnny Roland, one of the first to break the color line at the school, but I was fascinated by a Kansas frosh, Gale Sayers, a threat to score every time he touched the ball. Sayers went on to become a two-time All-American for the Jayhawks, coveted in the pros by both the Kansas City Chiefs of the fledgling AFL and the Chicago Bears. Chiefs owner Lamar Hunt personally courted Sayers and brought him to New York, where I met Sayers at the Manhattan Hotel. He was a young man of few words. Sayers said laconically, "I felt funny having a millionaire open doors for me." He signed with "Papa Bear" George Halas for $150,000 over three years, unprecedented money in 1961. He was immediately brilliant and scored an NFL rookie record twenty-two touchdowns carrying the ball, catching passes, returning kickoffs and punts. Shades of Red Grange: on a rainy December day in Chicago, I saw him score a record six touchdowns against the San Francisco 49ers. The average-sized running back had an innate ability to writhe through defenses with shifty speed and lateral, spooky moves. His NFL career was meteoric but also comet-like. His record lists seven seasons, but in the last two, with his knees failing him, he appeared in only a pair of games. Yet he was voted into the Pro Football Hall of Fame, the shortest-tenured Canton honoree. His fame came equally from an acclaimed movie, *Brian's Song*, inspired by Gale's autobiography *I Am Third* that depicted his close friendship with Brian Piccolo, the Bears' fullback who was diagnosed with terminal cancer—they were roommates, a rare pairing of white and black in that era—and how their relationship grew in handling the tragedy. I authored a coffee table book called *The Running Backs* that featured Sayers in action on the dust jacket and which he signed for me.

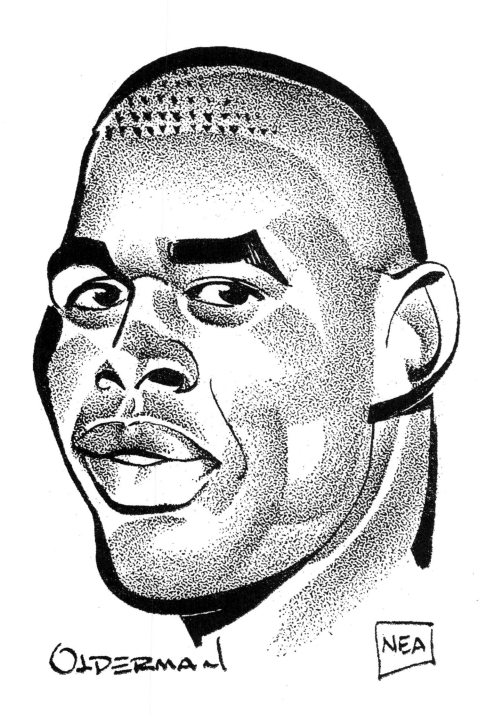

OLDERMAN

NEA

Dolph Schayes

A TRIP TO the Maccabiah Games in Israel in 1997 gave me the chance to know Dolph Schayes, scrunched together on an El Al flight carrying the U.S. contingent to Tel Aviv. Over the years, I had seen lots of Dolph scoring scads of NBA points with his patented two-hand over-the-head set shot or driving determinedly to the basket, but had him pegged as whiny and dour, always complaining about something, wearing a perpetual scowl. My perception, I found out, was totally awry. He turned out to be one of the sweetest, gentlest persons I have met in sports, considerate and upbeat, always smiling. For the cramped overseas flight, the only concession Dolph asked for was a seat with room to stretch out his knees, battered from a younger lifetime of basketball. He resided outside Syracuse, where he starred for fifteen pro seasons in more than a thousand games and had become successful in post-career business ventures. A schoolboy star in the Bronx, a collegian at sixteen, and a 1948 honors graduate of NYU, Dolph seemed a natural fit for the New York Knicks, then a member of the Basketball Association of America. They offered Dolph $6,000 a year. Syracuse of the National Bas-ketball League signed him for $7,500, plus a $6,500 bonus. The leagues merged into the current NBA the next year. Discounting a twenty-four-game hitch as player-coach of the Philadelphia 76ers, Dolph tallied virtually all his 19,247 points for Syracuse, a record exceeded by Wilt Chamberlain more than a decade later. He was voted into the Basketball Hall of Fame in 1972. Everywhere we went in Israel, from the Wailing Wall in Jerusalem to the International Jewish Sports Hall of Fame at Netanya overlooking the Mediterranean Sea (Dolph was an inductee there, too, and this was one of his regular pilgrimages back), the natives swiveled their heads when Dolph's imposing 6'8" figure passed by with our group. He was a man of great equanimity, satisfied with the honors that came his way, but eager to talk about his current connection to basketball. His son, Danny, a seven-footer, was playing in the NBA as a reserve center. "He's getting $1.5 million," said Dolph with fatherly pride as NBA salaries were escalating. "My highest salary for one year was $15,000. Danny's making more than five times as much money in one season as I made my entire career." The old man smiled contentedly.

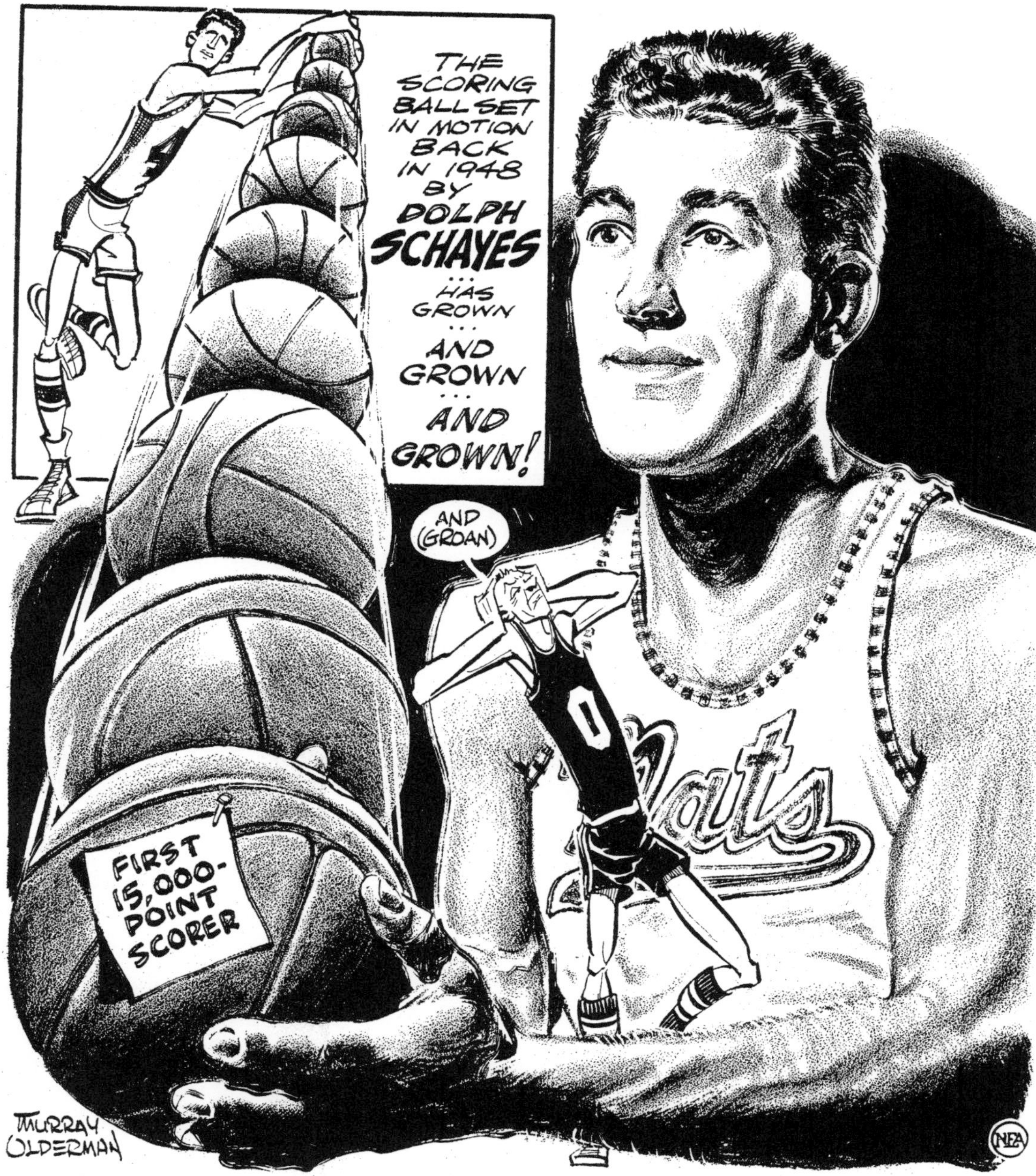
THE SCORING BALL SET IN MOTION BACK IN 1948 BY DOLPH SCHAYES ... HAS GROWN ... AND GROWN ... AND GROWN!
AND (GROAN)
FIRST 15,000-POINT SCORER
MURRAY OLDERMAN
NEA

"Like a Snowball"

Tom Seaver

EARLY IN HIS pitching career with the New York Mets, Tom Seaver visited the sports office of my syndicate in mid-Manhattan, giving me a chance to reveal that when I was starting out with the McClatchy Newspapers in California, I had drawn a cartoon of his father for the *Fresno Bee*. Charlie Seaver was a legendary amateur golfer at Stanford who settled in the San Joaquin Valley and grew grapes. Tom was just a scrawny mediocre schoolboy pitcher who joined the U.S. Marines at seventeen, filled out in a year, and after one collegiate season at USC, the New York Mets were awarded the rights to him in a draft lottery. In his first big league season with a sub-.500 team, Tom won sixteen games and was named Rookie of the Year. With a plodding gait, he made himself a great pitcher through hard work and intelligence. He figured out the nuances of getting a ball by a batter, with a strong and limber arm. "Baseball's not brain surgery," said "Tom Terrific." Pitch counts define modern baseball, with starting hurlers generally limited to one hundred pitches. "I regularly threw 135 or more," he revealed. And that was over twenty years, with 311 career wins, 231 complete games, five twenty-victory seasons, and three Cy Young Awards. He once struck out ten straight batters to end a winning effort. He led the lowly expansionist Mets to a World Series triumph with twenty-five wins in 1969, his third season. His image was squeaky clean; he was a no-nonsense straight talker, and some teammates branded him "insensitive." The Seavers, Tom and Nancy, were A-list celebrities while New York was going gaga over its sports heroes in the 1960–70s—Mantle, Namath, Gifford—and the Big Apple was shocked when he opted out of his contract over a salary dispute after eleven seasons and signed with Cincinnati. He also pitched for the Chicago White Sox and Boston Red Sox and established himself among the elite right-hand starting pitchers in baseball history. He was elected to the Baseball Hall of Fame in 1992 with the highest percentage of votes in the history of the Cooperstown shrine. The articulate Seaver did several stints as a TV baseball analyst, then moved back to his native California and bought a vineyard in the Napa Valley to create his own vintage wines. At his hilltop spread above Calistoga, he tended the grapes himself.

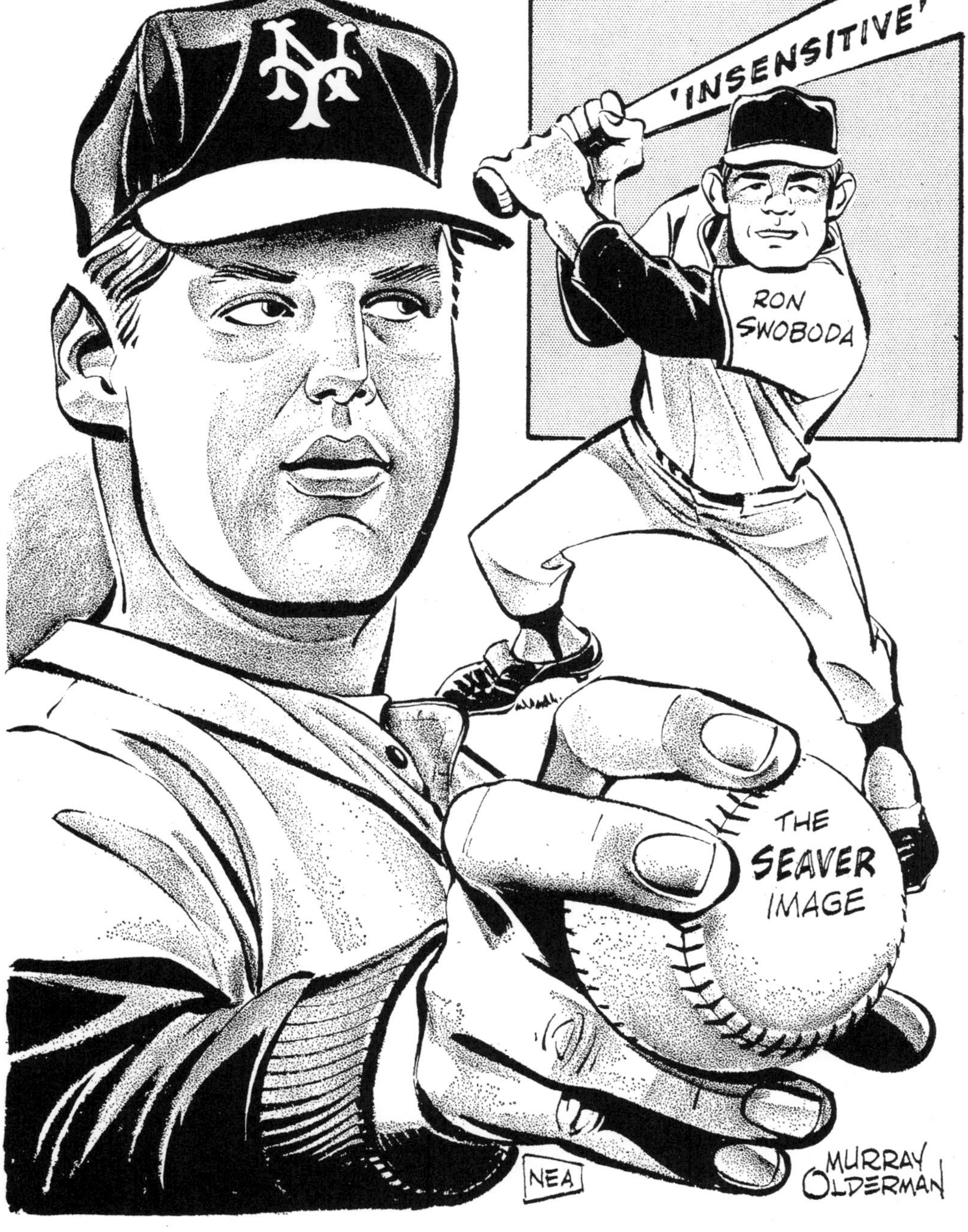
'INSENSITIVE'
RON SWOBODA
THE SEAVER IMAGE
NEA
MURRAY OLDERMAN

"Taking a Whack at It"

Bill Sharman

WE HAD A long, friendly conversation in the dugout of the Brooklyn Dodgers, with Bill Sharman in baseball uniform as an outfield prospect, because we had a common interest in central California. I had worked for Mc-Clatchy, whose newspapers covered the area from Sacramento to Bakersfield. Bill was from Porterville in the heart of that agricultural belt. I had done cartoons of him when he went on to star on the USC baseball team, but you won't find "Sharman" anywhere in the Encyclopedia of Baseball since he never once got into a game, though he had the distinction of being thrown out of one when the entire Dodger dugout was ejected during his only stint in the majors. Instead, basketball became his métier. I first saw him play in Sacramento on a visiting AAU team with Alex Hannum—both were USC basketball All-Americans, both excelled in the pros, both became winning NBA coaches—and found

Bill to be genuinely warm and approachable. He joined the Boston Celts in 1951 and teamed with Bob Cousy for ten years to form one of the greatest backcourts in basketball annals, was a consistent twenty-point scorer, and perhaps the top foul shooter in NBA history, leading the NBA in free throw percentage seven times. As a coach, he collected an ABA title at Utah in 1971, took over the Lakers and led them to their first Los Angeles title in '72, with an astounding win streak of thirty-three straight games. He devised the morning shoot-around on game day that became standard NBA practice and let me in to talk to the players. He later became general manager and then president of the Lakers until voice problems made him scale back. He was inducted into the Naismith Basketball Hall of Fame twice, as both player and coach, an honor accorded to only three men—John Wooden and Lenny Wilkins were the others.

BILL SHARMAN

L.A
LAKERS

NEA

MURRAY
OLDERMAN

"Soaring"

Willie Shoemaker

I NEVER MET a jockey who didn't look middle-aged. Even if diminutive, man wasn't meant to go through life never weighing more than 115 pounds. The constant struggle to make weight leaves jockeys with hollow cheeks, wrinkles around their eyes, and tight lips. Yet strength and agility is demanded to control neurotic thoroughbreds that weigh more than 1,000 pounds and not fall off in the chaotic bumping of a horse race. So yes, they have to be athletes. Willie Shoemaker went against the grain. He was born in a little West Texas town weighing two-and-a-half pounds, and there's a legend that he was put in a shoebox near a stove to keep him warm and survive. His father moved him to Southern California, and Willie (later "Bill") "grew" up to 4'11" and weighed ninety-eight pounds, so staying within the parameters of jockey size never was an issue. At seventeen, he mounted his first horse for money and finished when he was fifty-nine, having ridden in 430,350 races. He won 8,833, third all time behind Russell Baze and Lafitt Pincay Jr. They said he had "soft" hands to which horses responded. He won eleven Triple Crown races, including two Kentucky Derbies, and was forty-four, aboard Ferdinand, for the sec-

ond Run for the Roses triumph. He became a successful trainer, even from a wheelchair after he rolled an SUV over one evening and was paralyzed from the neck down. Shoemaker, rather taciturn, was one of the celebrity jockeys that I was aware of—along with Eddie Arcaro, who ran against type as a garrulous hanger-on at Toots Shor's, and Willie (again call me "Bill") Hartack, against whom I played ping-pong in the large press room at the Kentucky Derby. Jockeys for some reason also attracted the most beautiful women. But horse racing wasn't a priority interest in sports for me, though it provided a great free load, permissible in my journalistic generation. Horace Wade, running Gulfstream Park in Hallandale, Florida, used to charter a plane and fly a bunch of sports writers from New York to Miami each spring to drum up interest in the Florida Derby. A day at Santa Anita just south of Pasadena was a pleasant experience, mingling with the Hollywood crowd. I saw the great Secretariat run there, and as a kid I heard about Man o' War of the "Golden Age Twenties," supposed to be the best thoroughbred of all time. Somehow, Red Grange made more of an impact on me.

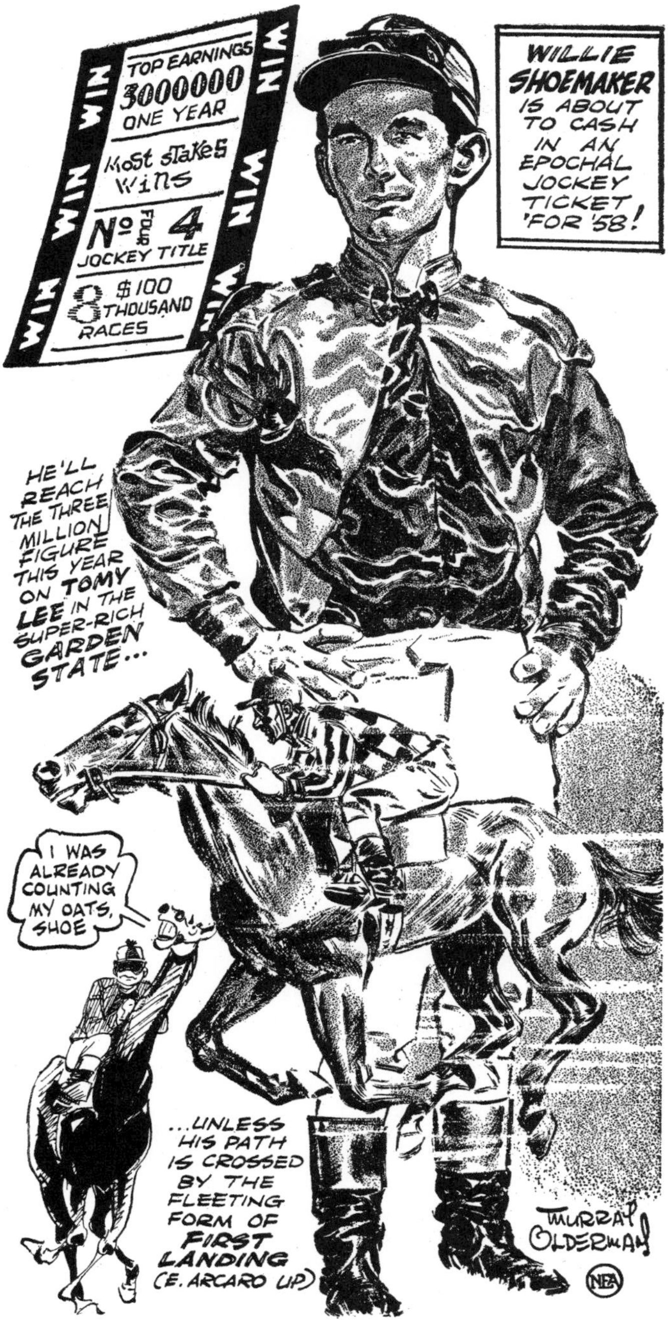
TOP EARNINGS 3000000 ONE YEAR
MOST STAKES WINS
No FOUR 4 JOCKEY TITLE
8 $100 THOUSAND RACES
WIN WIN WIN WIN
WIN WIN WIN
WILLIE SHOEMAKER IS ABOUT TO CASH IN AN EPOCHAL JOCKEY TICKET 'FOR '58!
HE'LL REACH THE THREE MILLION FIGURE THIS YEAR ON TOMY LEE IN THE SUPER-RICH GARDEN STATE...
I WAS ALREADY COUNTING MY OATS, SHOE
...UNLESS HIS PATH IS CROSSED BY THE FLEETING FORM OF FIRST LANDING (E. ARCARO UP)
MURRAY OLDERMAN
NEA

"The Right Ticket"

Don Shula

HIS JAW WAS wired shut because he'd broken it playing defensive back for the Baltimore Colts. That's how I met Don Shula on a Colts' season-ending West Coast swing, when he went along because, as linebacker Bill Pellington told me, he was "the smartest football man on the team and knows more than any of the coaches." He mapped their defensive plans. He was also a straight arrow, the designated chaperon of dates for the partying Colts until they sneaked out after bed check. At twenty-seven, traded to Washington, Don recognized he lacked the requisite speed for an NFL secondary and turned to coaching. I'd see him in press boxes, scouting future opponents, and get updated on football strategies like rotating zone defenses. After the Colts finished the 1962 season in Los Angeles, owner Carroll Rosenbloom invited me to fly back with him to New York on a redeye instead of returning to Baltimore on the team plane. Settled in his seat, Carroll made it plain he was going to fire Weeb Ewbank as head coach and mentioned some assistants around the NFL as successors. "There's another guy in the league," I said, "that everybody's high on." "Who's that?" he asked. "Don Shula," I answered. "You once

had him on your team." I mentioned his work as defensive coordinator of the Detroit Lions, who shut out four opponents and yielded just one touchdown in two other games. At thirty, Shula was younger than many of his players. Carroll nodded and napped the rest of the flight. In January '63, I was passing through Grand Central Station and ran into Jim Kensil, the NFL P.R. director. "Boy," said Kensil, "you must have done some selling job on Rosenbloom." What do you mean? Kensil responded, "The Colts are announcing a new coach tomorrow. It's Shula." I called up Wellington Mara, the Giants' owner for a reaction. "That guy doesn't have the disposition to be a coach in this league," he said, referring to a play when Shula on defense for the Redskins "knocked one of our guys over the sidelines and then hit him while he was out of bounds." In February, on Colts' stationery, Don sent me a note of thanks. Over the next thirty-three years, Shula won more games, 347, than any coach in NFL history, including Super Bowl V with Baltimore and Super Bowl VII with Miami as the Dolphins concluded the league's only perfect 17-0 season. A bona-fide football great.

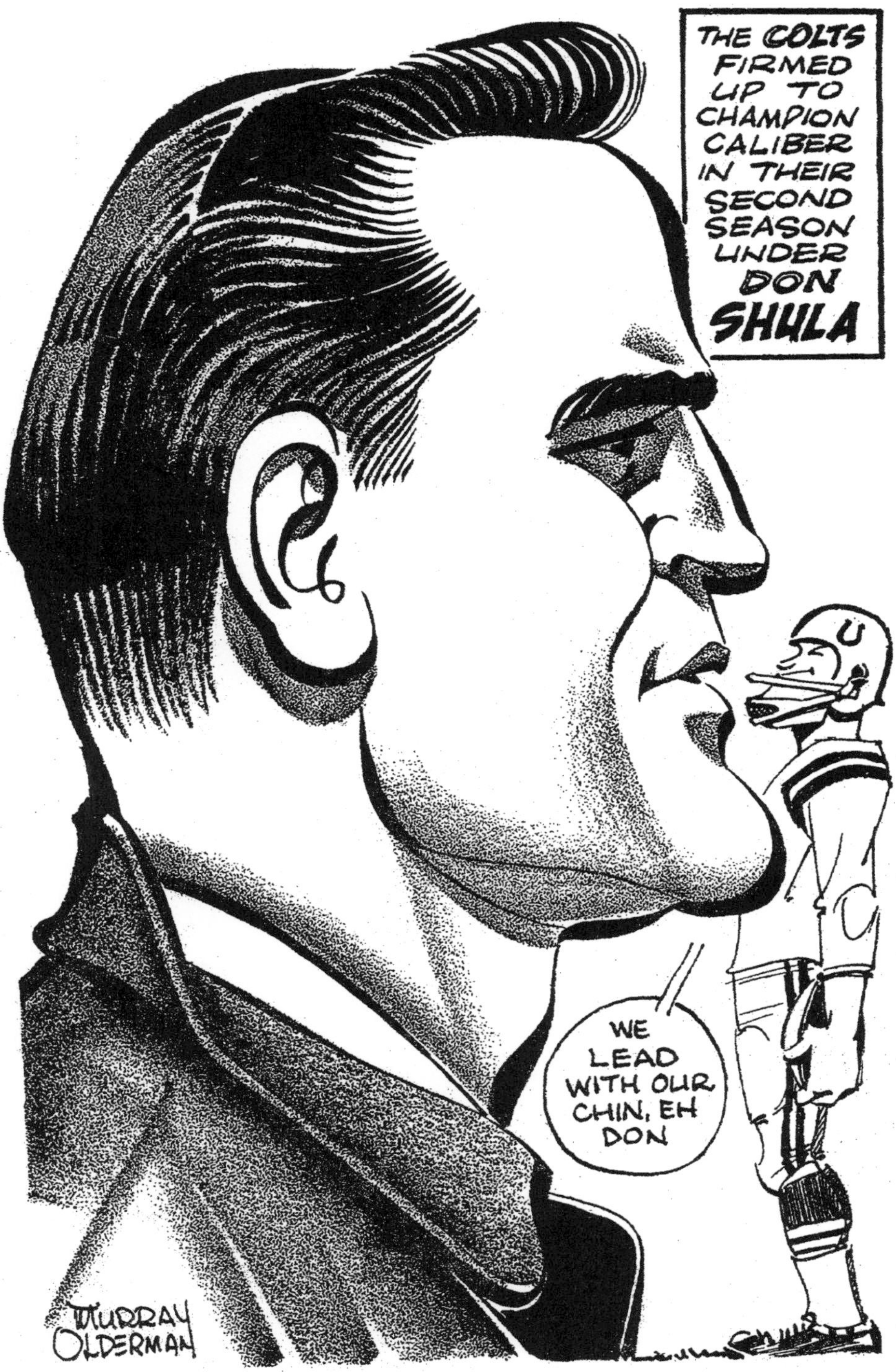
THE COLTS FIRMED UP TO CHAMPION CALIBER IN THEIR SECOND SEASON UNDER DON SHULA
WE LEAD WITH OUR CHIN, EH DON
MURRAY OLDERMAN

O.J. Simpson

IN THE PLAYERS' dormitory at Niagara University, O.J. Simpson was in a dilemma. He didn't know what tie to wear for the ride to town and his first exhibition game as a Buffalo Bill in 1970. "All the guys'll be wearing sweaters," said roommate Ben Gregory. But O.J. wore a shirt and tie to go with his blue blazer and dark gray slacks. On the way, in Gregory's Buick, Simpson kicked up the stereo to sing along with Junior Walker and the All Stars' "What Does It Take?" "My soul song," explained O.J., a twenty-two-year-old without a care in the world. O.J. was personally signed by owner Ralph Wilson for $215,000 over four years, plus a $100,000 loan, a huge deal then. The Heisman-Trophy-winning All-American from USC was a commodity in demand: Chevrolet with a three-year $250,000 deal, Royal Crown with a minimum $120,000 over the same period, and under contract with ABC. I was doing a profile on him for *Sport*, and Roone Arledge, head of ABC Sports, told me, "I would have hired him even if he hadn't been a superstar. I met him when he was a junior in college and was struck with his poise and intelligence." He was charming, handsome, exuberant, and infallibly cooperative. Over a ten-year period, as he became the finest running back in the NFL, whenever and wherever I saw him, he was cordial and eager to please. At a Pro Bowl game, I presented him with the Jim Thorpe Trophy as NFL MVP. At the height of his fame, however, there was no secret about his philandering. His marriage on the rocks, he openly consorted with stunning Nicole Brown and married her. A knee injury led to his trade to hometown San Francisco, and a tough little running back, Paul Hofer, beat him out as the starter. He was making $733,000 a year to soothe his ego. But his public persona declined. A 911 call by Nicole on New Year's Day 1992 was gossip fodder. He told me on a visit to my tennis club, "That was just a domestic quarrel. I never hit her." She left him. I spent the summer of 1995 recovering from surgery and watching the televised O.J. murder trial and acquittal. I was certain that Simpson, always amiable and forthcoming, but frustrated, a man who had never experienced rejection, committed the crime.

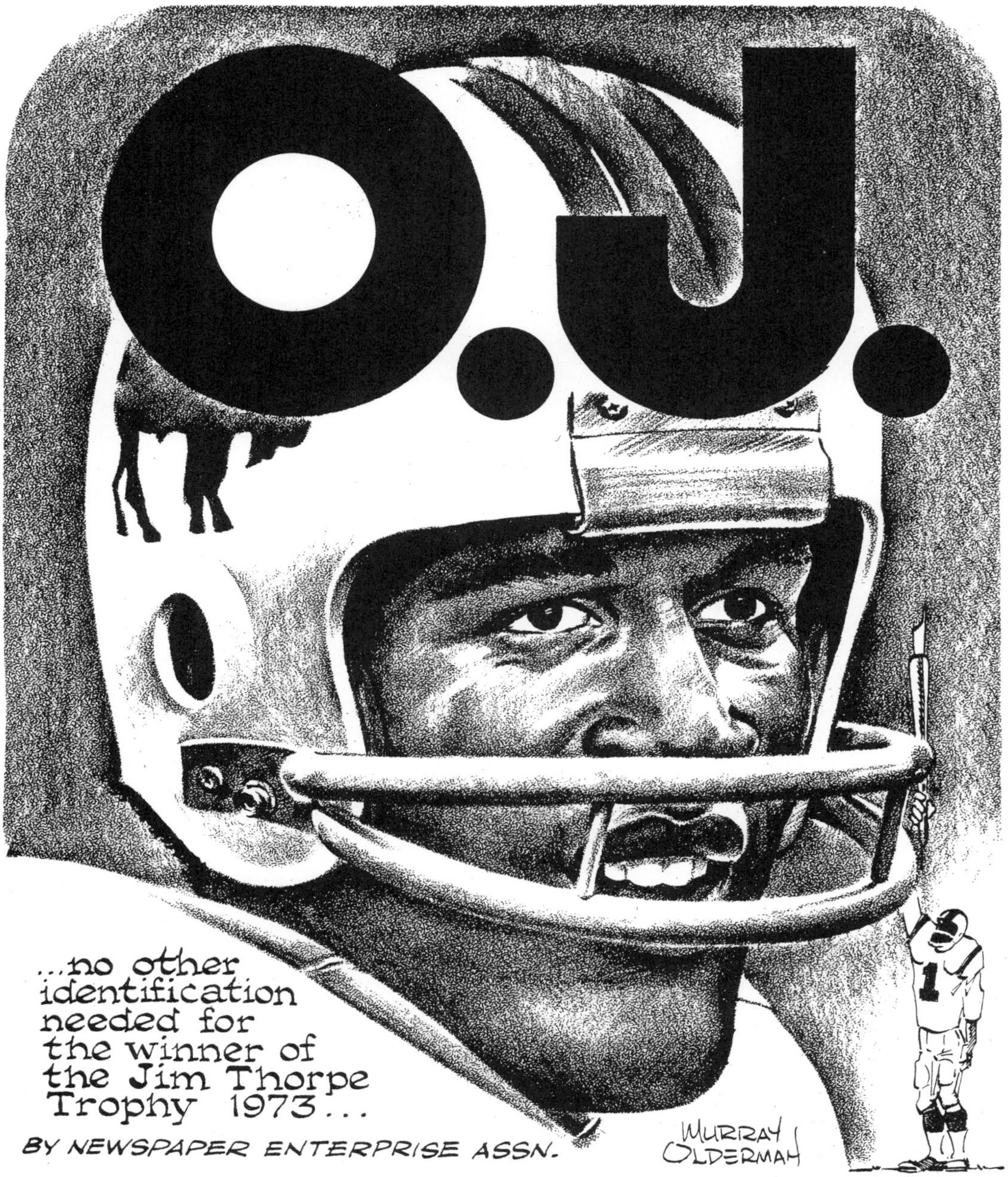
O.J.
...no other identification needed for the winner of the Jim Thorpe Trophy 1973...
BY NEWSPAPER ENTERPRISE ASSN.
MURRAY OLDERMAN
1

"Brand Name"

Warren Spahn

"SPAHN AND SAIN and pray for rain" was the mantra for the old Boston Braves in the late 1940s. The doggerel line was lifted from a poem written by Gerald Hern in the *Boston Post* as the Boston Braves won the 1948 National League pennant on the arms of veteran righthander Johnny Sain, a twenty-four-game winner, and Warren Spahn, who won more games, 363, than any lefthander in modern baseball history. Spahn was more than a clever southpaw who lasted twenty-one seasons and was a twenty-game winner for thirteen of them. The Buffalo, New York, native had come up to the Braves in 1942, but left to join the army and become an authentic World War II hero. He fought in the Battle of the Bulge and got a Purple Heart. As a combat engineer, he was in the first unit to cross the bridge at Remagen over the Rhine River into Germany, under heavy fire, and received a battlefield commission. He felt the three years in the service actually elongated his mound career, all but one season with the Braves in Boston and later Milwaukee. He was twenty-five and physically mature when he came back from the war. The six-footer had a distinctive high leg kick that masked the ball from the batter, much like Juan Mar-

ichal of the San Francisco Giants. They had a memorable pitching duel when "Spahnie" was forty-two years old, each going the distance in a scoreless game that only ended in the bottom of the sixteenth inning when Willie Mays hit a walk-off homer. That same season, Spahn's record was twenty-three wins and seven losses. "I don't think Spahn will ever get in the Hall of Fame," said Stan Musial slyly. "He'll never stop pitching." Of course, he did make the shrine at Cooperstown. To Spahn, baseball was simple. "Hitting is timing," he said. "Pitching is upsetting timing." He also broke the mold as a pitcher who could hit. He swatted thirty-five home runs during his career, exceeded in the record book only by Wes Ferrell's total of thirty-seven. In his final season, with the New York Mets, he was managed by Yogi Berra, who briefly donned pads to catch him. "I don't know if we're the oldest battery ever," said Yogi, "but we're sure the ugliest." Spahn had been hit on the nose by a line drive that left him with a distinctive hooked schnozz. He bought a ranch outside Broken Bow, Oklahoma, and became a hardworking cowboy on his spread between seasons.

...AND
WARREN
SPAHN
THE MAN:
BALDING,
BATTLE-
SCARRED
ATHLETIC
MARVEL
AT 43!

"A Man and His Legend"

Bart Starr

HE HAD THE ideal name for a sports hero, but deep down he felt it was a misnomer. His father, Master Sgt. Ben Starr, a career soldier, doted on younger brother Bubba and his superior athletic skills, with Bart deeply resenting it. One Sunday after church in Mobile, Alabama, Bubba ran outside barefoot, and his heel was pierced by an old bone. Three days later, he was dead from a tetanus infection, and Bart felt guilt that lasted for years. As Bart showed facility for throwing a football, the critical old master sergeant taunted him for every mistake, "Bubba would have . . ." Yet in his sophomore year, he led Alabama to a Cotton Bowl, was out his junior year with a back strain, and as a senior sat on the bench while the Crimson Tide lost ten straight games. Green Bay drafted him in the seventeenth round. Bart was downgraded for lack of assertiveness. Vince Lombardi took over the Pack in 1959 and immediately traded for Lamar McHan, a journeyman QB. McHan was injured, and Bart took over. A burly Chicago Bears linebacker sacked Starr, stood over him, and gloated, "I'm going to do that every play, you pussy." Starr wiped the blood from his mouth, looked up, and retorted, "Fuck you, Bill George." Guard Jerry Kramer gaped and said, "Until then, I never heard Bart say anything stronger than 'golly gee.'" Over a dozen seasons, Starr passed Green Bay to five NFL championships (including Super Bowls I and II) and then coached the Pack, less successfully, for eight years. His popularity in Wisconsin was undiminished. He asked me to collaborate with him on an autobiography for the William Morrow publishing house. "It'll be like talking to the Pope," scoffed author Dick Schaap. I was a guest at the Starr home in Green Bay. He and his wife Cherry flew out to Incline Village, Nevada, for a week at my place at Lake Tahoe. The extent of his celebrity surprised me when strangers flocked to him in the coffee shop at the Reno airport. I used the George incident to keynote the manuscript. The Starrs never told me that their younger son had died tragically months earlier of a drug overdose. A week before publishing deadline, the Starrs completely rewrote the book, cutting out the George anecdotes and eliminating any earthy references common to pro football. It was their prerogative. The Bart Starr squeaky-clean image carefully cultivated over the years was preserved.

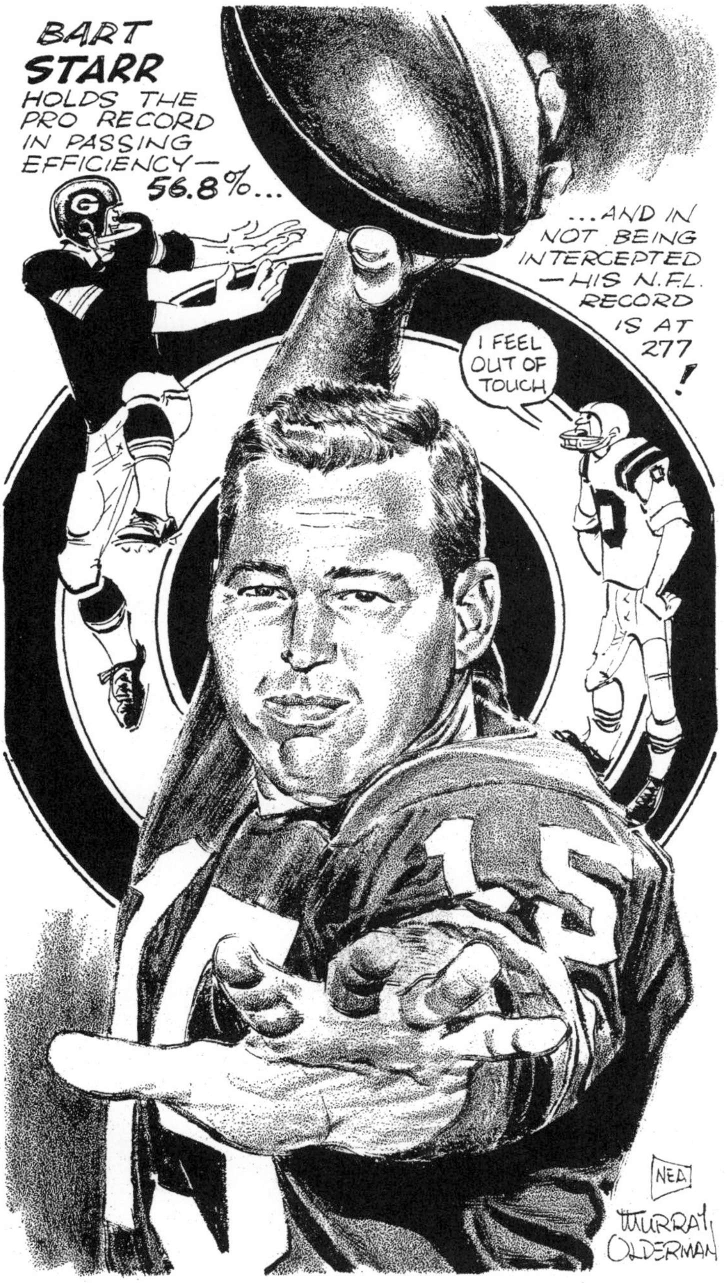
BART STARR HOLDS THE PRO RECORD IN PASSING EFFICIENCY— 56.8%...
...AND IN NOT BEING INTERCEPTED —HIS N.F.L. RECORD IS AT 277!
I FEEL OUT OF TOUCH
NEA
MURRAY OLDERMAN

"On Target"

Casey Stengel

HE NURTURED A reputation as a clown and buffoon over six decades as a player and manager. He was anything but. C harles Dillon Stengel became "Casey" because he was from Kansas City, aspiring to be a left-handed dentist. He became a good major league outfielder, but better known for hilarious stunts. He made a fine running catch, stopped and doffed his cap to the fans. A bird flew out. The ultimate Casey was a calculating, cranky old man, a tyrant to his players. By manipulating media, 'The Perfesser' craftily built an image of a kindly geriatric character engaged in amusing double-talk. I sat with bug-eyed Walter Alston, the new Brooklyn Dodgers manager, listening to Casey at a New York luncheon. "I figured here was a smart fellow," Alston told me, "and I might learn something. When the S.O.B. got through, I'll be damned if I could remember or understand a thing he said." At a spring training banquet in St. Petersburg, I overheard Casey counsel Red Schoendienst, the new manager of the St. Louis Cardinals, how to handle himself at the podium: "Never stop talking when you're up there, no matter what you say. They'll never know the difference." But Yankee pitcher Whitey Ford said, "There was no double-talking in his clubhouse. You always understood every word he said." When fast-baller Bob Turley was in a slump, Stengel muttered, "He don't smoke, drink, or chase around, but I get better pitching out of a drunk." He was astute enough to revolutionize modern baseball by platooning his players. He simply ignored their feelings. He motivated through fear—of being benched or traded—and won ten American League pennants and seven World Series in twelve years. Casey got his job after abysmal stints managing the Boston Braves and Dodgers and was skipper of Oakland in the Pacific Coast League when Del Webb, the Yankees' co-owner, saw him doing a kids' morning clinic and was impressed by the old man's zeal. The cartoon opposite is a takeoff of General Douglas MacArthur's comeback in the Pacific in World War II.

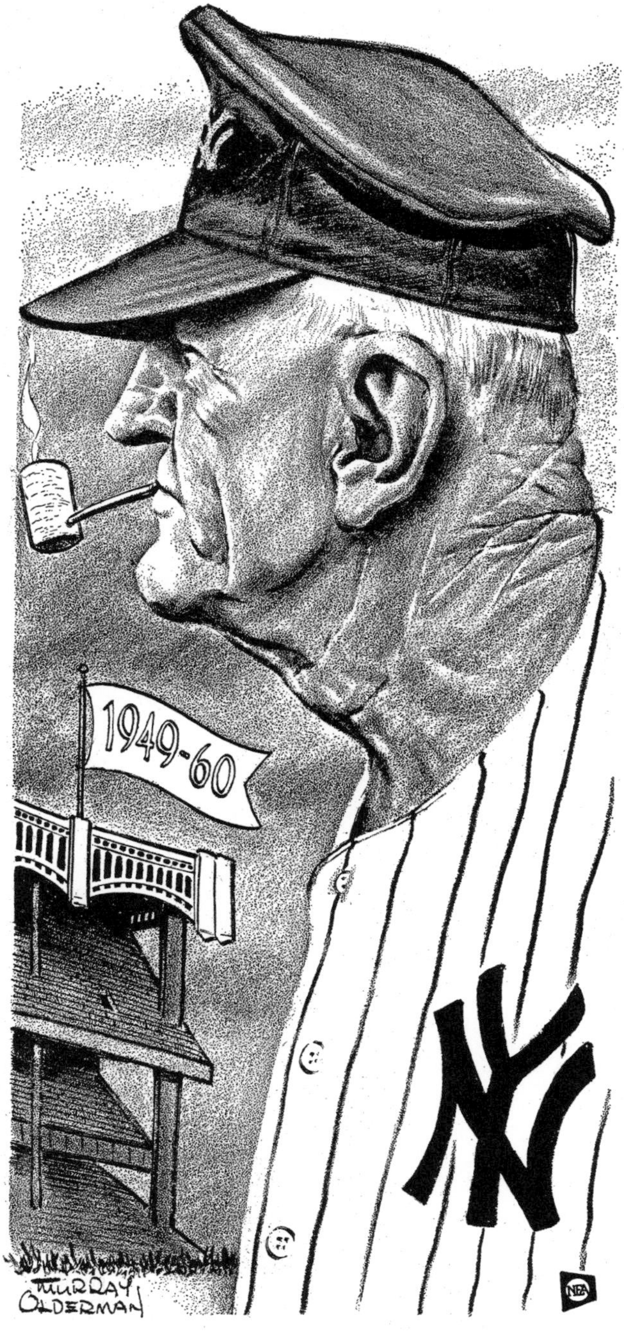
1949-60
MURRAY OLDERMAN
NEA

"But He Won't Fade Away"

Fran Tarkenton

FRANCIS ASBURY TARKENTON, the son of a Methodist minister, had a devilish side he didn't really try to hide. In a training camp drill his rookie year with the Minnesota Vikings, Tarkenton was handing the ball off, but the fullback made the wrong cut and botched the play. Norm Van Brocklin, the Vikings' testy coach, blistered the running back with four-letter profanity and added seven and ten-letter obscenities as well. Tarkenton, the preacher's son, repeated to me verbatim every word in Van Brocklin's tirade. He was a feisty, resourceful quarterback who lasted eighteen NFL years on his wits and wile. Listed as six feet tall, he was probably a shade less than 5'11". He had small hands and didn't throw projectiles, but his nimble feet and instincts made him the best scrambling quarterback ever. By his fifth season, chafing under Van Brocklin's restraints—he preferred to have his quarterback stay in the pocket—Fran confided to me at an NFL Players Association convention in Florida that he was going to retire at twenty-seven rather than return to the Vikings. He was traded to the slumping New York Giants, where I found Tarkenton refreshing and exuberant, as well as loquacious. He playfully called me "Murray the

K" after a New York radio disc jockey. I hired him to write a weekly post-game column for my syndicate for the grand sum of seventy-five dollars a column, which he dictated to me. I'd call and say, "This week we're going to write about play-action passes." Half an hour later, I'd say, "OK, Francis, that's enough." He never ran out of words for three years. I took him to see Danny Kaye in a Broadway show and afterward watched them yuck it up in Danny's dressing room. The night before a game, Francis would burrow into his hotel room with a big cigar and a beer. The preacher's son liked his pleasures. He raised the Giants to within one game of the Eastern Conference title. He also wangled his way back to Minnesota and led the Vikings to three Super Bowls in four season, was the NFL MVP at thirty-five and set new career records for yards passing and touchdowns that held up for two decades until eclipsed by Dan Marino. He was equally nimble as a talker and doer post-football and even put in a stint with Howard Cosell in the Monday Night Football booth. "Most inane thing I've done in my life," he said. He returned to his Georgia roots and gained prominence as a small business advocate.

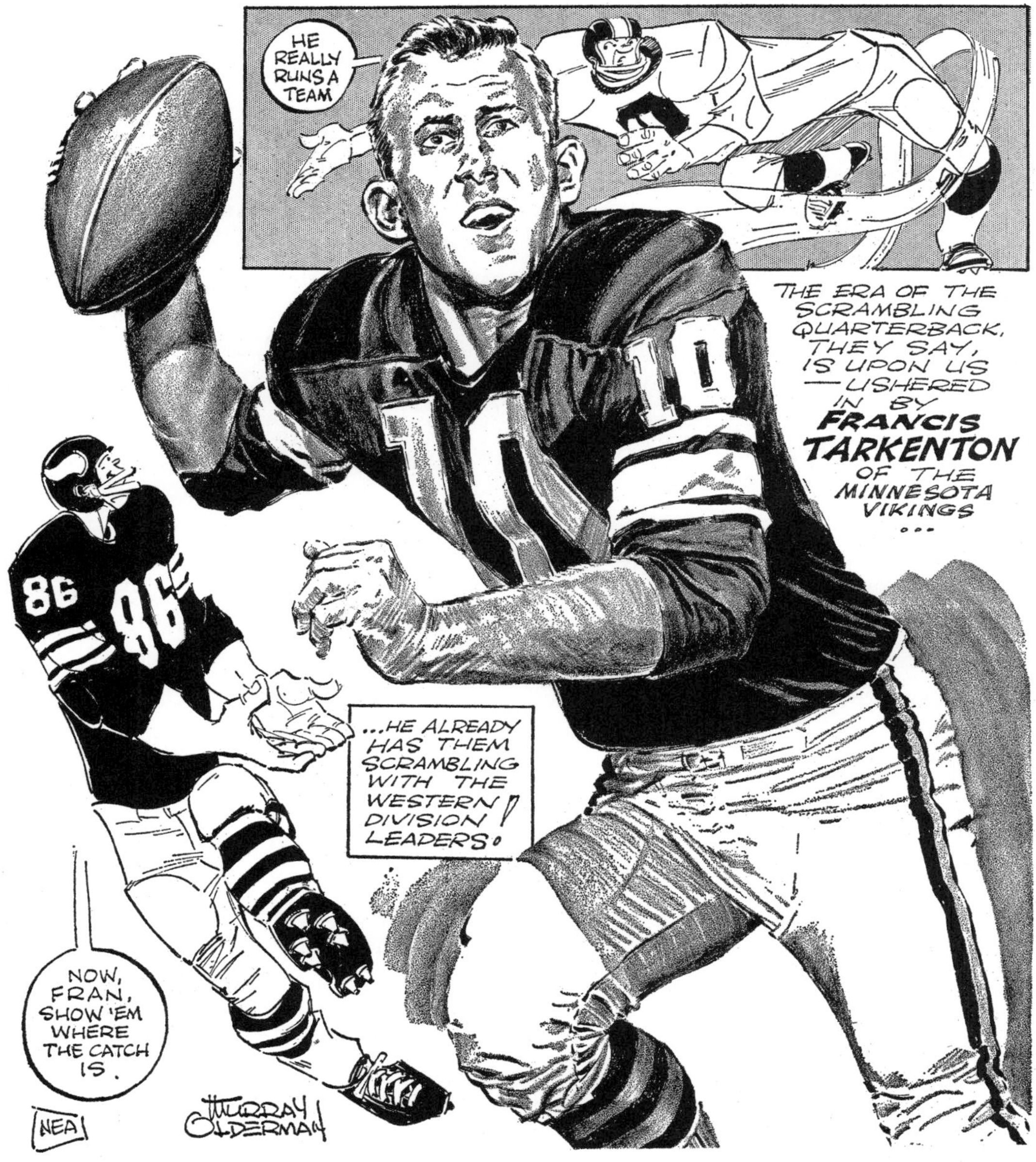
HE REALLY RUNS A TEAM
THE ERA OF THE SCRAMBLING QUARTERBACK, THEY SAY, IS UPON US —USHERED IN BY FRANCIS TARKENTON OF THE MINNESOTA VIKINGS ...
...HE ALREADY HAS THEM SCRAMBLING WITH THE WESTERN DIVISION LEADERS!
NOW, FRAN, SHOW 'EM WHERE THE CATCH IS.
NEA
MURRAY OLDERMAN

"Title Scrambler"

Jim Thorpe

AS A TEENAGER in the late 1930s, I got behind the wheel of an old DeSoto and drove seven miles east to Nyack, a hamlet on the Hudson River, there to see the most legendary athlete of the twentieth century. The Jim Thorpe All-Stars were featured in a sandlot baseball exhibition and, already writing a sports column for the weekly *Rockland County Leader*, I didn't want to miss the great Sac and Fox Indian, even if he was fifty years old. I can't claim to have known him, but I did see Jim Thorpe perform in a sports uniform. He was the whole package. His first renown was on a football field when he led Carlisle Institute, a small Indian industrial school in western Pennsylvania, to an 18–15 victory over vaunted Harvard, the national collegiate champion, scoring all the points on a touchdown and four field goals. A year later, he was competing in the decathlon at the 1912 Olympic Games in Sweden. "You,

sir, are the greatest athlete in the world," said King Gustav, presenting him the gold medal. Thorpe simply said, "Thanks, King." Later, it was revealed that Thorpe played semi-pro baseball one summer in North Carolina, for fifteen dollars a week, and he was stripped of his Olympic medal. He spent parts of seven seasons in the majors, starting with the New York Giants. In 1920, he stood on the running board of a car in a Canton, Ohio, auto dealership and helped launch the first professional football league that two years later became the NFL. He served as its first president and starred with the Canton Bulldogs. He wasn't imposing by today's standards, but he was huge in dominating any sport he tried. I met his daughter Grace in New York when the Thorpe family strove to revive memory of his heroics—a town in Pennsylvania, where he was interred, was named for him. In 1982, his gold medal was reinstated posthumously.

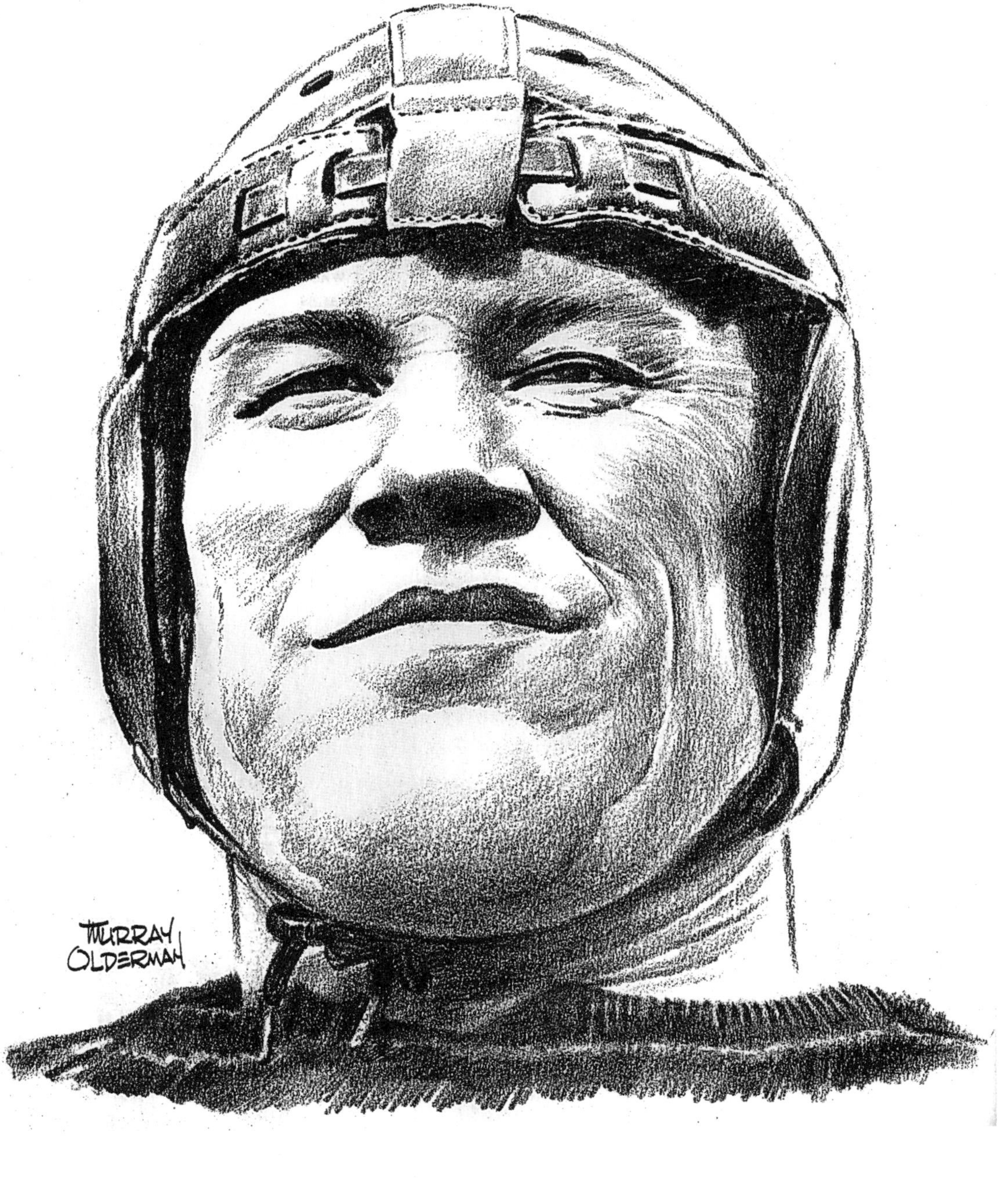
MURRAY
OLDERMAN

Lee Trevino

AT A U.S. Golf Open at Baltusrol, New Jersey, in the late 1960s, I heard about this Tex-Mex kid—a rarity in the country club sport—who was staying at a cheap motel, but couldn't get in the dining room because he didn't have a necktie. Lee Trevino walked along the highway to a pizza parlor. The $6,000 he earned for finishing fifth launched him on the PGA Tour. "I learned to play golf with a broomstick," he said, "swinging at horse apples." The next year, I was at Oak Hill in Rochester, New York, when he won the prestigious Open. "I'm the happiest Mexican alive," he gushed. "I'm going to buy the Alamo back and give it to Mexico." He was a self-made super star. His six major titles—a repeat Open, two PGA championships and consecutive British Open victories in 1971–72—testify to that. He titillated galleries with witty ripostes, a chatterbox who played to the crowd and built an image as a funny man. But off the course Trevino was often snippy and surly and a loner, always, however, with a quick quip. Wives number two and three were both named Claudia. He didn't, he said, have to change the bath towels. He grew up in a shack on the outskirts of Dallas and sneaked onto golf courses to play instead of going to school. He enlisted in the U.S. Marines and served four years, and claimed that golfing with officers got him promoted to lance corporal. He wound up with a club job in El Paso, Texas, and hustled all comers, sometimes using a coke bottle in lieu of a golf club to beat them. He conquered a tendency to hook shots by hitting controlled fades, left to right. Playing in a Western Open in Chicago, he was struck by lightning that inflicted spinal injuries on his lower back and required surgery. He said that in a future storm he'd brandish a 1-iron because "God can't hit a 1-iron." "Super Mex," as he called himself, recovered to amass twenty-nine PGA titles and was equally successful on the Seniors Tour after he turned fifty.

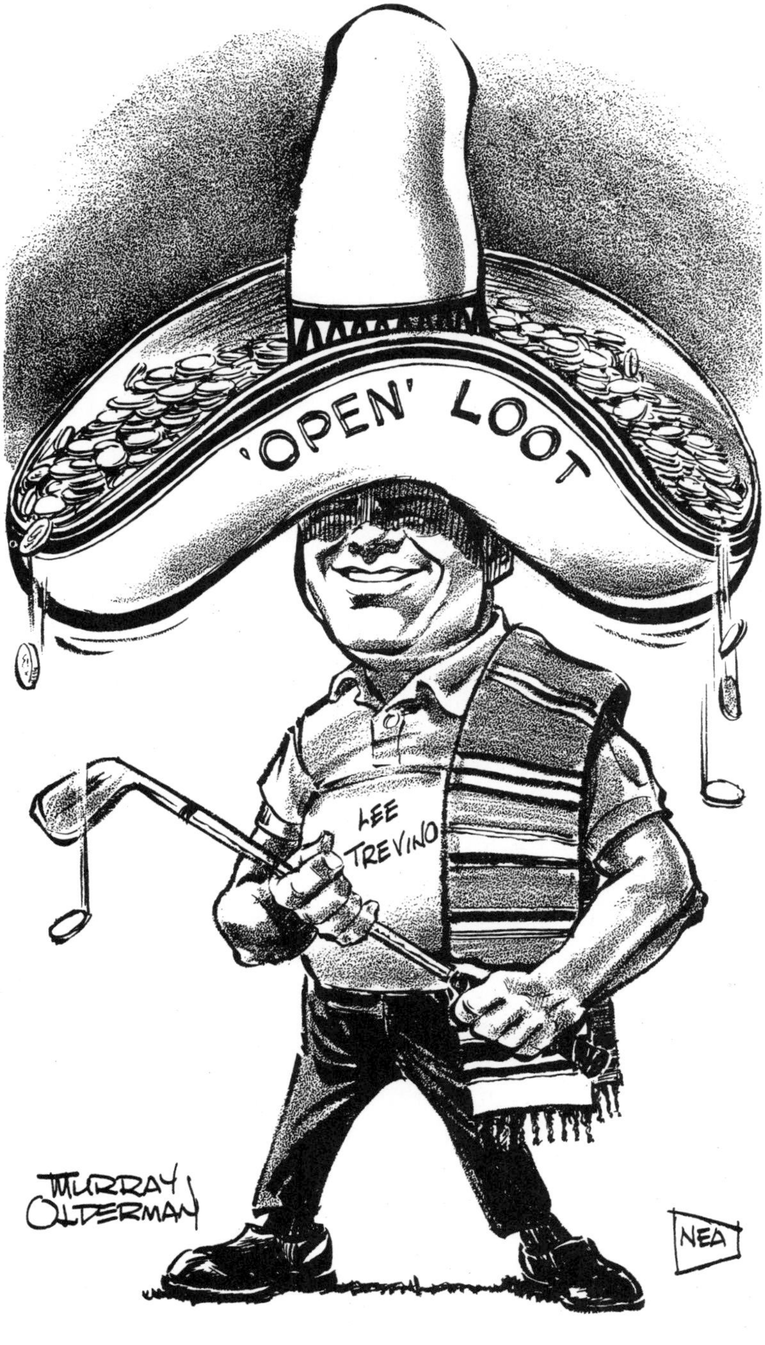
'OPEN' LOOT
LEE TREVINO
MURRAY OLDERMAN
NEA

"Peon's Happy Birthday"

John Unitas

EVEN SIX DECADES ago, he was a throwback. "Johnny U" wore high top football shoes like they did before World War II. He had a flat-top haircut that you could skate off. His jersey had long sleeves. Drafted and discarded by his hometown Steelers, he was plucked off a Pittsburgh sandlot, where he was getting six dollars a game for the semi-pro Bloomfield Rams, working as high man on a pile-driving crew, with a pregnant wife at home. A fan sent a letter about him to the Baltimore Colts, and general manager Don Kellett made an eighty-cent phone call, inviting him to a Baltimore tryout camp. Unitas caught on as the backup to George Shaw, who tore up a knee in the fourth game of the 1956 season, and the ascendant Colts had their quarterback for the next eighteen years. Many consider him the best ever. Lean and angular, he had tremendous will and the strong, accurate arm to throw long passes under fire. In his second year, I brought him to New York to present him with the Jim Thorpe Award as the MVP of the NFL. In his third year, he led the Colts to a title in the famous "sudden-death" overtime game in Yankee Stadium, a benchmark for pro football. The final sequence typified

Unitas. I never met a player who was more confident in himself. The Colts were on the Giants' six-yard line. All they needed was a field goal to seal the victory. Instead, Unitas on his own called for a dangerous pass across the field to right end Jim Mutscheller, who caught the ball and fell out of bounds at the one-yard line. (Alan Ameche plunged for the winning TD on the next play.) Questioned about the risk of being picked off, Unitas shrugged: "When you know what you're doing, you're never intercepted." The Colts repeated as champs the following season, but hit a slump in the early 1960s as Lombardi's Packers took over. I persuaded Unitas to talk about what had gone wrong in a story for *Sport*. The subhead read: "Is the Colt quarterback washed up?" Unitas, twenty-nine and in his prime, was furious when he saw it and blamed me for the headline, which distorted the thrust of the story—he said there was a philosophic difference on how to run the offense between him and Coach Weeb Ewbank, who was fired. He refused to talk to me. I'm not sure he even read the actual text of the piece. I never had a decent interview with him again.

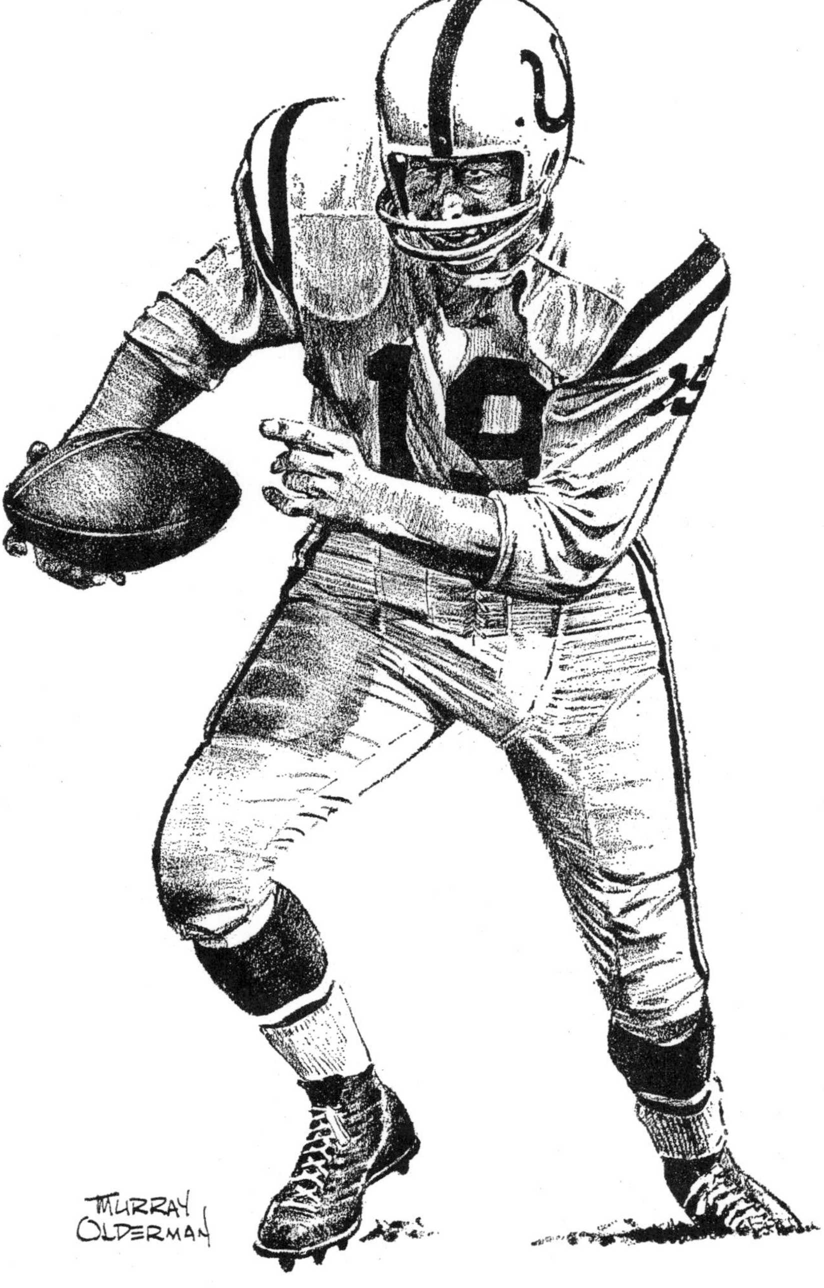
19
MURRAY
OLDERMAN

"Master of All"

Norm Van Brocklin

"THE DUTCHMAN" WENT through a dozen Hall of Fame years with brilliant passing skills and a biting tongue. As the seasons piled up, he was asked, "Would you want to be a coach?" "No," he snapped, "I want to be a sportswriter, like the rest of you idiots." Caustic was part of his nature. He described an offensive lineman as master of the "look-out" block. "He misses his man," explained Van Brocklin, "and he turns around and yells, 'Look out, Dutch.'" Van Brocklin was truculent Bobby Knight before there was a Bobby Knight. Just after a fitting finale as Philadelphia's quarterback, leading the Eagles to the 1960 NFL title, he immediately announced he was quitting. At the Pro Bowl, as he was pulling off his grimy jersey for the last time, a radio guy stuck a live mike in front of him and asked, "Is this really your last game as a player?" "You're fucking goddamn right it is," the Dutchman spluttered. He was asked what his plans were. "To get the fucking hell out of L.A. as fast as I can." He had first made his mark as a quarterback for the Rams, racking up 554 passing yards one Sunday against the old New York Yanks in 1951, still the all-time NFL record for one game. He also connected with Tom Fears for a seventy-three-yard TD that beat the Cleveland Browns in the final minutes for the NFL title. He was not a classic athlete. At Oregon, he was a slow-footed fifth-string tailback converted to quarterback by new coach Jim Aiken. He immediately led the Ducks to a Cotton Bowl. "He runs like a woman trying to get out of her girdle," an opposing coach said. But he could throw a football long and accurately with a super-quick release. In 1958 he announced his retirement because Coach Sid Gillman insisted on calling the plays, was traded to the Eagles, and became a virtual coach on the field for two seasons, ending with a championship over Green Bay. He became coach of the newly created Minnesota Vikings. Some years later, at a gab session before a Vikings game, I brought up the Pro Bowl interview and replayed it verbally for him. "You got it wrong," he scowled. "I never used any profanity." I retorted, "I was right there." He snorted, "You're like those L.A. writers." Coaching expansion teams in Minnesota and then Atlanta was a losing proposition for the fiercely competitive Dutchman.

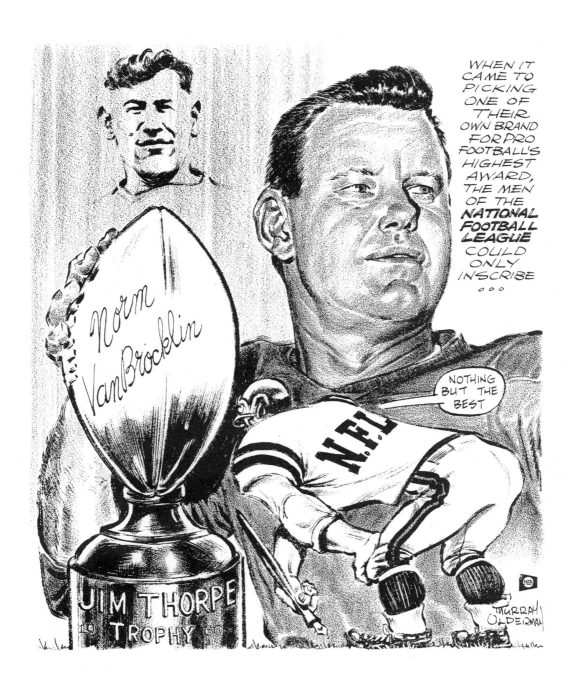

"Most Valuable Autograph"

Doak Walker

HE SPOTTED ME in the hotel coffee shop, attending a National Football Foundation dinner in New York. "Hey," he said with a broad smile, "you did it!' Did what? "We got married," beamed Doak Walker. Each winter a ski instruction series was distributed nationally by my syndicate, generally authored by a skiing celebrity like Stein Erikson. This one winter I tried something different. I knew that Walker, the legendary football player, now lived in Colorado and occasionally ventured down a ski run. I arranged for Skeeter Werner, an Olympic downhiller based in Steamboat Springs, to give Walker lessons on the slopes that would be our illustrated national ski series. So that's how they met. And then eloped to Las Vegas. Driving through Colorado later, I visited the happy couple in their Steamboat Springs domicile. Doak was a football marvel. A two-time All-American, a Heisman Trophy winner at Southern Methodist, he was the key ball carrier for the Detroit Lions when they won NFL championships in 1952–53. He never gained as much as 400 yards rushing in a single season. He never caught more than thirty-five passes in a sea-

son, doubling as a flanker. He was quick and elusive, but not exceptionally fast. He played only six years in the NFL, retiring before he was twenty-nine. And yet he was voted into the Pro Football Hall of Fame! Of course, he also punted, kicked field goals, returned punts and kickoffs, threw option passes, and managed to come up with the big play when it counted, like a 67-yard touchdown run from scrimmage that sealed the '53 title game over the vaunted Browns. On the Lions, he was reunited with his old Highland Park high school teammate, quarterback Bobby Layne, who was as flamboyant as Doak was reticent. On his title-clinching run against Cleveland, Doak whispered to Bobby that the Browns' defensive left tackle was chasing the Lions' pulling right guard on running plays and paying no attention to Doak as he dove into the line. So Layne slipped him the ball, and Doak sneaked through the vacant hole and sprinted untouched to the goal line. He was that type of player who maximized his natural skills with intuitive feel for the game that let him compete with the big boys. His name still comes up with the greats of all eras.

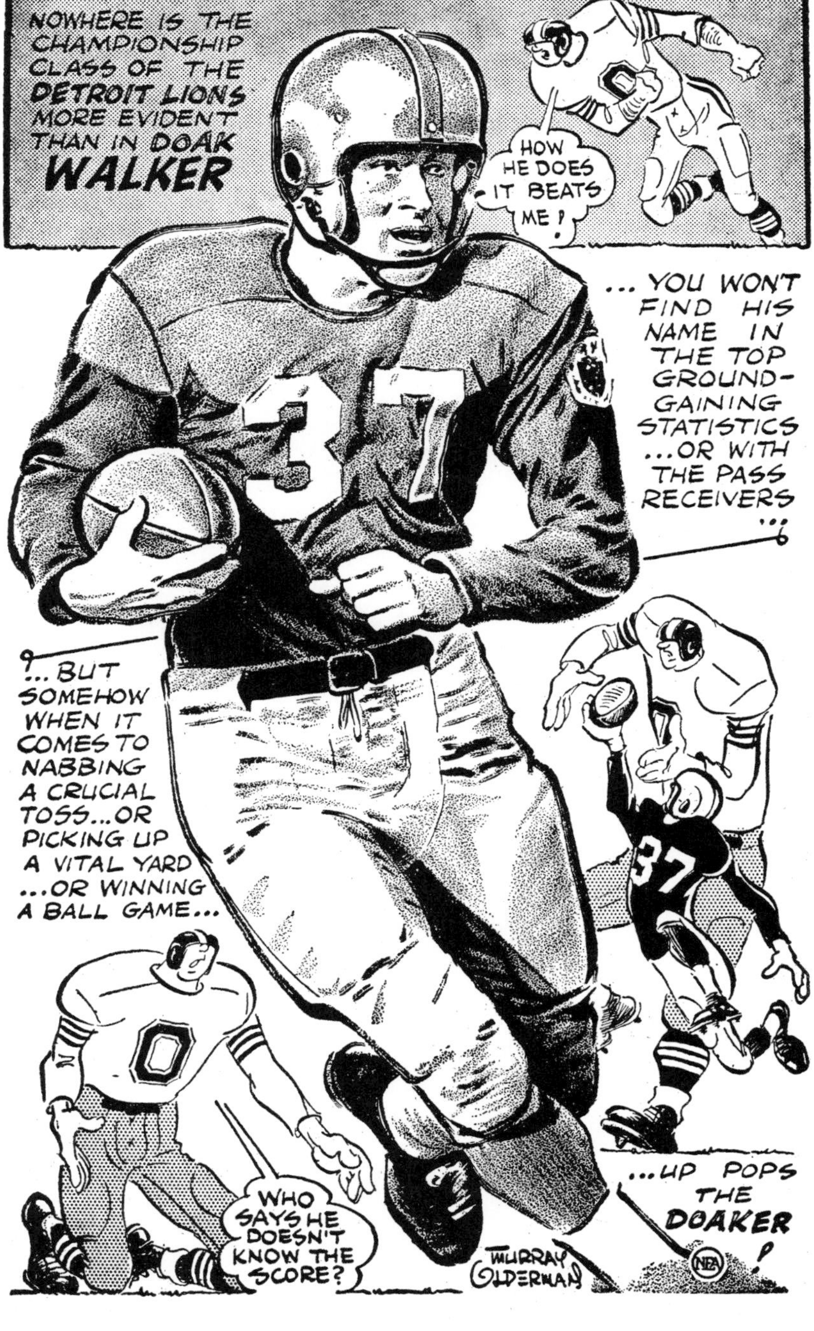
NOWHERE IS THE CHAMPIONSHIP CLASS OF THE DETROIT LIONS MORE EVIDENT THAN IN DOAK WALKER
HOW HE DOES IT BEATS ME!
... YOU WON'T FIND HIS NAME IN THE TOP GROUND-GAINING STATISTICS ...OR WITH THE PASS RECEIVERS ...
... BUT SOMEHOW WHEN IT COMES TO NABBING A CRUCIAL TOSS...OR PICKING UP A VITAL YARD ...OR WINNING A BALL GAME...
...UP POPS THE DOAKER!
WHO SAYS HE DOESN'T KNOW THE SCORE?
MURRAY OLDERMAN
NEA

"Winning Ways"

Paul Warfield

GROWING UP IN Warren, Ohio, an hour east of Cleveland, Paul Warfield's sport was going to be baseball until a charismatic high school coach turned him on to football. At Ohio State as an eighteen-year-old freshman, he was fielding punts in practice and flubbed one. An irate, fuming Woody Hayes raced out on the field and berated him, taking off his cap and stomping on it, then ripping it to shreds before Paul's gaping eyes. Years later, when he was in personnel for the Cleveland Browns, one of Paul's scouts visited Hayes's office and saw the Buckeye coach pull out a drawer full of caps, with the seams carefully slit by a razor—Woody's cap-tearing trick was an act. Meanwhile Warfield, a number one pick of the Browns in the 1964 draft that produced eleven Pro Football Hall of Fame players, became the best wide receiver in football. Cleveland needed a quarter-back, targeted Mike Phipps of Purdue, and Joe Thomas of the lowly Miami Dolphins, picking next in the 1970 draft, insisted on Warfield for the right to Phipps. Within four years, with Warfield a key cog, the Dolphins were in consecutive Super Bowls and had an historic 17-0 run, capped by victory in Super Bowl VIII. Paul, Larry Csonka, and Jim Kiick shocked pro football by jumping to the upstart Memphis team in the World Football League. The Warfields, Paul and Beverly, ultimately moved to Rancho Mirage, California. We had become friendly at between-seasons golf junkets. Beverly called and said they wanted to join Mission Hills Country Club next door. So I sponsored them. Still in great shape in his 70s, Paul bicycled every morning at 6:30 to our fitness center to work out. Despite a graying thatch on top, he looked like he could still suit up.

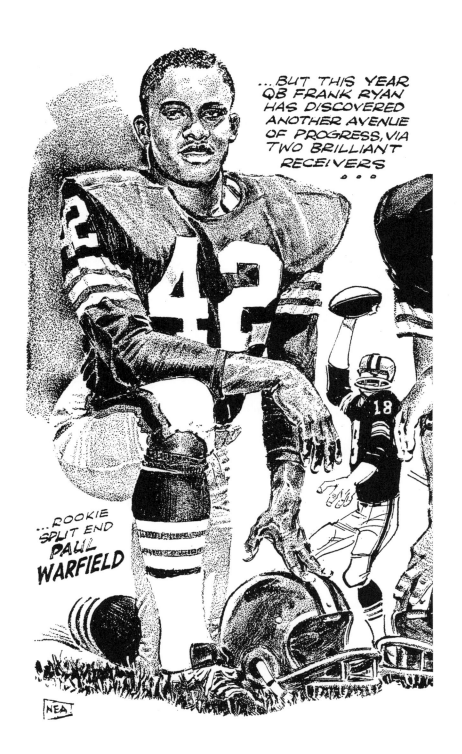

...BUT THIS YEAR QB FRANK RYAN HAS DISCOVERED ANOTHER AVENUE OF PROGRESS, VIA TWO BRILLIANT RECEIVERS...

...ROOKIE SPLIT END PAUL WARFIELD

Bud Wilkinson

CHARLES "BUD" WILKINSON was one of the most imposing men you'd want to meet: Hollywood handsome, tall, and articulate. He was in the vanguard of a wave of post-World War II college grid coaches whose tremendous success and popularity transcended the game. Bud had been a guard and blocking quarterback in the single wing for Bernie Bierman's mighty Minnesota Gophers, national champions three straight seasons in the 1930s. In the Navy during WWII, Bud also served as assistant coach at Iowa Pre-Flight School under Don Faurot, inventor of the split-T formation, and learned the complexities of that pass-run option offense, implementing it when, at thirty-one, he became the head coach at Oklahoma. Over seventeen seasons, 1947–63, he won three national championships and thirteen conference titles, with a streak of forty-seven straight victories that's still the collegiate record. He was a great recruiter and motivator. A flattering moment came when I received a note from Bud, requesting the original of the cartoon about his son Jay, a back at Duke. Proud Pop retired from coaching, changed his first name legally to Bud and ran for the U.S. Senate from Oklahoma on the Republican ticket the next year. He'd already had a taste of public life as the first director of the President's Council on Physical Fitness, appointed by John F. Kennedy. Caught in the landslide presidential defeat of Barry Goldwater in 1964, Bud lost his race narrowly and never again ran for office. He turned to television as a sports show host and the first color analyst on ABC college football telecasts. NFL teams had long courted Bud and been ignored. After being away from the sidelines fifteen years, he surprisingly became head coach of the St. Louis Cardinals, rumored to impress his new young wife. It was a disaster. He was fired in the second season.

"...and I pledge a return to free substitu---er-r--I mean enterprise."

WILKINSON FOR SENATOR

John Wooden

THE PRIM, MINISTERIAL man who wrote poetry, shunned profanity, and went to church regularly made basketball his real religion. Its shrine was an arena on the UCLA campus in west Los Angeles during his record run of twenty-seven years. Pauley Pavilion should have been called Wooden Tabernacle. On a visit to his college office, I saw tacked to the wall, a poster in the form of a word pyramid, topped by "Success." On the bottom corners were the words, "Enthusiasm" and "Industriousness." Between them was the verbal foundation: "Condition, Fundamentals, Teamwork." Wooden explained to me, "Success is not winning. I never told my team to go out and win. It is peace of mind, self-satisfaction in knowing you've done your best." Homilies are fine. Results are the proof of their wisdom. No other basketball team had the blanket domination of the college sport that UCLA achieved during Wooden's coaching tenure on the Westwood campus, 1948–75. In the last dozen seasons, his Bruins won ten NCAA championships, seven of them in a row, and had a streak of eighty-eight consecutive victories! He won with a team whose tallest player was 6'5" tall and he won with the likes of the towering Bill Walton and Lew Alcindor

(later to be Kareem Abdul-Jabbar). I watched a couple of his practice sessions at UCLA. He drove the kids hard and sternly in relentless drills. Wooden was the ultimate proponent of team play against the strong modern trend of solo performances by young hotshots. "I tell my players when they come on the floor each day," he said, "they are no longer individuals. They are part of a basketball team. Soon as practice is over, they are now individuals to me." Disparate personalities such as Walton, the flower child of the hippie era, and Alcindor, aloof and reclusive, bought into his program. You looked at the school-masterish, under-sized John Wooden and didn't realize he was also inducted into the Basketball Hall of Fame as a player. He was an All-American guard on a national championship team at Purdue in 1932. He was also a high scorer in the National Basketball League, forerunner of the NBA, at the same time he began his coaching career, on the high school level. This icon of bygone days was held in awe and respect into his nineties, long removed from the game. Walton called his old coach twice a week until Wooden died at the age of ninety-nine.

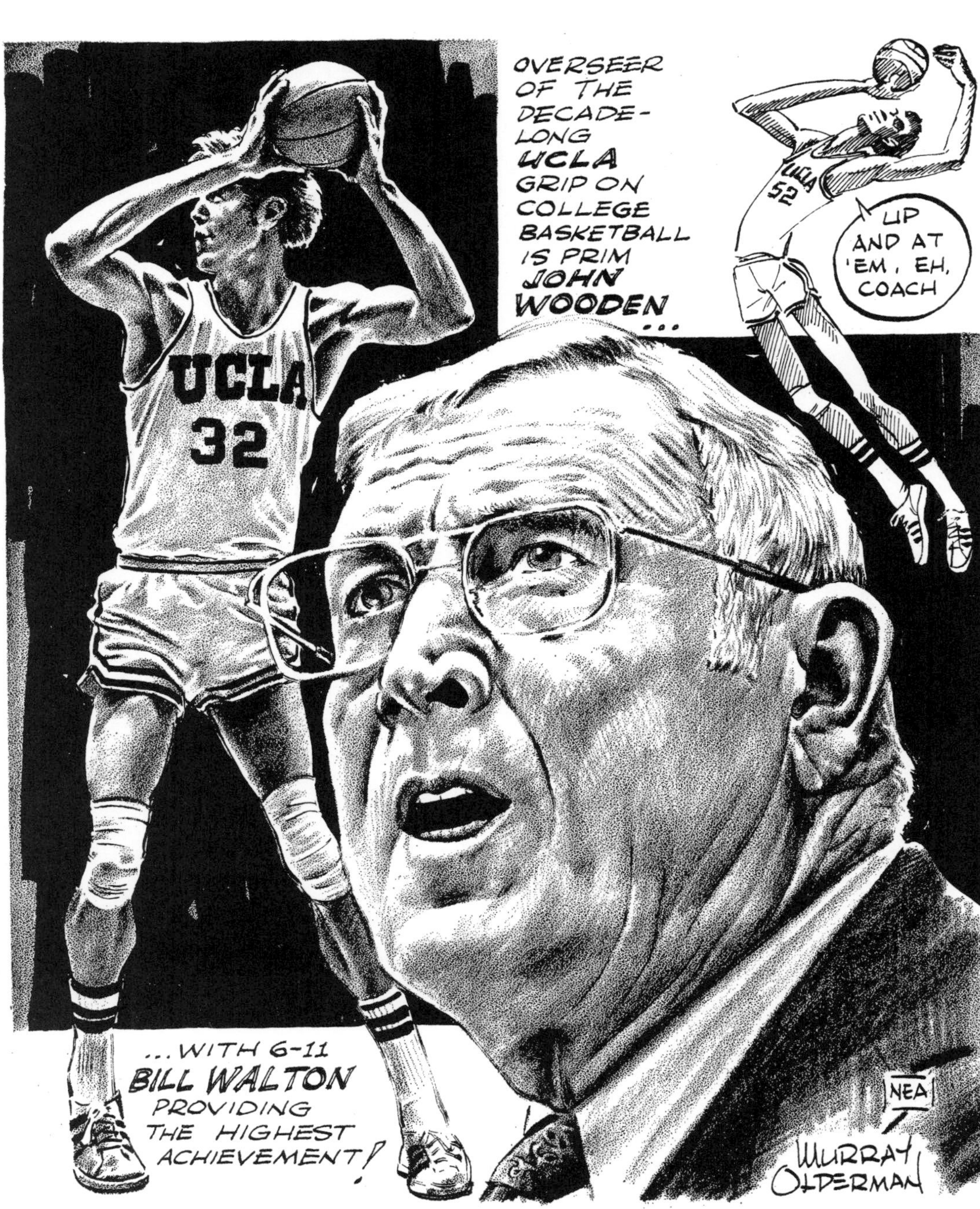
OVERSEER OF THE DECADE-LONG UCLA GRIP ON COLLEGE BASKETBALL IS PRIM JOHN WOODEN...
UP AND AT 'EM, EH, COACH
UCLA 52
UCLA 32
...WITH 6-11 BILL WALTON PROVIDING THE HIGHEST ACHIEVEMENT!
NEA
MURRAY OLDERMAN

"View from the Top"

Carl Yastrzemski

BASEBALL, MORE THAN other sports, thrived on a succession of heroes to provide a continuous flow of sentimental memories for its ardent fans. In New York, Babe Ruth was followed by "Joltin' Joe" DiMaggio, who was overlapped by Mickey Mantle. In Boston, too, the "Splendid Splinter" Ted Williams, was succeeded immediately in front of the Green Wall in left field by Carl Yastrzemski, whose name was unpronounceable (it's ya-STREM-ski) until the Beantown faithful shortened it to "Yaz." Williams retired in 1960, and Yaz moved into Fenway Park in 1961 and stayed with the Red Sox for twenty-three years, playing 3,308 games, second most in baseball history (behind Pete Rose). The compact slugger was signed with a $100,000 bonus off a farm outside Southampton in eastern Long Island. Unlike Williams, who played left field with diffidence, Yaz was a great defensive outfielder with a strong throwing arm, but his métier was hitting with power when it counted. In his third season, he led the American League in batting. In 1967, he won the hitting Triple Crown—batting average, home runs, runs batted in—and was voted the league's most valuable player while pacing the Red Sox to the World Series. He played in seventeen All-Star games. He didn't have the most colorful personality and was never controversial. He simply was a guy who delivered hits consistently and effectively until he was forty-four years old.

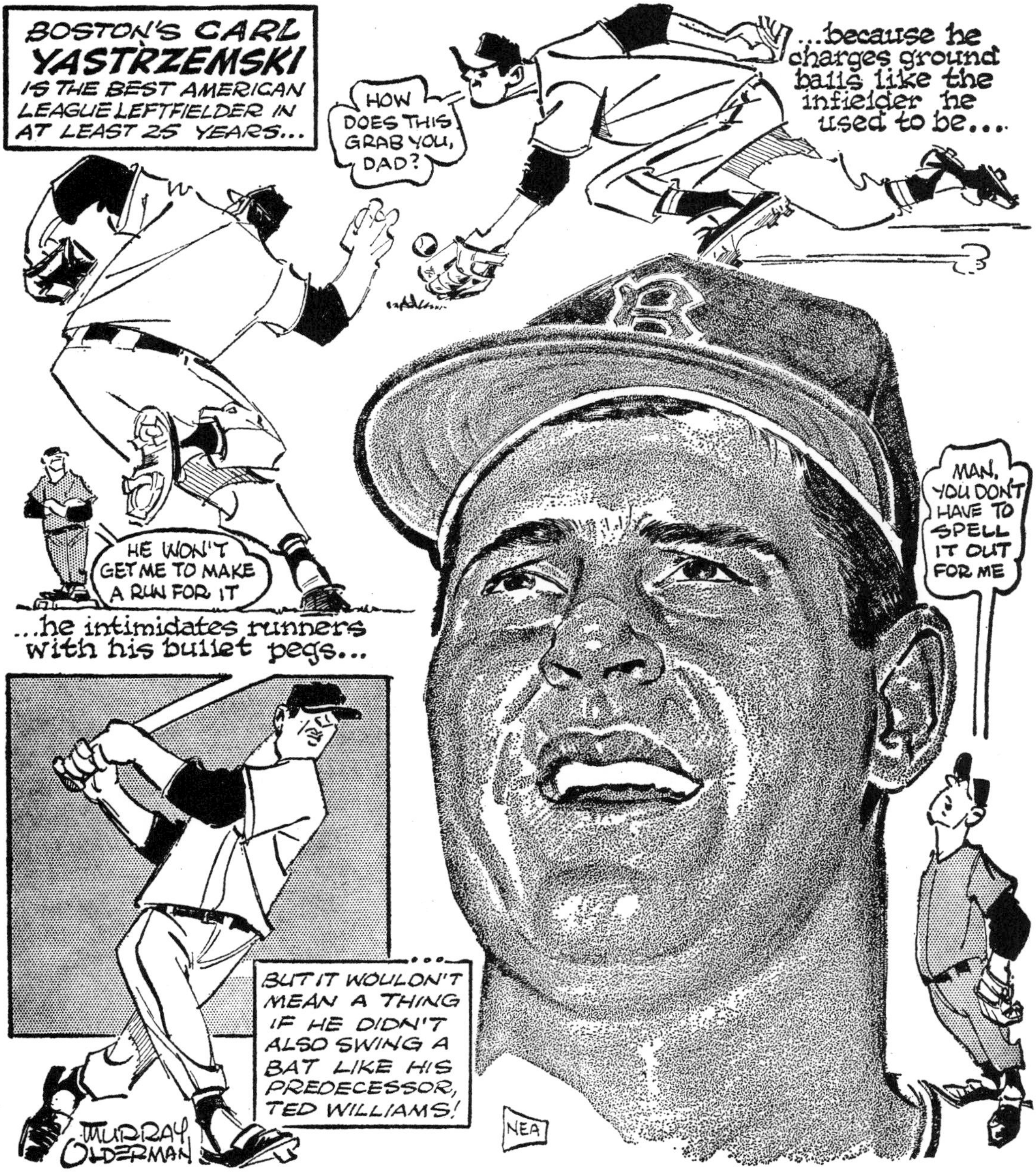
BOSTON'S CARL YASTRZEMSKI IS THE BEST AMERICAN LEAGUE LEFTFIELDER IN AT LEAST 25 YEARS...
HOW DOES THIS GRAB YOU, DAD?
...because he charges ground balls like the infielder he used to be...
HE WON'T GET ME TO MAKE A RUN FOR IT
...he intimidates runners with his bullet pegs...
MAN, YOU DON'T HAVE TO SPELL IT OUT FOR ME
...BUT IT WOULDN'T MEAN A THING IF HE DIDN'T ALSO SWING A BAT LIKE HIS PREDECESSOR, TED WILLIAMS!
MURRAY OLDERMAN
NEA

"A Hit in Every Way"

Babe Zaharias

SHE WAS VOTED the Female Athlete of the Year a record six times by the Associated Press, but not always as a golfer, the sport for which she became most famous. Mildred Ella Zaharias—known as "Babe" growing up in Port Arthur and Beaumont, Texas—was an illuminating sports prodigy: an AAU basketball All-American; gold medalist in hurdles and javelin, plus silver medal in high jump, at the 1932 Olympics. And just as proficient in bowling, diving, roller-skating, tennis, softball, and throwing a baseball. But golf was a way to make money, and she took it up seriously in 1935. Five years later, she won a women's major, the Western Open, as an amateur. At the 1938 L.A. Open, a men's event, the Babe was partnered with George Zaharias, a wrestler-promoter, and later married him. Chain-smoking and brash, yet she also excelled as a clothes-designing seamstress. Babe turned golf pro in 1947 and was a founding member of the LPGA, won three U.S. Women's Opens, and was the Arnold Palmer of her day in popularity. I did the drawing on the opposite page when she was diagnosed with colon cancer in 1953. Yet she competed in and won major LPGA tournaments the next two years. She passed away in September 1956, at the age of forty-five.

BABE DIDRIKSON **ZAHARIAS** TEES OFF IN THE GREATEST MATCH OF HER LIFE ...

....with the sports world in her gallery and her own indomitable spirit as an ally against illness.

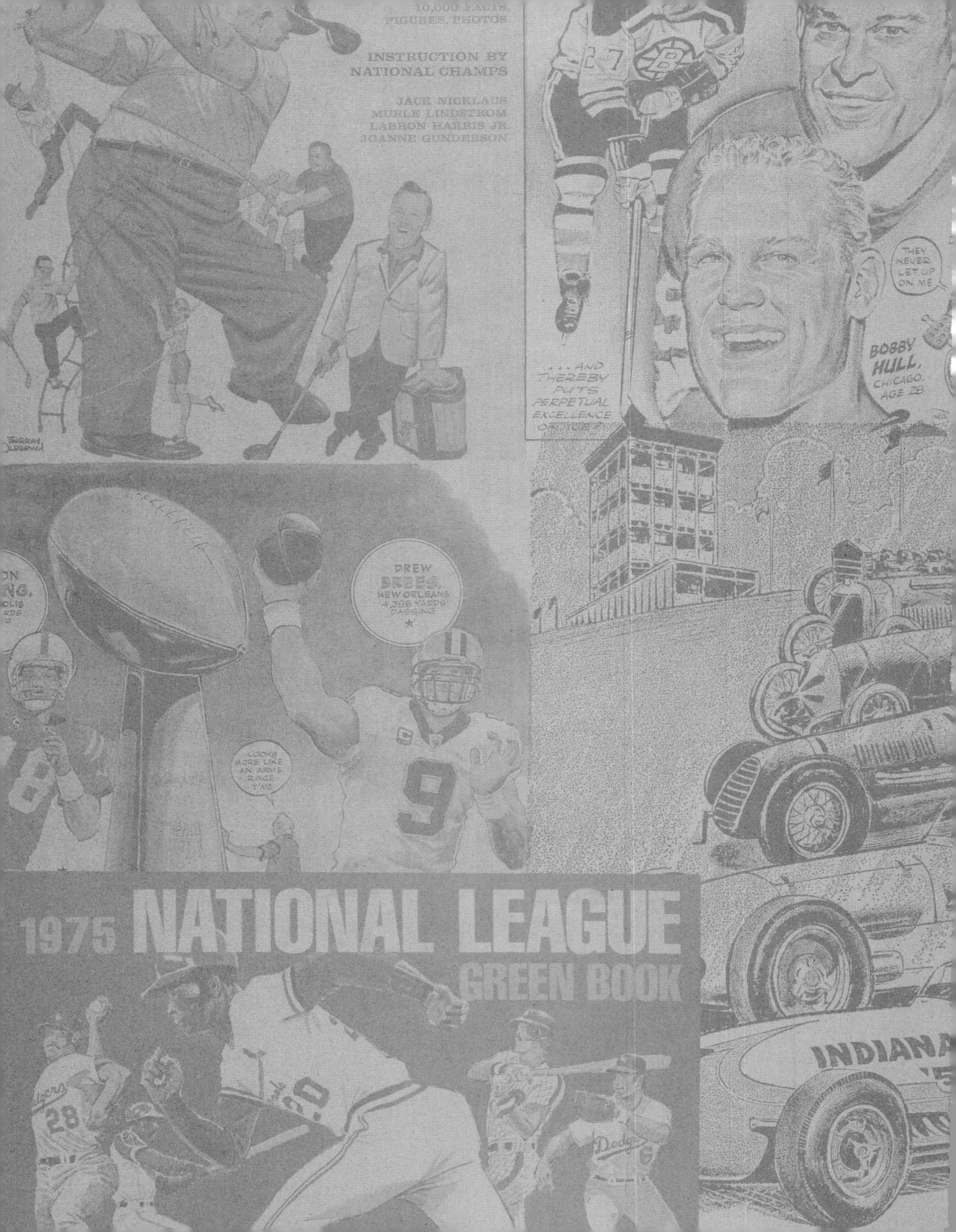
10,000 FACTS, FIGURES, PHOTOS
INSTRUCTION BY NATIONAL CHAMPS
JACK NICKLAUS
MURLE LINDSTROM
LABRON HARRIS JR
JOANNE GUNDERSON
THEY NEVER LET UP ON ME
BOBBY HULL, CHICAGO, AGE 28
DREW BREES, NEW ORLEANS 4,388 YARDS PASSING
LOOKS MORE LIKE AN ARMS RACE T'ME
1975 NATIONAL LEAGUE GREEN BOOK
INDIANA

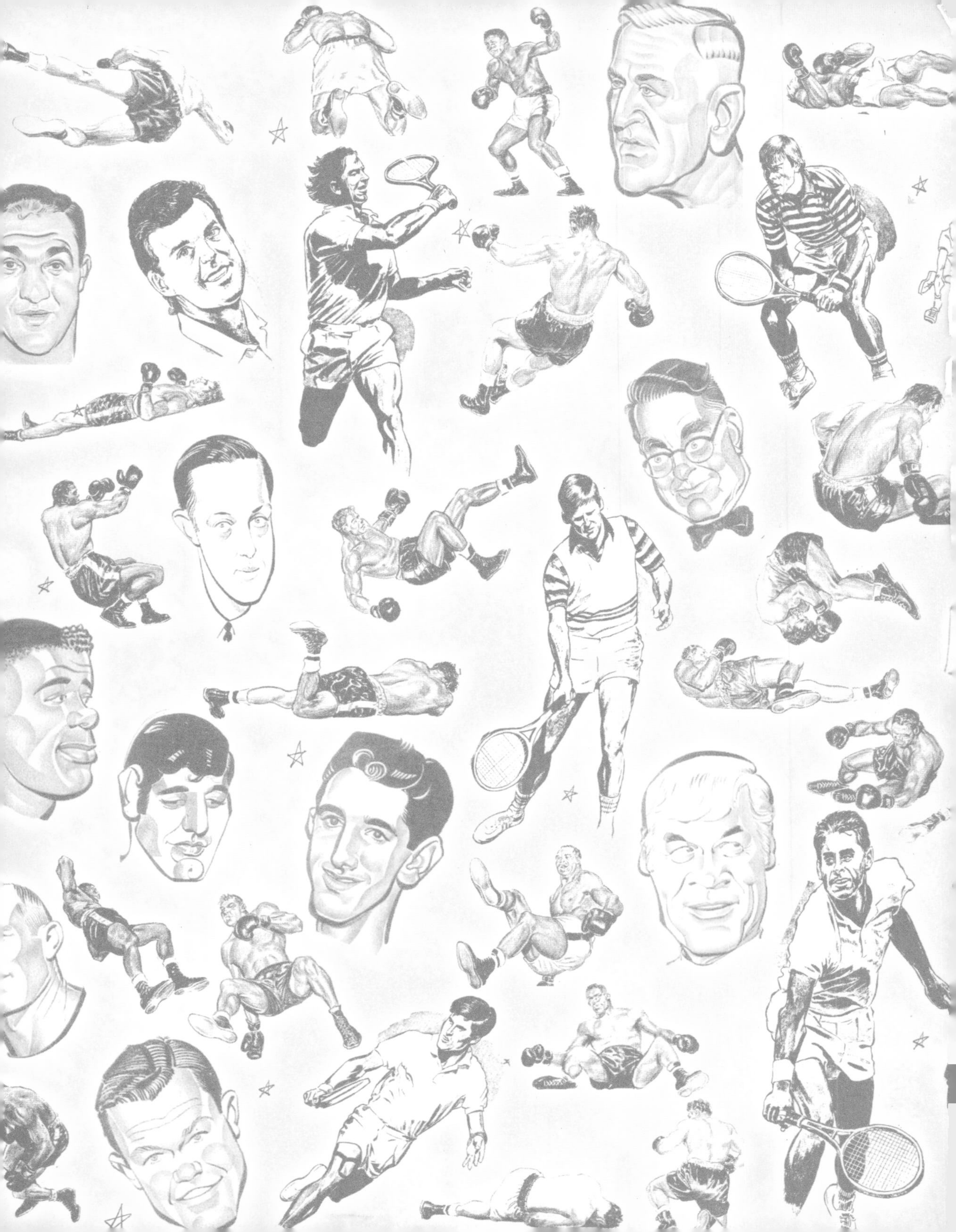